Doing Qualitative Educational Research

Also available:

Doing Qualitative Educational Research

A Personal Guide to the Research Process

Geoffrey Walford

CONTINUUM
London and New York

Continuum

The Tower Building
11 York Road
London SE1 7NX

370 Lexington Avenue
New York
NY 10017–6503

First published 2001

British Library Cataloguing-in-Publication Data
A catalogue record for this book is available from the British Library.

ISBN 0–8264–4701–5 (hardback)
      0–8264–4702–3 (paperback)

Typeset by YHT Ltd, London
Printed and bound in Great Britain by TJ Internatonal, Padstow, Cornwall

Doing Qualitative Educational Research

A Personal Guide to the Research Process

Geoffrey Walford

CONTINUUM
London and New York

Continuum
The Tower Building   370 Lexington Avenue
11 York Road   New York
London SE1 7NX   NY 10017–6503

© 2001 Geoffrey Walford

First published 2001

British Library Cataloguing-in-Publication Data
A catalogue record for this book is available from the British Library.

ISBN 0–8264–4701–5 (hardback)
     0–8264–4702–3 (paperback)

Typeset by YHT Ltd, London
Printed and bound in Great Britain by TJ Internatonal, Padstow, Cornwall

Doing Qualitative Educational Research

A Personal Guide to the Research Process

Geoffrey Walford

CONTINUUM
London and New York

Continuum

The Tower Building	370 Lexington Avenue
11 York Road	New York
London SE1 7NX	NY 10017–6503

© 2001 Geoffrey Walford

First published 2001

British Library Cataloguing-in-Publication Data
A catalogue record for this book is available from the British Library.

ISBN 0–8264–4701–5 (hardback)
     0–8264–4702–3 (paperback)

Typeset by YHT Ltd, London
Printed and bound in Great Britain by TJ Internatonal, Padstow, Cornwall

Contents

Preface

Over the past fifteen years I have edited a series of books in which well known educational researchers have presented personal descriptions of the process by which they conducted particular pieces of research (Walford, 1987c, 1991a, 1994c, 1998a). In each of these volumes I included a chapter that related to my own research, and I have written accounts of my research in some other similar volumes edited by other people. Along with new material, this book brings together modified versions of some of these previously published writings and presents a personal view of many elements of doing qualitative educational research. It is not a comprehensive account of all of the elements of any qualitative research process, but provides a series of essays on various aspects of doing qualitative research about education. Together, these essays provide a coherent reflexive account of aspects of the research process built upon my own experience over more than twenty years as a university-based educational researcher.

The overall aim of the book is to get 'beneath the surface' (Fletcher, 1974) of some of the ways in which research is currently conducted. It reflects not only upon the trials and tribulations, problems and promises of conducting particular pieces of research, but on the links between what is possible in research and personal idiosyncrasies and circumstances. Research is revealed as a much more complicated process than many would expect, sometimes more messy and disorganized, sometimes constrained in ways unexpected, but always challenging to the researcher and, hopefully, to the reader.

This book brings together in modified form several of my previous essays. I acknowledge permission given by the publishers to reproduce parts of the following:

'Research role conflicts and compromises in public schools'. In Geoffrey Walford (ed.), *Doing Sociology of Education*, Lewes: Falmer, 1987, pp. 45–65 (Chapter 5).

'Researching the City Technology College, Kingshurst'. In Geoffrey Walford (ed.), *Doing Educational Research*, London: Routledge, 1991, pp. 82–100 (Chapter 2).

'Ethics and power in a study of pressure group politics'. In Geoffrey Walford (ed.), *Researching the Powerful in Education*, London: UCL Press, 1994, pp. 81–93 (Chapter 9).

'Political commitment in the study of the City Technology College, Kingshurst'. In David Halpin and Barry Troyna (eds), *Researching Education Policy: Ethical and Methodological Issues*, London: Falmer, 1994, pp. 94–106 (Chapter 8).

'Compulsive writing behaviour: getting it published'. In Geoffrey Walford (ed.), *Doing Research about Education*, London and Washington, DC: Falmer, 1998, pp. 184–98 (Chapter 11).

'Research accounts count'. In Geoffrey Walford (ed.), *Doing Research about Education*, London and Washington, DC: Falmer, 1998, pp. 1–10 (Chapter 12).

'First days in the field: whose agenda?' Paper given at the Ethnography and Education Conference, University of Oxford, 7–8 September 1998 (Chapter 4).

'Children learning: Ethnographers learning' (with Alexander Massey). In Geoffrey Walford and Alexander Massey (eds), *Children Learning in Context, Studies in Educational Ethnography, Volume 1*, Stamford, CT and London: JAI Press, 1998, pp. 1–18 (Chapter 1).

'Selling your way in: gaining access to research sites'. In Alexander Massey and Geoffrey Walford (eds), *Explorations in Methodology, Studies in Educational Ethnography, Volume 2*, Stamford, CT and London: JAI Press, 1999 (Chapter 3).

The various research projects that are discussed in this book were funded by the ESRC, the Nuffield Foundation, the Spencer Foundation and the Universities of Aston and Oxford. I am most grateful for their support but the responsibility for any comment here is mine alone.

— 1

Introduction

REFLEXIVE ACCOUNTS OF RESEARCH

I have been active in educational research for over twenty years. A great deal has changed in educational research over that time, yet the introductory books on social and educational research methods only partially reflect these changes. The well known textbooks, such as those by Moser and Kalton (1982) and Cohen and Manion (1994; Cohen *et al.*, 2000), are still widely used on undergraduate and postgraduate courses in universities and colleges and have been regularly reprinted to serve successive cohorts of students. They have been modified, but the thrust of these texts is still to present research largely as an unproblematic process concerned with sampling, questionnaire design, interview procedures, response rates, observation schedules and so on. They still present a largely idealized conception of how social and educational research is designed and executed, where research is carefully planned in advance, predetermined methods and procedures are followed and 'results' are the inevitable conclusion. In essence, such books take what they perceive to be the methods used in the natural sciences as their model, and seek to present social and educational research as being equally 'scientific' in its methods.

In practice, however, it is now widely recognized that the careful, objective, step-by-step model of the research process is actually a fraud and that, within natural science as well as within social science, the standard way in which research methods are taught and real research is often written up for publication perpetuates what is in fact a myth of objectivity (Medawar, 1963). The reality is very different. There are now several autobiographical accounts by scientists themselves and academic studies by sociologists of science that show that natural science research is frequently not carefully planned in advance and conducted according to set procedures, but often centres on compromises, short-cuts, hunches and serendipitous occurrences.

One of the earliest and most well known of these autobiographical accounts on natural science research is that by Nobel Prize winner James Watson (1968), who helped to unravel the helical structure of DNA. His revelations of the lucky turns of events, the guesswork, the rivalries between researchers and personal involvement and compromise gave a totally different view of how natural science research is conducted from that given in methods textbooks. The personal and social nature of science research (and of writing about that process) is underlined by the somewhat conflicting account of the same research given later by Watson's Nobel Prize co-winner, Francis Crick (1989). Various sociologists of science have also looked in detail at the process by which scientific knowledge is constructed. The ethnographic study of the everyday world of the scientific laboratory by Latour and Woolgar (1979), for example, shows clearly how scientific 'facts' are not 'discovered', but are the result of an extended process of social construction.

Yet, while it is increasingly recognized that the individual researcher in natural science does not behave as an objective automaton, social and educational research has traditionally tried to justify its own research procedures by making them as 'scientific' and 'objective' as possible, and by apeing what have been perceived to be the methods of the natural sciences. Many social science and educational research methods textbooks still abstract the researcher from the process of research in the same way as have natural science textbooks. The social dimension of research is largely omitted and the process is presented as an analytic practice where any novice researcher can follow set recipes and obtain predetermined results. It is little wonder that when the novice researcher finds unforeseen difficulties, conflicts and ambiguities in doing research he or she will tend to see these as personal deficiencies arising from insufficient preparation, knowledge or experience. While it might be argued that these idealized models of research presented in traditional textbooks are a necessary part of understanding research, they certainly do not prepare novice researchers for the political and social realities of the actual research practice. They need to be supplemented by rather different accounts of the research process in action.

The limitations of traditional research methods textbooks have gradually been recognized over the past decade or more, and there has grown a range of 'alternative' books for students and practitioners, which aim to present more realistic accounts of the particular research practices that led to specific research reports. In these books the researchers themselves have written semi-autobiographic reflexive accounts of the process of doing research, in the hope that others will benefit from this sharing of practical experience. Sociologists, and in particular those engaged in more qualitative research, have tended to be the most forthcoming in their accounts, and Whyte's (1955) appendix to his ethnographically based *Street Corner Society* is widely regarded as a classic. During the 1980s the most widely known and used collections of such accounts were those edited by Colin Bell and Howard Newby (1977), Colin Bell and Helen Roberts (1984) and Helen Roberts (1981). All these collections, in their different ways, gave accounts of the 'backstage' research activities and unveiled some of the idiosyncrasies of person and circumstances which are seen as being at the heart of the research process. Anthropologists have written similar accounts of their fieldwork for some time (see, for example, Wax, 1971). In contrast, it is noticeable that psychologists have been more reluctant than sociologists to move away from the security of their natural science research model, and there are few similar collections of reflexive accounts on key psychological works.

Few of the articles in these early general collections on sociological research methods were concerned with sociology of education. Indeed, the only article on education intended for inclusion in Bell and Newby (1977) was not published due to possible libel action, and a modified version only appeared much later (Punch, 1986). Nevertheless, there has now been a minor flood of such volumes which present the practical, political and personal side of educational research. In Britain, the first of these was the collection edited by Marten Shipman (1976), who managed to persuade six authors of highly respected research reports to write about the origins, organization and implementation of their projects, including the personal and professional problems that they had to overcome. He was unusually fortunate in being able to include authors of longitudinal quantitative research as well as detailed case studies and qualitative work. As with all such collections, the authors responded with differing degrees of candour, but some of the accounts were eye-openers to students trained only in the 'scientific' method.

During the mid-1980s there was an outpouring of four books edited by Robert Burgess which gathered together similar revelatory autobiographical accounts by educational researchers.

The most important of these was *The Research Process in Educational Settings* (Burgess, 1984b) which presented ten first-person accounts of research experience in ethnographic or case study work and became an Open University set book. Burgess produced three rather similar collections in 1985 (Burgess, 1985a, b, c), which discussed strategies and tactics for research, and examined methods of investigation in relation to theories, problems, processes and procedures. The relationship between research and policy and practice was also given prominence.

The rise of evaluation work within educational research has brought its own literature on methodology. This has mainly consisted of 'how to do evaluation' books and articles, but there have also been several reflexive accounts of the evaluation process. An early collection was that of David Smetherham (1981), which included sensitive accounts on a diverse range of evaluation studies. This was followed by Clem Adelman's (1984) *The Politics and Ethics of Evaluation*, which brought ethical questions to the fore. More general ethical issues have also been addressed in a collection of essays edited by Burgess (1989).

The present book seeks to place itself in this tradition of books which explore the practical and social aspects of doing research in education, but it differs from them in focusing on the work of just one author over several different qualitative studies. The majority of the chapters examine particular segments of the process of a research project that led to a major book. In doing so, it is hoped that readers will be better able to assess the validity, reliability and generalizability of that particular research, but it is also hoped that these discussions of specific research projects will help students and others involved in conducting and reading research to understand the research process more fully. The chapters have different emphases. Some give general discussions of particular aspects of research, others elaborate the day-to-day trials and tribulations of research, while yet others are concerned with the process of publication of findings and the ethics of research.

With all such accounts, there is always some self-censorship. Some of this will be done to avoid harm to others or because there might be a threat of libel action, but the majority is likely to be the result of the reluctance on the part of the researcher to reveal quite all that occurred. It is only very recently, for example, that there has been any comment on any sexual relationships that may have been a part of the research process (Kulick and Willson, 1995), and I have not included any such discussion here. Perhaps the best that anyone can expect is that the second worst (or perhaps second best) thing that happened will be discussed. Thus, this book does not pretend to present 'the truth' about research or even about the research process that was followed in the particular studies discussed, but it gives a further perspective on the ways in which research can be and is conducted. It is hoped that it will help readers to reflect critically on research methodology, and may provide a source of comfort to students and fellow professional researchers setting out on their own research projects.

One of the interesting aspects of these collections of reflexive accounts is that they have tended to emphasize accounts relating to qualitative rather than quantitative research. A critical reader might gain the impression that the 'flexibility' of method and the effect of the personal on the way in which research is conducted is a feature only of qualitative methods, and that the 'harder' quantitative methods escape from these problems. This is certainly not correct for, fundamentally, doing all research is a profoundly pragmatic and down-to-earth activity which is broadly similar whether quantitative or qualitative data are being generated. Individuals and groups try as best they can to grapple with the innumerable problems that confront them in their task, working within practical, personal, financial and time constraints imposed upon them to produce research reports which are as sound and propitious as possible. Where textbooks on research methods usually give normative advice on how research should proceed in an 'ideal' environment, the real world of research is one of constraint and compromise. The nature of the various compromises to be made will vary with the research project and may well change in importance as the research progresses. Finance is nearly always a major constraint which necessitates some compromise to be made between what the researcher would ideally wish to do and what is possible. In social survey research, for example, the amount of funding crucially influences the possible sample size, but it also constrains the amount of pilot work conducted, the efforts made to reduce non-response, the depth of analysis of the data that is possible and so on. In a somewhat similar way, in ethnographic research financial compromises can determine the amount of time spent in the field, the extent to which interviews can be fully transcribed and the extent to which the observer can truly participate in the lifestyle of those he or she is studying. Time is also a fundamental constraint that impinges on all research. This is not just time in the field or time gathering data, but also extends into the analysis stage, the development of theory and the writing and publication of research reports. It is always possible for the researcher to generate more data, follow up more references, do more detailed statistical analysis, refine a developing theory, rewrite a chapter draft once again and so on, but in each case a line has to be drawn and a decision taken to stop, or no report would ever get published. Few researchers are ever entirely happy with their own work once it is in cold print, for they recognize that a trade-off had to be made in terms of quality for their work ever to get to that stage. This particular stark conflict faces all researchers, whether involved in qualitative or quantitative work, and perhaps especially those involved in the development of 'grand theory'. Providing they have a good library, the latter, however, are not usually faced by the myriad of practical problems that beset those involved in empirical work. The researcher is often overwhelmed by the daily round of research problems, each one of which, although trivial, must be overcome or dealt with in some way. For an ethnographer the problem of access may be personified by the teacher who refuses to allow the observer into the classroom, while for those involved with social surveys it may involve the construction of an adequate sampling frame or the threat of a boycott of questionnaires by a trade union's members. With longitudinal work, whether it be qualitative or quantitative, the researcher is forced to deal with the inappropriateness and inadequacies of data generated in an earlier social context and often for different purposes than those for which the data are now to be used. Here, as elsewhere, decision and compromise are the essence of the research process.

Further compromises that must sometimes be made if research is to be conducted and published involve complicated questions of politics and ethics. Here it is not simply a matter of the choice between 'overt' and 'covert' research, for such a dichotomy is a gross simplification of the reality of the continuous decision-making process that accompanies research. Even in the most 'open' of research procedures, where there is sustained negotiation between researchers and researched, it is quite impossible to avoid all political and ethical problems. The essence of research, after all, is concerned with the uncovering of what is not known, and that cannot be predicted in advance. Should the researcher only publish what those researched wish to be known, or might there be some occasions when the public's 'need to know' has priority? Indeed, some authors go further than this, agreeing with Becker (1964) that

'A study that purports to deal with social structure ... inevitably will reveal that the organization or community is not all it claims to be, not all it would like to be able to feel itself to be. A good study, therefore, will make someone angry.' Such dilemmas have only recently begun to be discussed in research methods textbooks, yet, as I have experienced it, they are at the heart of the research process.

THE STUDIES DISCUSSED AND THE NATURE OF ETHNOGRAPHY

Over more than twenty years as an academic researcher I have inevitably been involved in many different research projects. Being an academic researcher in a permanent position throughout this period has given the privileges of time and choice that many contract researchers would envy – and I have taken full advantage of both. Most of the projects I have been involved with, and certainly those discussed in this book, have been long-term projects of my own choosing where funding has been obtained in response to particular suggestions for research that I have made to funding bodies. However, external funding has never been particularly large, the most important funding being the largely invisible costs of my own time which I have been able to squeeze from a regular teaching schedule. The universities that have employed me have, in fact, been the largest funders of my research.

That I have not required very much extra financial support is mainly due to the type of qualitative research that I have chosen to conduct – most has been ethnographic, with me as the single ethnographer involved. As ethnography has had such a part to play in my research it is worth outlining what I believe ethnography to be (following Massey and Walford, 1998). For me, for a study to be called an ethnography, it needs, at the very least, each of the following seven elements:

A study of a culture
Ethnographers stress that we move within social worlds, and that to understand the behaviour, values and meanings of any given individual (or group), we must take account of some kind of cultural context. In this respect, ethnography balances attention to the sometimes minute everyday detail of individual lives with wider social structures.

The word 'culture' is notoriously difficult to define, but it is hard to avoid in a discussion of ethnography. A culture is made up of certain values, practices, relationships and identifications. The ethnographer tries to make sense of what people are doing by asking 'What's going on here? How does this work? How do people do this?' and hopes to be told by those people about 'the way we do things around here' (Deal, 1985).

Multiple methods, diverse forms of data
Cultures are complex and multifaceted. To reach even a rudimentary understanding of them requires an openness to looking in many different ways. Different situations must be sampled many times – including the now widely accepted parameters of people, place and time – to establish what and who counts as being part of a culture.

Data may consist of written documents, the researchers' own fieldnotes (including records of discussions, chance conversations, interviews, overheard remarks, observational notes), audiotapes and videotapes; quantitative data may also be included, such as survey or experimental findings. Gold (1997, p. 393) suggests that the fieldwork phase of an ethnography is complete only when 'both the ethnographer and his or her informants have exhausted their ability to identify other kinds of informants and other sorts of questions of relevance to the research objectives'.

In order to 'develop the story as it is experienced by participants' (Woods, 1994, p. 311), and gain a multidimensional appreciation of the setting, the ethnographer must be prepared to consider many different types of data. These can be generated only through the use of multiple methods, which may include interviewing, observing, quantitative work and assembling cultural artefacts. It makes sense, then, that a study which uses only one field technique (however exhaustively) does not constitute an ethnography, since it can generate only one kind of data.

Engagement
The ethnographer believes that 'observation of culture *in situ*' (Denscombe, 1995, p. 184) is the best way of getting to know it intimately. Hence Woods's (1994, p. 310) description of the 'most prominent features of an ethnographic approach' as 'long-term engagement in the situation as things actually happen and observing things first-hand'. Ethnographers work on the premise that there is important knowledge which can be gained in no other way than just 'hanging around' and 'picking things up'.

The principle of engagement by the researcher contains two elements: human connection with participants, and an investment of time. There is an assumption that, as the researcher becomes a more familiar presence, participants are less likely to behave uncharacteristically. Gold (1997, p. 394) explains: 'The fieldworker uses face-to-face relationships with informants as the fundamental way of demonstrating to them that he or she is there to learn about their lives without passing judgment on them'. The idea is that participants 'perform' less, and, as trust builds, reveal more details of their lives.

Researcher as instrument
Denscombe (1995) points out that much detailed and useful background information on a setting is often subjectively informed, echoing Woods (1994, p. 313), who describes an ethnographer as 'his or her own primary source of data'. Whether the researcher's subjectivity is a weakness or strength is not the issue. It is seen simply as an inevitable feature of the research act.

The ethnographer must aim to keep an open mind about 'what is going on here' and what might be the best ways to talk or write about whatever is being studied. But recognizing the presence of subjectivity is not the same as saying 'anything goes'. Somehow a balance must be struck between suspending preconceptions and using one's present understandings and beliefs to enquire intelligently. Dey (1993, pp. 63–4) puts it this way:

> there is a difference between an open mind and empty head. To analyse data, we need to use accumulated knowledge, not dispense with it. The issue is not whether to use existing knowledge, but how. ... The danger lies not in having assumptions but in not being aware of them.

To achieve such awareness, the ethnographer must constantly review the evolution of his or her ideas, reflecting on why particular decisions were made, why certain questions were asked or not asked, why data were generated a particular way and so on. Above all the ethnographer must try to articulate the assumptions and values implicit in the research, and what it means to acknowledge the researcher as part of, rather than outside, the research act. For Hammersley and Atkinson (1995, p. 192), reflexivity, which demands 'the provision of ... a "natural history" of the research' as experienced and influenced by the researcher, is a 'crucial component of the complete ethnography'.

Participant accounts have high status

Each person's account of the world is unique. What the researcher offers is an account which can be examined critically and systematically because the means by which it was generated are clearly articulated. It is often in the nature of ethnography that participants' accounts and actions appear to be in the foreground, and that the researcher has managed to 'get out of the way', acting only as 'information broker' (Goodson and Mangan, 1996, p. 48). However, whether easily visible or not, it is the researcher who remains the highest authority, who selects from what has been seen and heard, and constructs the final account.

An ethnographic approach is no automatic protection against an overly 'researcher-centric' view of a culture, but it does at least allow the possibility of including multiple perspectives.

Cycle of hypothesis and theory building

The openness which has underpinned many of the elements so far is particularly evident in the ethnographer's constant commitment to modify hypotheses and theories in the light of further data. Gold (1997, p. 395) describes it as the 'running interaction between formulating and testing (and reformulating and retesting)'.

In this type of enquiry, developing a theory is often not so much an event as a process. As new data emerge, existing hypotheses may prove inadequate, the ethnographer's sense of what needs to be looked at and reported on may change and explanations of what is going on may be supplanted by ones which seem to fit better. Sometimes this process goes on far beyond the data generation stage. Such an approach is consonant with emergent design, another distinguishing feature of ethnography.

Intention and outcome

The ethnographer aims 'to discover how people in the study area classify or label each other, how they find meaning in activities they care about in life, and how they engage in processes in which they individually and collectively define (antecedents and consequences of) their situations' (Gold, 1997, p. 391). Any attempt to generalize findings beyond the case itself should be regarded as suspect, since statistical random sampling is rarely a feature of ethnographic research. Rather, as with other kinds of qualitative work, the intention is to achieve some kind of understanding of a specific case, whether it be a culture, people or setting.

In describing the outcome of this kind of research, Denscombe (1995, p. 182) draws attention to the 'storytelling' aspect. An ethnography contains descriptions of local places, snapshots of people's lives and relationships, their inner thoughts and feelings, their outward appearances, anecdotes of personal triumphs and disasters, rules, contradictions and meanings. And at the end of all of this, through a judicious blend of empirical experience, systematic activity and appropriate theory, the ethnographer hopes to construct a coherent story that takes the reader into a deeper and richer appreciation of the people who have been studied.

The above seven features are not meant to provide an exhaustive definition of ethnography, but they do give an indication of the more specific focus of ethnography compared with qualitative research in general. While some of the research discussed in this book is simply qualitative in a broad sense, most of my work has moved towards this tighter idea of ethnography.

The earliest major project that is discussed in this book was an ethnographic study of two university physics departments where I interviewed research students and their supervisors and tried to observe the relationships between them (Walford, 1978, 1980a, 1981a). This particular research was conducted originally as part of a higher degree, and it followed a period when I was myself a physics research student. As I discuss in Chapter 7, this was an example of a research topic chosen in large part in order to understand my own experience and to place it in the wider context of the experience of others.

This was also partly true for the second major study I discuss here of two public (or private) boarding schools (Walford, 1983a, 1984, 1986a). I spent a month in the first and a term in the second of these schools trying to understand various aspects of how the schools operated. By the end of the study I was particularly interested in issues of gender and the lives of schoolteachers, but the broad choice of topic, far from unusually, was related to my own history. I had not attended such a school as a boy but, as I explain in Chapter 5, I had taught briefly in one of the major boys' private boarding schools before undertaking an MPhil in sociology at Oxford University. I had found it a fascinating 'total institution' which I far from understood. My experience of high level sociology stimulated a greater and more academic interest in the ways that these schools acted to reproduce class differences, and in their cultures. The study was driven in part by my desire to understand better my own prior experience.

In date order, the third study to be discussed here (mainly in Chapter 7) resulted from a similar desire to understand and describe my own experiences, but here they were those of an academic in a rapidly changing university. As a result of large and swift cuts in government funding, the University of Aston, where I was working, underwent massive changes in the period 1980–6. Departments and faculties were closed, courses cut and the number of academic staff reduced to about half. This was accomplished through the introduction of highly managerialist strategies which included the threat of compulsory redundancy for many staff. In order to try to understand this experience, and because I (correctly) saw what was happening at Aston as an indication of what could occur later elsewhere, I researched the process. I used documentation, interviews with staff and participant observation to construct an account of the process and to begin to theorize about its effects (Walford, 1987e).

The interest in the private sector of schooling, together with a growing interest in the potential equity effects of educational policies that the Conservative government was making, led to the next major project to be discussed in this book (mainly in Chapters 2 and 8). This was a study of the first City Technology College to be opened in Solihull. These new secondary specialist schools were to be officially independent or private schools, yet were to receive most of their funding from the state. I was working in nearby Birmingham at the time, and the equity implications of this particular scheme encouraged me to conduct an ethnography of the Solihull College as part of a far wider study of the scheme conducted by others (Walford and Miller, 1991). For a variety of reasons the constraints on me were such that this had to be a 'compressed ethnography' where only two or three days a week were available for research for a period of a term. As is shown in Chapter 2, there were particular problems of gaining access to this research site which show clearly the constraints under which such research has to be conducted.

This was followed by a project which was qualitative, but not ethnographic. My next excursion into the private sector concerned a group of about 60 small private evangelical Christian schools which had been started mainly because parents and churches believed that the state-maintained schools had become too secular for their own children. The research focused on the nature of the schools and the activities of a related political pressure group in its attempts to obtain state funding (Walford, 1995b). This pressure group activity did, in fact, lead to legislation such that these schools and other faith-based schools were eligible to apply for state funding. My next research followed the process of implementation of this legislation, both before and after the general election of 1997. In the end, no new evangelical Christian schools were successful, but a variety of Roman Catholic, Jewish and later Muslim schools applied and passed into the state-maintained sector. I followed the process through interviews, documentation and visits to schools and other organizations (Walford, 2000a). This research is discussed mainly in Chapters 4, 9 and 11.

My current comparative project between the Netherlands and England developed from these previous studies. In it I am trying to understand the ways in which these two countries provide schooling for religious minorities and the way in which so called 'policy borrowing' can occur. This study involves compressed ethnographies of several schools in both countries, documentation and extensive interviews with policy-makers and others involved in policies on schooling. This research has contributed mainly to Chapters 2 and 6.

All these studies, and others that I have not discussed here, have added to and challenged my understanding of the nature of educational research.

Choice of research site and problematic access

SELECTION OF RESEARCH SITES

From my reading of numerous qualitative and ethnographic accounts of schools and classrooms, it appears to me that insufficient concern is often given to the choice of research site. Most ethnographic studies do not name the educational institution in which the research has been conducted, yet it is frequently evident (either from internal evidence or from personal communications) that a study was undertaken in a particular location simply because it provided a convenient site for the researcher. Often, a local school is know to the researcher, or contacts can be made through colleagues or friends. Researchers settle for a research site to which they can easily gain convenient and ready access rather than thinking through the implications of particular choices. The result is that there are far too many ethnographic studies of schools and classrooms where the choice of site does not appear to be closely related to the objectives of the study. Further, while adequate justifications for the choice of site are often not given, many authors explicitly or implicitly make claims not only about that site, but also about a broader, usually non-defined, population of schools, classrooms, teachers or students.

Of course, it is understandable that academics and research students should include convenience in their consideration of which sites to approach to try to gain access. There are time, financial and personal costs to be considered, and a distant location may involve accommodation away from home. Additionally, and obviously, ethnographic research can only proceed where access has been achieved, and this is not always straightforward. There is an obvious temptation to accept a site that appears to be readily available rather than work harder to try to achieve access to the most appropriate site. As is discussed in Chapter 3, I do not believe access is as difficult as some would have us believe but, however difficult it is, it is crucial that obtaining access is seen as a separate consideration from locating an appropriate site.

THE DILEMMA OF GENERALIZATION

A fundamental and longstanding dilemma within qualitative and ethnographic research is that the method requires a focus on a very small number of sites, yet there is often a desire to draw conclusions which have a wider applicability than just those single cases. Within the ethnographic literature about education there is a plethora of examples where schools, or particular groups of children or teachers within schools, are researched because they are seen as 'typical', or because they can offer 'insights' into what may be occurring in other schools. Thus, for example, we have many studies of single schools where racism and sexism have been shown to occur. Strictly, such studies can only show that events that have been interpreted as racist (usually by the researcher alone, but sometimes by those involved as well) occurred in that one particular school, with those particular teachers and students, at a time that is often many years before the publication of the academic article or book. Such studies cannot provide information about what might be happening now even in that same school and, most importantly, cannot provide any evidence about what is happening or what might have been happening in any other schools.

I do not intend to attempt to cover the much debated problem of generalizability. Classic contributions include those by Becker (1990), Schofield (1990) and Stake (1995). There are several standard attempts to deal with this dilemma. The first is to argue that, while strict generalizability is not possible in the statistical sense, for one (or a small number of cases) cannot possibly be an adequate sample drawn from a wider population of schools or classrooms, ethnographic and qualitative studies can achieve 'transferability' through 'thick description'. If the authors give full and detailed descriptions of the particular context studied, it is claimed that readers can make informed decisions about the applicability of the findings to their own or other situations. However, in order to be able to judge whether a particular finding from an ethnographic study in one school is applicable in another, it is actually necessary to know as much about that second school as about the first. Lincoln and Guba (1985, p. 316) follow their logic through and argue that this means that one cannot generalize from a case study to a wider population unless one makes unwarranted assumptions about the wider population.

The second main way in which commentators have tried to deal with the problem of generalizability is to argue for theoretical generalization. Numerous authors (e.g. Bryman, 1988; Silverman, 1993; Yin, 1994) have sought to move away from statistical or empirical generalization from case studies, and have proposed that the wider significance of findings from a particular ethnographic study can be derived through the strength of logical argument for each case. A case is significant only in the context of a particular theory, and logical inference replaces statistical inference. An extrapolation can be made between a particular case and a wider population only if there is a strong theoretical or logical connection between them. The strength of the theoretical reasoning is seen to be crucial. This means that the selection of the case to be studied is crucial. Rather than attempt to find a school or classroom that is 'typical' or for which 'there is no reason to believe it is untypical', theoretical generalization requires a clear theoretical basis for the choice. This may be seen as a version of Glaser and Strauss's (1967) theoretic sampling, applied here to the initial choice of research site rather than the individuals and situations to be sampled once the site has been chosen. However, the attempt to by-pass empirical generalization through the idea of 'theoretic generalization' is, in the end, a failure. For there to be a convincing theoretical argument for extrapolation, there needs to be empirical evidence about the wider population. This requires a great deal of empirical work with the wider population as well as with the case study school. Indeed, one problem is usually defining what any 'wider population' actually is in relation to the cases studied.

So how should sites be chosen? One answer, and perhaps the most acceptable answer, is that cases should be chosen because they or the activities in them are intrinsically interesting or important in themselves, for themselves. Generalization, whether it be empirical or theoretical, need not be the goal at all. There are two possibilities here. First, it might be that particular cases are selected because they are important to understand in the light of their unique significance. This might be, for example, their role within policy formulation and development. Second, it may be that the activity that is observed in a particular ethnography case study is so important that it is sufficient to be able to show that particular events have occurred in *any* school or educational institution. Thus, if we are able to show that incidents that can be interpreted as racist have occurred in one school, many people would see this as an important finding in itself. The extent to which similar activities might be present in other schools is secondary – it is enough that they can be found in one school. The problem with this second argument is that it is dependent upon something 'important' actually occurring – which cannot be known until after the case has been selected. It offers little help in making the initial choice of site. Choosing a site that is interesting or important in itself is the only safe way to ensure that results have meaning beyond the particular case selected. This usually means that the site has to be named in any publication – an act that brings its own problems.

SOME EXAMPLES OF SITE SELECTION

Most of my previous ethnographic research has focused on sites that I believed were seen as important and of interest to a far wider group than those immediately involved in the organization (although book sales suggest that my judgement was not always correct!). My study of boys' public (private) boarding schools was careful about the issue of generalizability but, in the end, claimed that a limited generalizability was possible. Although the book was given the very general title of *Life in Public Schools* (Walford, 1986a), I made it clear that any generalization could only be made to the limited wider population of 29 schools then members of the Eton and Rugby groups of schools. I explicitly excluded Eton, bringing the population down to 28, and argued that there was sufficient information available on all of these 28 schools for me to be able to assess generalizability. I spent four weeks in one school and a term in another, made visits to several of the others in the two groups and was able to interview members of staff who had previously been teachers in practically all of them. The frequent meetings between teachers within the two groups meant that all schools were well known to teachers in the others. I now believe that it would have been better to have restricted my account to the two schools and have made no further attempts at generalization. However, in this example, had I done this, it still would not have been possible for me to have named the two schools. The headteachers made it clear that the identity of the schools would have to be concealed in any publications. This was a condition that, at the time, I readily agreed with, for I felt that the many issues of class and elitism that surrounded these schools were sufficiently interesting to a wide and diverse enough audience to make the work worthwhile.

In contrast, my next major study was of a named institution – my own university at that time, Aston University in Birmingham (Walford, 1987e). Aston was one of the universities most badly affected by the cuts in government funding implemented in 1981, and I recognized that there was an important story to tell about the ways in which the institution was being restructured. There was no question about generalization, as this was a study of the reactions within one particular university. Its wider interest was simply that the severity of the reductions in government funding were such that extreme changes were being made. It was an indication of what _could_ happen, but not a prophesy of what _would_ happen within other universities.

My following study was of a named school: the City Technology College (CTC), Kingshurst (Walford, 1991b, f; Walford and Miller, 1991). This ethnography was undertaken as part of a linked project to a wider study of the CTC initiative (Whitty *et al.*, 1993) but, again, there was no intention of making generalizations about other CTCs from the study of this one. The school was important in itself, simply because it was the first of this new type of school to be established and because it was at the centre of the initial controversy over funding and selection of children. I expected that there would be a wide audience for an account of selected aspects of 'what it was like'. In this case there were pressures put on me by the publishers to make generalizations about the whole scheme. In particular, they wished the book to be called *City Technology Colleges* and to include a detailed account of the wider initiative. I stuck to the singular title, *City Technology College*, to emphasize the restricted nature of the study.

More recent work, which has been qualitative but not ethnographic, has focused on a group of small private evangelical Christian schools and their involvement as a pressure group in influencing government legislation (Walford, 1995a, b). This was then followed by a somewhat similar linked study that examined the implementation of the particular aspects of the 1993 Education Act that made it possible to obtain state funding for some private schools (Walford, 1997, 1999b, 2000a). In both cases the work involved visits to schools where interviews with headteachers, teachers and others were conducted and documentary material collected. Only 15 schools eventually benefited from the legislation and achieved state funding, and the success of each school was widely publicized in both the local and national press. Each story was, in itself, worth telling.

Thus, my qualitative and ethnographic work is unusual in that most of it has dealt with named schools, for it was impossible and undesirable to conceal their identities. The choice of site was made because these particular schools were of interest in themselves, and not because I had any expectation of being able to generalize from them.

SELECTION OF SITES IN AN INTERNATIONAL COMPARATIVE PROJECT

My current research builds upon my past work on government policy on sponsored grant-maintained schools and on the schooling of religious minorities. It is a comparative project which involves ethnography, interviewing and document analysis in England and the Netherlands. It is funded by the Spencer Foundation for three years, and is examining and comparing the two countries' current state policy and practice on faith-based schools. The particular focus is on Muslim and fundamentalist Christian schools, both of which are fully funded by the state in the Netherlands. In contrast, following the sponsored grant-maintained legislation of 1993, only two Muslim schools are state-funded in England, while no evangelical Christian schools have yet been supported.

The comparison between Britain and the Netherlands is particularly appropriate as recent British policy on the funding of religious minority schools, in the 1993 Education Act, drew in part on the Dutch experience through a process of so-called 'policy-borrowing'. The research examines the possibilities and limitations of this particular case of policy-borrowing, and considers wider issues associated with the practice of policy-borrowing. Information is being gained about current government policy and practice through published documentation and a series of interviews with politicians, officials and religious leaders in each country. In addition to broad issues of policy, these interviews focus on the potential and real equity effects of state-funded faith-based schools.

The ethnographic aspect of the research consists of a series of case studies of schools and their local environments in each country. Four case studies are being conducted in each country – two of Muslim schools and two of fundamentalist Christian schools. These case studies selected for more intensive study are being chosen because of their particular historical role in the development of policy rather than any statistical significance or opportunity for generalization. There was no intention of looking at 'typical' schools, but at specifically chosen schools which are important in understanding the implementation of overall policy in each country. Their selection thus required substantial preliminary research on overall policy. Each school site is being visited for a total of three weeks over a period of about a year. Thus, I am using a form of 'compressed ethnography' (Walford, 1991b) to build an account of the nature of each school, and to try to understand the possible effects of state funding on the culture of each school. In order to indicate why I chose to select the schools that I have, it is necessary to describe some of the background to the project.

I will focus on the way the choice of two evangelical Christian schools in both countries was made. My aim was to choose schools which were important in their own right in the development of policy in each country and to have the possibility of limited cross-national comparisons. Again, there was never the intention that any findings about particular schools would be generalizable, such that 'what happens in English schools' could be directly compared with 'what happens in Dutch schools'. I expected the choice of sites to be relatively easy. In England I already knew a great deal about the evangelical Christian schools and the roles that some had played in campaigning for legislative change. Only one school had made an attempt to obtain sponsored grant-maintained status. This would have been one obvious choice and I had a very good relationship with the headteacher, but, sadly, that school had since closed. From my previous research I knew that no other evangelical Christian school had attempted to obtain state funding and I believed that this was largely as a result of the first school's failure. However, when I started to talk with schools again, I found that there were additional reasons for their limited interest. It was certainly true that additional funding was seen as desirable by several of the schools, but they were increasingly concerned about government control of the curriculum. The introduction of the literacy hour and numeracy hour, in particular, was seen as a possible 'first step' towards a highly centralized system which they believed would leave teachers with less space for Christian activities or for their own ways of teaching. In contrast to my initial expectations, I could find no Christian schools that were actively considering applying for state funding. I thus decided that I would look for schools that I judged would have a good chance of obtaining funding if they were to apply, and that were also important in themselves, in that their headteachers had been active in pressure group activity. I was able to select such schools because I already had extensive knowledge of the entire group through previous research. I easily obtained access to the two schools I selected.

I had two Dutch academics acting as consultants on the project, so my first attempt to locate suitable Dutch schools was through them. I found that definitions were problematic. What exactly did I mean by 'evangelical Christian'? There were various schools of different degrees of liberalism or conservatism within each of the educational groups, but, according to my colleagues, it was not possible to locate evangelical Christian schools as a group – no group existed.

Next I tried the Ministry of Education and Science, where a very helpful person spent several hours with me showing me maps and tables. He showed me the Catholic areas, the 'Bible Belt' and the various cities where there might be schools that had evangelical roots. But the only way I could find which, he suggested, was to visit many and see for myself which met my definition of 'evangelical Christian'.

In some desperation, I tried a different strategy. I went back to my contacts within the evangelical Christian movement in England and asked them for leads. One of these contacts gave me the name of a Dutch independent consultant who did work for Youth with a Mission (YWAM) and had been involved in setting up two Dutch Christian schools. YWAM is an international evangelical organiza-tion with which several of the schools in England have close links. It owns a building in Amsterdam that is opposite the central railway station and 'guards' one entrance to the extensive red light district. Near its roof the message 'Jesus Loves You' is displayed in neon in English and Dutch. Yes, that was what I meant by 'evangelical Christian'.

I eventually met this person and he explained to me that, while theoretically it was possible to start new schools if there was sufficient demand, the reality of establishing new evangelical Christian schools was very different. He had been involved in two schools. One in Amsterdam had been easily established ten years ago, but there had been a eight-year legal battle before a similar school had been started in Arnhem. Where the ever-liberal Amsterdam authorities had simply agreed, the far more conserva-tive local council at Arnhem had tried to avoid funding such a school. The case had eventually passed to the highest court in the Netherlands. Thus this Arnhem school was central to the practical development of policy in the Netherlands. Moreover, this small group of two schools was actively working together with two more evangelical schools to try to start a organization which would help the establishment and maintenance of similar schools. This putative group had many similarities with the Christian Schools Trust in England that I had researched but, rather than the Netherlands acting as a model for England, it was the English organization acting as a model for the Dutch. I visited both schools and staff later gave me access for a longer period.

IMPLICATIONS

I have argued that insufficient consideration has often been given to the selection of sites for qualitative and ethnographic research. Within the research methods literature (including my own contributions) far more attention has been given to the assumed difficulties of access, rather than to the far more important task of selecting appropriate sites.

I have argued that generalization, whether it be empirical or theoretical, is an illusory goal. Any generalization requires knowledge about a defined wider population which is rarely available. It may be more important, especially in ethnographies concerned with policy issues, to select research sites which are important for themselves (in this study for their historical role in the policy process) rather than for their supposed 'typicality'. This demands considerable research before sites can be selected. It is worth noting that it took over six months before I was happy that I had located appropriate schools in the comparative study. Perhaps it is also worth noting that I am in the privileged position of being funded so that I can travel and live anywhere in England and the Netherlands for the periods of compressed ethnography. While time and personal factors are still an issue, these have not led me to compromise over my choice of schools. Not everyone is so lucky.

GAINING ACCESS

Choosing an appropriate site is just the first step. The second is gaining access to conduct the research. This is far from easy, and is clearly one reason why so many studies do not appear to have been conducted in the most appropriate sites. While I was successful in obtaining entry to the evangelical Christian schools in my most recent research, entry to other sites has been far more problematic.

In this section I illustrate this by describing the way in which I gained entry to the first CTC in Solihull.

In October 1986, Kenneth Baker, then Secretary of State for Education and Science, announced the creation of a pilot network of twenty CTCs. These new secondary schools were to offer a curriculum strong in technology, science, business studies and practical work and were to be sited in inner-city areas. The intention was to establish a new partnership between government and industry for, while the CTCs were to be government funded, they were also to be non-fee-paying, independent schools run by educational trusts, with private sector business sponsors who were expected to make substantial contributions to costs.

An informed educational observer might be concerned that the CTC initiative seemed to be openly encouraging a process of privatization of education. The Thatcher government had shown its clear support for private education by establishing the Assisted Places Scheme and by its continuing financial and ideological support for private schools (Walford, 1987a). The CTCs could be interpreted as an indication of possible future intentions. Without any prior consultation with local education authorities, the government planned to introduce new, well funded and supported independent secondary schools into inner-city areas, where they would compete with local maintained schools for students. I, for one, saw this as privatization with a vengeance!

In February 1987, when the first site was confirmed in Conservative-controlled Solihull, I decided to conduct some serious research on CTCs. In addition to my longstanding interest in private schools, I had also published an article on an earlier unsuccessful attempt to reintroduce selective education in Solihull (Walford and Jones, 1986), and Aston University was near to the proposed site. I consulted with a colleague at Aston, Henry Miller, and we decided that we would approach the Economic and Social Research Council (ESRC) to fund a three-year project to look at the national, local and college effects of the CTC policy. A somewhat similar research strategy had been used by Tony Edwards and Geoff Whitty in their ESRC-funded study of the Assisted Places Scheme, so I wrote to them to see whether we could use their successful application for that research as a model for our own. It turned out that they already had the same idea as us, and were in the process of applying to the ESRC for funding for research on CTCs. So the final proposal to the ESRC from Tony Edwards and Geoff Whitty included Henry Miller and myself as 'consultants' to their project. The intention was that we would conduct the Kingshurst case study, looking at the two local education authorities (LEAs) involved, the local secondary schools in the CTC catchment area and the CTC itself. We planned to write a short, mainly descriptive, book about Kingshurst as rapidly as we could, as well as feeding our data into the national study. We did not then realize some of the practical and ethical problems of this decision: to conduct research on a specific, named school which was the centre of political controversy was very different from any research that either of us had previously undertaken.

The problem of gaining access to a research site is one which has been written about by many others in their reflexive accounts of the research process (see, for example, the collections by Shaffir *et al.*, 1980; Moyser and Wagstaffe, 1987), but this situation differed greatly from the norm, for we wished to investigate a specific school and its effect on other nearby schools. In this respect the research was similar to that of Punch (1977, 1986), who experienced considerable difficulties during his investigation and publication of his study of Dartington Hall School. Ideally, we wanted to interview local politicians, LEA administrators, the heads and some teachers from neighbouring schools, industrialists, parents and pupils; and to obtain access to the CTC itself, to conduct a mini-ethnographic study. We expected access to those on the political left and to the nearby LEA schools affected to be relatively easy, but anticipated difficulty in obtaining interviews with those on the political right and those within the CTC itself. We knew that the college principal, Mrs Valerie Bragg, was the primary gatekeeper who had to be prepared to give some degree of help for the project to be fully successful.

My first interview with Valerie Bragg occurred in March 1988, in the unrenovated building of Kingshurst School, which at that time still had its final year of local authority pupils. It had been relatively easy to arrange the meeting a few weeks earlier. I explained what the national and local study might involve and we talked for about an hour. It was made clear that I was far from the first person to ask for help. From the time of her appointment onwards, she had received a stream of people wanting to interview her, film her, conduct research on the college and so on. Local and national press, television and radio reporters jostled with educational researchers of various descriptions. She argued that the problem was over-exposure, and that the tasks of building a college from scratch and providing an education for the pupils had to be the first priorities.

She could not grant all requests from researches. Why should she help me rather than anyone else? And, more importantly, how could she ensure that her pupils and the college were not disrupted?

Although there were clearly difficulties, in general I felt that the meeting had been friendly and helpful, and that I would, probably, eventually be given some form of access. At her request, I sent a letter giving details of the project and waited for a reply. None came, but in early June, I received an invitation to attend a small ESRC information technology seminar for researchers and policy-makers. I wrote again to the CTC to try to interview someone about its plans for information technology. In the first interview Mrs Bragg had talked of the CTC becoming a 'catalyst for change' within the state-maintained sector, and I thought that she might see this as a chance to begin to influence future policy. Again, no reply came to the letter. After eight telephone calls from me intercepted by her secretary, Mrs Bragg returned with the answer that it would not be possible for me to talk to her or any of her current staff about information technology plans, simply because they were all too busy. This answer was one which I could quite understand, for the series of telephone calls had revealed just how busy they were (secretaries often inadvertently give away a great deal of informa-tion!). I asked vaguely about the possibilities for the general project, and it was made clear that the CTC's first priority was the children who would soon be arriving. Any research would have to wait. I was careful not to give her the chance to reject the project outright, but the discussion verged dangerously close.

While some of this exchange was clearly designed to put me off, I still felt that I would probably be able to obtain some form of access after the school had started. If the CTC was to act as a catalyst for change, then it seemed to me that a balanced account of what the college was doing was needed. Mrs Bragg had made it clear that she would support an independent evaluation of the college in due course, and that she wanted to know the effects of the CTC on the pupils. I decided that the best policy was simply to continue interviewing staff in neighbouring schools and other people involved with the CTC, and to try again later. I was still so optimistic that access would eventually be granted that, towards the end of 1988, Henry Miller and I wrote a proposal for our short book. The Open University Press gave us a contract in March 1989. At this point we had no idea just how important that contract would turn out to be in securing the success of the whole project.

Meanwhile, in addition to conducting interviews with the various external participants, I kept up a gentle stream of reminders to Mrs Bragg that I was still wishing to do research. An article on the CTC in the *Times Educational Supplement* in January (Fisher, 1989) conveniently included a quote from one of the staff which suggested that he would like someone to write about the college's curriculum. I wrote to Mrs Bragg saying that this was exactly one of the things I wanted to do. In February, I wrote volunteering to become one of the 'adults in residence' for a week, which had been advertised in earlier promotional literature on the college. No replies were received, and I was gradually becoming less optimistic about being able to gain access.

An imminent meeting with the ERSC national study team in April put pressure on me to show some progress. Within a two-week period I made about 40 telephone calls to the CTC trying to arrange an appointment with Mrs Bragg. Since she controls her own diary, it was necessary to talk directly with her. Again, I found out quite a lot about how busy she was, and was even given a message that she was 'not trying to avoid' me. Eventually, however, I received a message from her personal assistant that she could not see me in the near future. In response, I decided to risk putting on some more explicit pressure and sent a letter to Mrs Bragg explaining that I had been conducting research outside the CTC and had a contract for a book. I enclosed a copy of my *Life in Public Schools* (Walford, 1986a) and explained that reviewers of that volume and my *Restructuring Universities* (Walford, 1987e) had remarked on the degree of objectivity that I had shown. I said that I wished to do the same in the book on Kingshurst, but that this would be difficult if I was going to have to rely on second-hand information about what was occurring inside the College. All I asked at this point was for an interview with her, at least on curriculum and organizational matters. By this time I had learned (correctly) not to expect any rapid reply.

By September 1989, a further meeting with the national research team was imminent, which acted as another spur to activity. In the week preceding this meeting I telephoned the college some ten more times to try to make an appointment. The secretaries began to recognize my voice, but I got no nearer to arranging a meeting.

The world of British educational research is a small one. I knew that several other academics had tried to obtain access to the CTC, to conduct research or just to find out what the college was doing. None had got very far. At one academic conference I compared notes with a colleague. I was not doing any worse than him! He thought that no one was going to be allowed in for a few years. I was beginning to fear that this was correct, but, for a variety of reasons, I could not wait that long. First, in the summer of 1988 I had written a short book in which I had attacked the CTC concept as a stage towards privatization. Although I found it inexplicable that my publishers could take 16 months to publish it, I was somewhat glad of their tardiness as I felt that I would have even less chance of access after publication, due in January 1990. Second, the contract we had for the book on the CTC gave us until April 1990 to get the manuscript to the publishers. I had to make one final 'all or nothing' effort to get a meeting with the principal.

I decided to try to engineer a meeting with the principal by attending a British Educational Management and Administration Society Annual Conference in September 1989, at which Mrs Bragg was due to talk about 'Managing a CTC'. I sat through a rather dull three days of conference in order to hear, and possibly meet again, my primary gatekeeper. Luckily, on the Sunday morning on which Mrs Bragg was due to speak I opted out of the 'members' papers' sessions, and was the first person she met on entering the conference building. We talked for about fifteen minutes in the empty conference hall, and agreed to talk further after what turned out to be a very impressive presentation. Our discussion had been frank, open and friendly. I had already explained my main purpose in attending the conference to some of the organizing committee, so that they were not surprised to find me sitting with them, opposite Mrs Bragg, during the informal lunch. I made it clear that I already had a contract and a great deal of material for a book, and that I wanted to be able to present an objective and balanced account. On the other hand, quite understandably, Mrs Bragg did not want a book written about Kingshurst yet, and argued that if anyone was going to write one, it ought to be her. I agreed with her that she should do so, but that there was also a need for an outsider's account. A possibility of compromise developed, as both of us began to see that one way out might be for the book to include both an insider's and an outsider's account of developments. I suggested that she might write 15,000 words for the book with no editorial control being exercised by me, if she would give me access to the college and help with information. This is what we eventually agreed. In order that I should really understand the college and be able to write about it, she insisted that I attend for about two days each week and that I went to some of the special college events during the following term – exactly what I wanted to do!

Sadly, in the end, the book did not include this contribution by Mrs Bragg. In order for it to be topical and to make a contribution to the debate, the book had to be written quickly, and the period for writing coincided with the time that the college was preparing for its first post-16 intake. Mrs Bragg decided that developing new courses and planning for a virtual doubling of staff and student numbers were higher priority activities than writing. I guess that by that time she was also more confident that we would be honest and fair in the major part of the book, so the perceived need for her to contribute was lessened.

I have recounted the long process of gaining access to the CTC, not because I am proud of having been 'successful', or still less that I feel that it is a method to be emulated by others, but because I believe that such a description is necessary to an understanding of the nature of the research and the constraints under which it was subsequently conducted. I am well aware that the account can be read in several different ways, with far from all of them being complimentary. While some readers may see the process in terms of perseverance, others may see it as unwarranted harassment. There were certainly times when I felt that I was engaging in the latter, for it was obvious that Mrs Bragg would have preferred me to have just given up on the research, at least for a few years until the CTC was really established. At several points my own inclination was certainly to give up, for this method of badgering my way into the CTC was far from the ideal of 'informed consent' which I had tried to apply in my earlier research into private schools. Indeed, I felt this to be desirable in practically all research.

My initial reasons for trying to obtain access were innocent, perhaps even naive. I had a continuing research interest in private schools and privatization, and I had previously written about Solihull. I was against the idea of selection of children for particular well funded schools, whether by IQ tests or by motivation and aptitude, simply because I feared the effect of such selection on rejected pupils and other nearby schools. But I was genuinely interested to know how pupils' experiences in a CTC would differ from those of pupils in other maintained schools. It was an example of the simple 'nosiness' of the sociologist about how organizations structure themselves, and how these different structures affect the lives of those within them. I expected that there would be an interesting story to tell about the CTC, which many would wish to read. I recognized that Kingshurst, being the first CTC, was particularly in the public eye, and that the whole scheme was highly controversial politically, but I only came to appreciate the full implications of this highly exposed position as I tried to obtain access and, more directly, once I was in.

I recognized, of course, that it was politically important to the Secretary of State, and to the Conservative government, that some CTCs came into operation quickly. Industry had not responded as generously as had been hoped and there was pressure from the Labour Party and many others to abandon the scheme in the face of rising predicted costs to the Exchequer. What was less obvious to me at the time was that Kingshurst was the first school which the DES had ever directly funded from its start – those involved in establishing the college had little previous experience of setting up any school, let alone a CTC. It only opened on time in September 1988 by an army-like campaign and a tremendous amount of work by a small number of people at Kingshurst itself. All of the design and building for the college had been conducted within very strict time limits but, even then, the builders were still working in the college for the first few weeks of its existence, and among the teachers' first tasks was that of unwrapping the many boxes of equipment, most of which they had not themselves ordered. Only a few of the staff had been appointed more than a couple of months earlier, and there had been little time to plan details of the curriculum.

In any other newly established school it would be expected that 'teething problems' would occur and that these would be gradually overcome in the first few years, but Kingshurst was expected to be a showcase from the very first day. Newspaper and television reporters demanded to see what the college was doing, industrial sponsors wanted to get their money's worth in advertising, and the government wanted to receive publicity and praise for its new venture. From the very first day, through the official opening by Kenneth Baker in November and onwards into 1989, a constant stream of VIPs of one description or another visited the CTC. In many of these cases their visits were clearly of benefit to the CTC and their presence welcomed, but a visit of an hour or two, which might mean a discussion with the principal followed by a tour of the college, is very different from allowing an outsider open access for a term. A researcher staying for such a long period inevitably finds the problems as well the strengths of any school, and while these problems would not be newsworthy in most schools, they certainly would be for Kingshurst.

Once I was inside the CTC, I recognized the total unreasonableness of my desire to conduct any ethnographic research. The risk to the college of allowing me to sit and watch teaching and to talk to students and staff was enormous – not necessarily because anything startling was taking place, but because I could have exaggerated any incident of disruption, misdemeanour or sexism into something 'newsworthy'. Activities common in any school could have been presented in a highly potentially damaging way. Moreover, the college would have found it difficult to defend itself against any possible published comments. I had simply not recognized the risks that I was asking the CTC to take.

The principal's reluctance to allow a researcher into the CTC was compounded by several previous bad experiences with the media. For example, in one particular television documentary an 'industrial tutor' was shown teaching a class of children who looked bored and mystified by what he was saying. In fact, he was not an 'industrial tutor', and the shot of the children was engineered by the programme-makers by telling the children to look sad. While I was at the CTC I witnessed several other media misrepresentations. As articles appeared about the college in the national press, photocopies were circulated in the staff room, and I watched as teachers checked off the errors. It made me recognize even more clearly the need for a balanced account, but also made clear why it had been so difficult to gain access.

Yet, before I gained access, it had seemed to me that there was some public 'right to know' what the CTC was doing (Barnes, 1979; Pring, 1984). It was at the centre of a political controversy where there was little unbiased evidence, and where the taxpayer was paying far more towards the costs of the college than anyone had anticipated. Surely there was some 'right to know' which was more important than the problems that any research would cause the college? I recognized that such a right was not absolute, and that it had to be conditional on not causing 'too much' harm to individuals involved, but it seemed to me that the potential gain to public interest in this case was great. There would be some intrusion into the private lives of those involved, but this could be justified in research on such an important policy issue as CTCs. Having done the research, I am now less happy with this justification than I was originally.

In the end, one of the major factors that led me to continue to harass (or persevere) to obtain access was simply that I knew no researcher was being allowed in. If anyone else had been allowed to do something I might well have given up.

ACCESS AS A PROCESS

One other important feature of the CTC research was that it showed me how important it was to remember that access is a process and not a once-only decision. Negotiating my way past the primary gatekeeper to the CTC was only the start of a long process of access to people and information which was to last throughout the term. In true independent school fashion, my presence at the college had not been discussed with any of the staff. I arrived at 8.00 a.m. on Monday morning, in good time for the daily 'briefing' at 8.10 a.m., to find that none of the staff seemed to know I was coming. They were surprisingly friendly, and those I talked to appeared unconcerned that I would be there for a good part of the term. At that first briefing meeting I wanted to make a short announcement to staff about what I was doing. Unfortunately, in introducing me, Mrs Bragg stated that I was going to be doing 'an evaluation' of the college, a term with which I was most unhappy. In the few seconds I had to decide, I chose to risk antagonizing Mrs Bragg by seeming to correct her, and to say that I actually thought of what I was doing as a 'study' rather than an 'evaluation'. I added that I thought it was rather too early to be thinking about a real evaluation – important though that was. An awkward moment!

I knew that for the first few weeks I would have to be careful not to antagonize anyone, and to try to become part of the background. For the first half of term I thus wanted to adopt the standard technique of following teachers and pupils in their daily tasks. For the first few days I felt very effectively 'managed', for I was assigned to be with only 'safe' and highly trusted teachers – my access was severely restricted. We were all testing the water, but as the weeks passed and I showed myself to be trustworthy, I was able to negotiate access with individual teachers to watch their classes. Towards the end, there were days when I was left to fend for myself completely. In the end, all the teachers I asked agreed to allow me into their classes and most were only asked on the same day as being observed (some with only a few minutes' warning).

To describe what the college was doing, I had to try to understand how it was experienced by the different groups involved. To me, the most important group was the students, and I somehow had to gain access to them as well. No general announcement was made to students about my presence, and I did not ask for such a statement, fearing that it might be accompanied by a demand to be always on best behaviour when I was around. Instead I relied on the student grapevine to spread the news and, in practice, it was some days before any but a tiny few knew who I was. It was four days into the study before any of the teachers in whose classrooms I was observing asked me if I would like to explain to the students what I was doing, and students did not at first ask me individually.

A problem which I had not anticipated was that both teachers and students were reasonably used to having visitors in the college, many of whom would tour the classrooms and ask both staff and students questions. These visitors might be industrialists, sponsors, governors, reporters, politicians and so on and, while teachers were usually given some warning that specific visitors would be around the college, the students generally were not. Indeed, so common were visitors that students identified them as a separate category of participants in the college and it was as if unwritten 'visitors' rules' applied when they were present. Students were often told of the importance of creating a good impression for the college at all times, but especially when visitors were present. It was only after a few days that they began to realize that my own position in the college was different, and began to ask me what I was doing. I always explained that I was independent of the college, that I was writing a book about it and that I wanted to find out what it was like for them to be there. I tried to make it clear that I would not be reporting back anything to teachers and that (generally against their wishes) no students would be named in the book. As the weeks passed, students whom I did not know would check who I was and ask me if I was really writing a book about them. The student 'bush telegraph' obviously worked, but more slowly than I expected: probably because I was simply not particularly interesting compared with the other things that were going on.

The problem with the semi-official status of 'visitor' was that I had to fight to try to indicate that I was not to be treated as a visitor. I was there to observe the college warts and all, and not to be the recipient of image management. This took a long time. It was four weeks before I saw more than the most minor rowdiness or misbehaviour in classrooms. Before that, the presence of a 'visitor' had been such that individuals within groups would sometimes chastise other students, by giving a look in my direction. They wanted to maintain the college's reputation if they possibly could.

However, eventually, I sat in wonder as a group of boys behaved as 12-year-olds do – hitting each other, moving from chair to chair, mock wrestling and then becoming innocent and busy workers at the approach of the teacher. Again I became amazed at the ability of children convincingly to change their topic of conversation mid-sentence as a teacher comes within earshot. The teacher knew little of what was going on behind his back, and I had achieved a little more access.

Pupils tested me, and came to recognize that I could be trusted not to interfere and to keep whatever I saw to myself. Doors were less often opened for me and I began to have to ease my way down crowded corridors, instead of the waves parting as mysteriously as the Red Sea. Pupils began to talk to me instead of my always having to make the running. But the process of becoming accepted and gaining access to their lives was slow, and I certainly would not claim that it went very deep. As late as the seventh week of research, a boy in front of me in the queue for lunch handed me a tray and cutlery in true 'visitor' form. I cursed him under my breath as I tactfully thanked him. I tried to negotiate a 'special' independent role for myself with the CTC, but it would be foolish to pretend that it was fully successful. Although I saw more of some groups than others, there was insufficient time to develop the sort of close relationships which have characterized the major studies of ethnographers such as Ball (1981), Measor and Woods (1984), Aggleton (1987) or Mac an Ghaill (1988). I retained the status of adult throughout, never approaching honorary studenthood, and thus never being privy to the secret world of childhood.

However, I do feel that I approached a desirable 'insignificant other' status with most of the students. They recognized that I existed, knew why I was there and assumed that I would do nothing to try to affect them. The status attained was very similar to that of most adults waiting at a bus stop with children who have just been released from school. The children will ignore the adult and continue to push and shove, shout and scream, on the assumption that the adult will do nothing about it. The wise adult will stay on the sidelines and not become involved unless one of the children is seriously threatened. But adult status will allow the 'insignificant other' status to be overthrown if the adult so desires. At any point during the research I felt I could easily have acted 'as a teacher' and the students would have acquiesced to this assumed authority.

—3

Gaining access to research sites

ACCESS AS A PROBLEM

Gaining access to research sites has long been one of the 'classic' topics within methodology books about ethnographic and qualitative research. Hammersley and Atkinson (1995), for example, devote a whole chapter to 'access', Burgess (1984a) has 'starting research and gaining access' for the title of his second chapter, while the even older book by Johnson (1975) has a chapter that discusses 'gaining and managing entree in field research'. Access is also a popular topic for ethnographers to consider in their reflexive accounts. The several collections of such accounts edited by Robert Burgess (1984b, 1985a, b) and my own similar edited volumes (Walford, 1987c, 1991a, 1994c, 1998a) have numerous examples of the genre. These accounts usually offer descriptions of successful and unsuccessful attempts to enter research sites such as schools and classrooms, and offer an array of tactics that have met with success in the past. It is always emphasized that access is fraught with difficulties and that, within ethnography, it is a continuous process. As I have argued in Chapter 2, even after those with power within a school have been eventually persuaded to give access, the researcher has continually to negotiate further access to observe classrooms and interview teachers and students. At a deeper level, access can be seen as a process of building relationships with people within the organization. The aim is that teachers and students learn to trust the researcher to the point where they are prepared to be open and honest about their perceptions and beliefs. Access is thus never total, but might be seen as an incremental continuum, where the researcher is gradually able to move from the initial permission to enter the buildings to a series of developed and trusting relationships with some teachers and students. Access is also always provisional, as permission and trust can be withdrawn at any time by headteacher, teachers, parents or students.

Geoff Troman (1996) has suggested that access to schools has recently become even more difficult than before. He argues that the macro-changes in the organization, management and content of schooling that have resulted from government legislation since 1988 have led to schools becoming more reluctant to agree to become a site for a research study. Among the changes that he notes as important are the intensification of teachers' work, the negative views that teachers hold about the usefulness of research, the increased fear of surveillance by external 'experts' that has resulted from Ofsted and Key Stage testing and the increasing numbers of other researchers already in the schools as a result of the growth of masters and doctoral students and students undertaking research as part of their more school-based initial teacher training. If Troman is correct that access is becoming more difficult and that these difficulties stem from macro-changes, it is increasingly important that the micro-level interactions that lead to access are effective. Researchers can do nothing directly to reduce the effects of these macro-level changes on schools, so the process of obtaining access needs to take these new constraints into consideration. Just as salespeople conduct research on the commercial environment within which they are selling, and take this into account in the way they promote their products, so educational researchers must take macro-changes in the educational environment into account in their approach to gaining access. They must learn to 'sell' themselves and their research more effectively.

SELLING YOURSELF AND YOUR RESEARCH

In this chapter I wish to argue that researchers have much to learn from salespeople and that obtaining access to research sites is much like selling a product or service. The many popular sales and marketing books that abound in bookshops offer numerous insights about how to gain and maintain access. I am not suggesting that any of these books should be followed slavishly, or that their 'tried and tested' 'secrets of success' or 'vital ingredients' that lead to 'the perfect sale' should be taken too seriously. But what these books do is encourage salespeople to think about the access process and how they are presenting themselves and their products or services to potential clients and purchasers. These books deal in hyperbole, but in advocating selling as 'the world's greatest profession' (Denny, 1997) and by claiming that 'Living life successfully *is* selling!' (Carmichael, 1994) these authors remind us that researchers need to take the process of gaining access seriously. We have to be clear how our research can be sold to those who can grant us access and clarify what the potential benefits are to them. In selling, it may have become a platitude to say that 'people don't buy products, they buy benefits', but it is none the less true. We need to be clear about what benefits researchers, the process of research and the research findings themselves can offer.

The type of book that I am suggesting might be useful is hardly likely to find a place on academic booklists. They largely lack any sophisticated theoretical or research base and tend to present anecdote and opinion as fact. Even business schools would be hesitant to recommend them, and most educational research methodologists would probably not see them as having any relevance. These books have titles such as *The Perfect Sale: All You Need to Get It Right First Time* (Thornely and Lees, 1994), *Selling 101* (McGaulley, 1995), which promotes itself as 'Expert advice for small business', *Selling to Win* (Denny, 1988, 1997), which is advertised as the 'UK number one best seller', *Four Square Selling* (Carmichael, 1994) or, perhaps the most 'respectable looking', *The American Marketing Association Handbook for Successful Selling* (Kimball, 1994). Even books with such titles as *Persuasive Business Presentations* (Robinson, 1993) or *Powerful Presentations* (Ehrenborg and Mattock, 1993) have many points of interest. I am suggesting that we swallow our pride and see how highly successful salespeople can help us gain and retain access.

APPROACH

Rather than following an exact formula from one of these many books, it is more useful to organize an account in terms of a very general structure. One very simple way of thinking about the selling process is through the somewhat unfortunate acronym AIDS, where the fourfold formulation is: Approach, Interest, Desire, Sale. In most of the following I use entry to a school as the main example, but the discussion and suggestions are equally applicable to the many other institutions and organizations where learning occurs. Equally, although much of the discussion is framed around the initial entry to a school that might be granted by a headteacher, it can also be applied to individual teachers and students within the school.

According to the 'selling' books, in trying to make a sale, the first step is to seek prospects who are likely to want to buy your product or service. A great deal of work is done before any direct contact is made, for it is necessary to approach the correct prospects, and not waste time and energy on those who are unlikely customers. Similarly, in making an approach to a school or any other organization to conduct research, the ethnographer needs to make sure that contact is made with the person most likely to be receptive to the research. Prospecting is the term used for looking for someone who might be sympathetic to whatever it is that you are selling. This requires research before making any approach. So, to obtain entry to a school to conduct an ethnography, it is worthwhile doing some preliminary research on people within a number of potentially suitable schools. The aim is to build a file of information on the key people in each school. One obvious possibility is to look for any university connections. Someone who has spent time doing his or her own research might be expected to be more likely to agree to outside research than someone who has not. It is relatively easy to find the academic qualifications of those in the senior management team of a school and the title of a dissertation for a masters or doctoral degree can often be found from the university or on the Internet. If someone has a doctorate, it is worth seeing if he or she has published anything – again, this is now easily done on the Internet. If a headteacher has researched and published on management structures or special educational needs, for example, this is certainly worth knowing before making any approach. The approach can then be framed to include elements that might be likely to appeal.

It is usually important that the person approached is 'qualified'. In this case the term means 'qualified to deal with the issue' – in other words, able to grant access. In schools this is usually straightforward as the headteacher will be the obvious qualified person. But this is not so in all schools – in some the chair of governors has a major say, while in others the senior management team may expect to be consulted. So it is wise to investigate these people as well as the headteacher and to try to discover where the power lies. Troman (1996) gives an example where the headteacher appeared to be enthusiastic about his proposed research, but where the senior management team (whom he did not talk to) rejected it. It is possible to see this as erroneously making his sales presentation to an individual when he should have insisted on making the presentation to the group.

Several of the books on selling emphasize that they are only systematizing what they regard as 'common sense'. But this act of systematizing and naming is useful, for it encourages us to think through various possibilities. A 'referred lead' is a possible new client who has been suggested by an existing client. In attempts to gain access to a research site this might be seen as the use of a mutual friend or colleague. If there is someone else in the school whom the researcher already knows, this person might be able to act as a 'link' and as a recommendation. Obviously, it is important here to contact the mutual friend or colleague first to ask for help and to try to ascertain the relationship between this person and the 'qualified' person. A further development of this idea is that it might be possible to exploit a shared experience or interest. Headteachers are more likely to give access if they can perceive the researcher as being 'one of us'. A researcher who is able to show some shared experience has a real advantage.

In my own early ethnographic work on boys' public boarding schools (Walford, 1986a, 1987d), I approached access in a rather haphazard way. I wrote letters to headmasters and had five refusals before one gave me an interview. I discuss that interview in more detail below, but one of the important aspects was that the Headmaster spent time checking the question 'Are you one of us?' As I had briefly taught in three of these schools, he was able to answer that question in the affirmative, but only after he had extracted the name of someone whom we both knew from one of the schools who could act as a 'referee' for me. In this case, I had not contacted this person beforehand and I was not even sure that he would remember me with any clarity. But evidently the reference he gave (alongside that from the academic referee that was also demanded) was convincing, for an invitation to conduct the research soon followed. I had been lucky, for I had not thought through these possibilities beforehand and had done very little prospecting. It is also worth noting that, once into the system, it was very easy to be given permission to conduct research in other boys' independent boarding schools. The first headmaster gave me permission to use his name as a 'referred lead' and the headmaster of the second school simply telephoned him for a reference. I was let loose in this second school for a whole term with hardly a question being asked about what I was going to be doing.

Another important term in selling is 'gatekeeper'. In ethnography, the term is often used for the person who is able to grant access to the research site but, in selling, the gatekeeper is the person who is able to give you access to the prospect. I have found that secretaries are well worth being good to. They are able to help or halt the research approach according to how they are dealt with. As described in Chapter 2, my route into the first CTC at Solihull was particularly tortuous. I made dozens of telephone calls to the college before I was eventually able to meet the principal, but the various secretaries were most helpful, and I gradually built up a great deal of information on the activities of the college and the principal before even setting foot in the buildings (Walford, 1991b; Walford and Miller, 1991).

One of the reasons why I probably had so much difficulty in gaining access to the boys' public boarding schools was that I misunderstood the purpose of my letter to the schools. Had I read any of the 'selling' books beforehand, I might have been clearer that the purpose of any letter is to gain an initial interview, and not to gain access. Instead of a short letter that raised interest in the proposal without giving too many details, I wrote fairly long letters that included far too much information. Every additional piece of information gives a chance for an objection or problem to be raised in the mind of the reader. Detailed letters make it far too easy to find a 'good reason' to object. Thus, if a letter is to be used, it should be brief. If it is possible to include a referred lead or some aspects of common experience, then this is useful. If a letter is to be used, it should indicate that a telephone call will follow to try to fix an appointment. Having sent such a letter, it may be possible to use this as a way past any secretary who screens calls.

Denny (1997) puts the purpose of letters and telephone calls succinctly: 'Remember that the purpose of writing a letter is to sell your telephone call which should, in turn, sell the appointment. Another great principle of salesmanship: *you can only sell one thing at a time*' (Denny, 1997, p. 72, emphasis and sexism in the original). In a similar way, Kimball (1994, p. 87) uses large lettering to stress 'The purpose of the telephone call is to get the appointment.' They both then go into great detail about how a telephone call might be conducted, giving ways of getting past secretaries and, most importantly, not getting into the position where a face-to-face appointment is unnecessary. They indicate ways of avoiding saying too much on the telephone, and making it seem imperative that a meeting occurs. If researchers are just after a single interview it might be possible to explain the need during a telephone conversation and obtain a positive reply. But no one is going to give permission for an ethnographic enquiry explained through a telephone call – the focus must be gaining a meeting.

Now much of this (once we have read it) does indeed seem to be 'common sense', but the selling books take far more care with approaches than most researchers. The use of the telephone is one area where 'selling' books have a great deal to offer educational researchers trying to gain access. Whereas most research guides have little to say on the issue, these 'selling' books are brimming with ideas. Consider (and perhaps reject) the 'handy hints' about using a telephone. It is obvious that one should plan the call, and be enthusiastic, but is it obvious that one should know what reaction is desired, that we might sound more decisive if we stand up when using the telephone or that it might be a good idea to smile while on the telephone to project a better manner (Denny, 1997, p. 79)? And why not tape-record any telephone calls to see how we sound and to learn how to improve performance (McGaulley, 1995, pp. 42–3)? And what is the best way of dealing with voice mail? What time should be suggested for a meeting? These selling books have more ideas on these matters than any educational or social research methods books I have read.

INTEREST

The objective of any telephone call is to get a face-to-face interview. Despite the increasing success of telephone sales, it is widely accepted that the best way to sell is on a face-to-face level. Only fools make large purchases from telephone sales, and educational researchers are not usually dealing with fools. Headteachers and others who can grant access to schools and classrooms are not going to do so without actually seeing the researcher face-to-face. The purpose of the telephone call is to create some initial interest and to fix a date for an interview. The prospect has to become convinced that a meeting is both worthwhile and necessary. On no account should the prospect be given the chance to say 'no' on the telephone.

Once an appointment has been obtained, the preparation for and conduct of that interview must also be taken very seriously. One of the central tenets behind any of these 'selling' books is that the good salesperson is not born, but made. These books promise that all moderately competent human beings can learn skills and improve their techniques such that they can become successful salespeople. I would suggest that the need for such skills might be greater for academics and researchers than for most 'moderately competent human beings'. In my experience, educational researchers tend to be apologetic about their research; they balk at the idea of selling themselves or their research to others. Yet this is what they must do if they are to gain access.

My early attempts to gain access to the boys' independent boarding schools are indicative:

> My interview with the headmaster of the first school to express interest lasted for only twenty minutes, but I experienced it as being far longer and more nerve-racking than any of the interviews I had for academic appointments. He was extremely sharp and shrewd and demanded precise answers to a range of questions about my purposes and methodology. I had envisaged presenting myself as an open ethnographer and had thus prepared only a fairly flimsy outline of the sort of areas in which I was interested – I intended, in true ethnographic style, to develop my research strategy once actually in the school. The headmaster, however, had a rather different view of how research should be conducted, where questions are tightly framed, questionnaires or interview schedules developed, and representative samples drawn from populations. It quickly became obvious that the role of 'open ethnographic researcher' was one which he would not entertain. (Walford, 1987d, p. 50)

I had done insufficient groundwork and I had allowed the prospect to control the situation. In this case I was able to retrieve the situation by showing considerable flexibility in my proposed research methodology, but I was very lucky. More thought about how to interest the Headmaster in the research would have greatly improved my chances.

Although there is now much greater concern about preparation for interviews, in particular where those interviews are with powerful people (for example, Fitz and Halpin, 1994; McHugh, 1994), I believe that many researchers would benefit from appraising some of the presentation skills suggested in 'selling' books. Most educational researchers are now aware of the obvious aspects of self-presentation at interviews. We think about how smart to look, what clothes to wear and what degree of formality to try to adopt. Of course, we do not always get it right:

> In my recent research on sponsored grant-maintained schools, for example, I went to interview the Headteacher of a Transcendental Meditation Primary school that wished to

obtain state funding, but whose application was eventually rejected. I dressed reasonably smartly, but not in a suit. With a tie in my pocket, I checked whether I should wear it with the local taxi driver who was driving me to the school. 'No, they're all very laid-back. It's all very informal' he informed me. In fact, the staff were all very smartly dressed – all the male teachers had ties, and all the children were in stylish uniforms! I looked and felt out of place with my open collar.

But such aspects are trivial compared with the care that good salespeople take with their interviews. The various 'selling' books have pages of ideas about how to make sure your position in the room is a good one, how to control and interpret body language, how to deal with presentation aids and how to sell yourself as much as the product or service. But two points of emphasis in many of these books are the use of questions and the need to listen to the customer. In Denny's (1997, p. 85) words, 'If you were to ask me what I consider to be the single most important skill in mastering the art of professional selling, I would say it is the ability to ask questions.' Kimball agrees and states:

> when a professional salesperson makes a presentation, he or she will listen more than speak. In a presentation, you should listen – with the prospect talking – at least 55 percent of the time. If you are doing more than 45 percent of the talking, it's time to pull back on the reins, talk less, and listen more. You aren't going to persuade the prospect with your brilliant oratory. On the contrary, you persuade the prospect by getting him or her to talk. (Kimball, 1994, p. 106)

While we should not take too seriously the exact percentages (they are hardly likely to be the results of systematic research), it is worth stopping and thinking about the general statement. My feeling is that it is unlikely that most educational researchers would try to interest anyone in their research in this way. For most of us, preparation for an initial interview means working out what we want to say; we hardly ever think of what our prospects might want to say. Yet, according to these 'selling' books, questions can enable us to tune into prospects and their thinking, and to identify their needs and motives. Questions can help to establish a greater rapport and, at the same time, give greater control to the person asking questions. They can help us to shape our presentation more carefully so that it is more likely to be accepted.

In my experience headteachers definitely like to talk. When an appointment is arranged by telephone, they are often careful to explain how busy they are and how little time they can spare but, once in the office, they seem to have far more time than expected. In my recent work on sponsored grant-maintained schools (Walford, 1997, 1998b), for example, when I interviewed headteachers and sponsors I usually asked for 45 minutes. None of the interviews was this short, and some went on for over two hours. A great deal of that time was spent in them talking about issues that were not directly relevant to my own concerns but, by listening to their agenda, I was able to obtain very full answers to my own specific questions.

In a similar way, when trying to gain ethnographic access, listening to the headteacher's needs and desires can mean that the research proposal can be framed more closely to be more attuned to those requirements. Listening gives the salesperson 'buying signals' and indicates potential hesitations and objections. For the researcher, listening can give similar information about potential concerns which, as discussed in the next section, can then be dealt with before they are even voiced.

The 'selling' books use a great deal of space on presentational aids. In this case, questions of how to ensure that overhead projectors and computer graphics actually work are important. How are high quality visuals created? Should the salesperson have leaflets and other promotional materials and, if so, what type, and at what point should they be handed out? They also remind us that the salesperson himself or herself is the prime presentational aid. Kimball (1994, p. 110) celebrates this as: 'Remember: It's show time! Your presentation is a performance, designed to interest, entertain, and persuade. To be successful, it needs to be completely and perfectly rehearsed. Note that I said rehearsed, not canned.'

Now, it is unlikely that educational researchers would wish to see themselves as actors on stage or to use sophisticated aids in any presentation, but it is worth thinking about the impression that we wish to make. Visual inputs can be particularly effective, so some simple aids might be worth considering. In particular, it is worth trying to build and present an image of success, so taking along an example of the results of previous research would be helpful. A book based on previous research also has the advantage of slightly deflecting the discussion away from the details of the particular research that is being planned in this situation. An important book written by someone else might also have a similar effect. However, the aim would not be to deceive, simply to indicate the type of academic 'end-product' that the research might lead to.

DESIRE

There are two main aspects to raising the desire to purchase an item or service: overcoming objections and stressing benefits.

Within an interview numerous doubts may arise in the prospect's mind. It is usually thought better to deal with the most obvious possible doubts before they have been voiced. This shows that the salesperson is considerate and recognizes that the prospect may have some misgivings. In research, the doubts that will probably most often come to mind are those that concern the smooth running of the organization and the investment of time that staff and pupils might be asked to make. After all, schools have purposes other than to act as research sites. An ethnographer is in a very good position to quell some of these doubts, as the objective is always to disrupt the everyday life of the organization as little as possible. Any interviews are conducted at times convenient to those interviewed, and any observations are designed, as far as possible, to have no effect on those observed.

In an increasingly market-driven system, headteachers are often concerned about any potential bad effects on the school's reputation. This is easily dealt with by discussing confidentiality and anonymity before these problems are raised. Troman (1996) provides a list of macro-changes in the school environment that are also indicators of potential objections. It is useful making a judicial consideration of how each of these may be relevant to the particular target school, and showing how the particular research will take account of these problems.

If it is correct that 'people don't buy goods and services, but buy benefits', it is essential that desire is developed by stressing the benefits of the research. If convincing benefits cannot be found, then the research should be abandoned. It is very unlikely that access to conduct an ethnography will be granted without a clear understanding and explanation of the potential benefits.

Academic researchers often think of potential benefits only in terms of the benefits that might eventually flow from the results of the study. Although this is of prime importance to the researcher, such benefits alone are unlikely to convince most headteachers.

They offer no immediate benefits to the school and, if there are any long-term benefits, then all schools will benefit whether or not they agree to take part in the research.

An alternative is to offer more direct benefits. Thus many ethnographers have been prepared to become supply teachers when necessary or to take a class or two on a regular basis (e.g. Lacey, 1970; Burgess, 1983). This trade-off has obvious benefits for the school as it saves money, and it can have benefits for the researcher as well: in that it can help in getting to know the school's culture and in providing a ready group of students. But the role conflicts can be great and the time involved in lesson preparation and marking can overwhelm the research. If this sort of benefit is to be offered, it is probably better to suggest help with sports or other extra-curricular activities.

What researchers often forget is the direct benefits to the school, its teachers and students that the process of research can bring. Just as headteachers can benefit from talking in confidence to someone else about the school, so teachers can benefit from discussions about their work and careers. Students, too, can benefit from the process of being asked to think about their learning activities, their examination preparation or their plans for the future. A good salesperson will ask past customers about what they liked and disliked about their purchases. If, at the end of any research, educational researchers were systematically to ask headteachers, teachers and students about what benefits they thought they had gained from the research process, future access procedures could be enhanced.

Of course, there is a need to be careful about the agendas of those with power. It is far from unknown for headteachers to suggest that researchers observe certain teachers whom they want information about. The teacher may not be able to refuse a request, but the researcher should be very clear that observations and interviews with teachers are confidential and will not be fed back to the headteacher. It is wise to resist any suggestion that the researcher's topic be shifted to one that focuses on a particular problem for the school. It might be highly tempting, but the problem of feeding back information to the headteacher and others with power will not only compromise the research, but also lead to severe ethical problems. As researchers, we often have to decide 'whose side we are on' (Becker, 1968) and it is worth remembering that students may form one of the 'sides'. However, appropriate feedback to the school is an obvious benefit that most researchers can offer. If the focus is on bullying, for example, the researcher may be eventually in a good position to offer an in-service training session. The researcher's breadth of reading about the issue will be usually far greater than teachers have time for, so much of any feedback session can deal with general findings as well as the findings from the school itself.

The researcher's greater knowledge of the academic literature about the broad area of research should not be underestimated, for it is possible for some ethnographers accurately to present themselves as consultants on particular issues. Where the study focuses on more than one school, the researcher might offer the benefit of knowledge about other (obviously anonymized) schools and about general structural features. Such information can be of great benefit.

SALE

The final stage is the 'sale'. The prospect agrees to pay for 10,000 widgets or, in our case, the headteacher agrees to grant access in return for the benefits that he or she believes will follow. The 'selling' books have many tactics that might be used to bring a discussion to a successful conclusion. Many of these suggestions may involve far more 'pressure' than most researchers would be willing to use, and are unlikely to be appropriate within the education system. But the 'selling' books' viewpoint of seeing 'objections as your friends' and the reminder that 'your objective is to close the sale, not to complete the presentation' (Kimball, 1994, p. 175) are well worth consideration.

There comes a time in all sales presentations when it is best to start closing the sale. This time might be before the salesperson has completed all that could be said, and before some features of the product have been covered. Thus, in an access interview, it may be better to move to a decision at an unexpected time. When there are strong 'buying signals', it may be best to ask for a decision at that point. In the research context, such signals can vary considerably. They might include questions on the details of procedures to be followed, indications of who it might be thought desirable for the researcher to meet or even comments on a more collegial basis. Such signals need to be interpreted with care, and equal care needs to be taken with the method chosen for closing the agreement.

If the researcher has really generated a desire to take part in the research, it may be possible to use the 'scarcity' tactic. As Kimball

(1994, p. 176) states, 'People are motivated to buy when they feel the opportunity to buy may be lost.' Only a very limited number of schools will be involved in any ethnographic study, and the researcher selects particular schools to offer the opportunity to take part. The chance to be part of the research is limited, for the researcher does not have unlimited time or other resources. Is it too far fetched that researchers could generate a feeling that schools would be privileged to take part?

Another possibility, which may have only limited applicability, is the idea of the 'assumed close'. When the prospect has offered no objections, it might be possible to simply ask: 'When shall I start? Would next Tuesday be OK, or next Wednesday? Even said lightheartedly, it might well work in some cases. Another possibility, when there are signs of uncertainty, is to 'pass down the hierarchy'. If entry to a particular school is very important, and the headteacher is showing indecisiveness, pressure to make a decision may just go the wrong way. In many ways it is easier to say 'no' than 'yes', and our objective should be to avoid giving the chance of a 'no'. A suggestion that it might be a good idea to talk with the deputy head or other appropriate members of the senior management team might be one way of avoiding the 'no'. The advantage is that once the research has been discussed with that person, it may be possible to 'pass down the hierarchy' again so that several members of staff become involved with the research before any decision is made. The school may drift into a positive decision without knowing it.

There is also the possibility of some negotiation on the 'price' to be paid by the school in return for the benefits expected. The decision to grant access is not a simple yes or no. Just as salespeople are prepared to reduce their price and offer 'special discounts' to particular customers, so the researcher can negotiate the extent of access desired. In my rather chaotic negotiations for access to the boys' independent boarding school, I originally asked for six weeks (which I actually thought was too short) unstructured access. I was granted four weeks, under more tightly specified conditions. Perhaps if I had asked for eight I might have been granted six. If the cost to the school of granting access can be reduced, yet the same potential benefits are perceived to be forthcoming, then a deal might be easier to strike.

IS IT ETHICAL?

I have suggested that a selective and critical reading of some of the 'selling' guides might be of benefit to researchers wishing to gain access to research sites. The enthusiasm and care with which good salespeople approach selling should be a challenge for our own often rather poorly thought through tactics. If we don't take their suggestions too slavishly, these books can offer many insights. Not only can they give ideas about how to gain initial access to the buildings of an organization, they can help researchers with the continual process of gaining and maintaining access to the various people who work there. In ethnography, there is a continual need to find 'ways-in and to stay-in' (Beynon, 1983), and a study of selling might help ethnographers to develop their own procedures.

But is such selling ethical? Denny (1997, p. 10) asks the reader to consider the old saying 'A good salesperson can sell anything', and then goes on to say, 'It is rubbish. A good salesperson can only sell anything if he or she believes in it. Product belief is essential.' Being positive about the research that you wish to conduct, and being able to show the benefits that could be obtained from being involved in the research, does not involve lying or even being 'economical with the truth'. I believe that if we can't find convincing benefits, then we should not be doing the research.

Selling has a bad name, but good selling is concerned with selling not just to one-off customers, but also to the 'repeat buyer'. It is widely recognized that repeat buyers need to be cultivated, and the easiest way of doing this is for the product to be of a high quality. People do not purchase twice a product that has not given them the benefits that were claimed for it, or which has actually cost them more than they originally expected. They do not recommend to friends services that have failed to deliver.

But, of course, there are some occasions when the major benefits of doing research do not accrue to the school, teachers or students who are the subjects of the research. There are times when potential benefits are gained by the wider society or wider social group, rather than those directly involved in the research. In many cases researchers can still obtain access by selling the benefits of feeling altruistic and of acting in such a way as to develop teaching as a research-based profession. However, it is still probably easier to gain access to study teachers' working conditions and the possible intensification of work practices than it is to study classroom management techniques.

As I explained in Chapter 2, my research on the Kingshurst CTC is an example where the direct benefits to the school were very low and the potential threat that research presented was great. I recognized that the research might actually cause some harm to the college, and that there would have to be some intrusion into the private lives of those closely involved, but I believed that there was a public 'right to know' about how this important policy initiative was working in practice (Barnes, 1979; Pring, 1984). My attempts to gain access spread over many months, culminating in an unexpected (for her) meeting that I engineered with the principal away from the college. My selling was hard, if not crude. She did not want a book written about the college during its early years but, if one was to be written at all, she felt that she should write it. The bargain we eventually struck was that I would give her the immediate benefit of space for a 15,000 word unedited chapter written by her in the book that I intended to publish. Importantly, in order for me really to understand the college and be able to write about it, she also insisted that I attend for about two days a week for a term and that I go to some of the special college events. This was exactly what I wanted to do. My actions reduced the potential costs of granting access, and introduced some direct benefits.

CONCLUSION

While the 'problem of access' has long been a classic topic within methodology books about ethnographic and qualitative research, I have not found any that examine the insights that might be gained from the business of selling. Commercial salespeople live on their ability to sell, and they have developed a range of techniques that they can draw upon to help them. These techniques may well not be based upon systematic research and may be idiosyncratic but, at least in some circumstances, they work. I have argued that ethnographers and qualitative researchers might benefit from knowing about some of these techniques and I hope that, next time readers are in a bookshop with an array of business books in front of them, they will invest a little time and money in reading one of these books on selling. Most of them only take an hour or two to read from cover to cover.

First days in the field

INTRODUCTION

My title for this chapter is rather presumptuously copied directly from Blanche Geer's classic chapter first published in 1964. That chapter was one of eleven included in Phillip E. Hammond's path-breaking edited collection *Sociologists at Work*, which was the first to present case histories of the research process that lay behind major research projects. As Howard S. Becker is quoted as saying on the cover of the paperback edition (Hammond, 1967), 'As every researcher knows, there is more to doing research than is dreamt of in philosophies of science, and texts in methodology offer answers to only a fraction of the problems one encounters.' That edited collection was the first to present what have come to be known as 'confessional tales' (van Maanen, 1988) about the sociological research process.

Geer's contribution is about an educational research project. With such famous names as Howard S. Becker, Anselm L. Strauss and Everett Hughes, she had just finished working on the project that had led to *Boys in White* (Becker *et al.*, 1961) and was setting out on a new, but related, project on the culture of college life that culminated in *Making the Grade* (Becker *et al.*, 1968). In her chapter, Geer examines the fieldnotes that she took in the first eight days of fieldwork among new undergraduates at the University of Kansas who were attending introductory 'preview' days. Her concern is with the relationships between initial fieldwork experiences, her thinking before entering the field and her final understanding achieved at the end of the research process. She shows the way in which strategies and concepts developed before entry to the field can quickly change during the initial stages of fieldwork, and shows how some tentative hypotheses that developed in the first days became major themes in the subsequent research. She argues that, while early fieldwork reaches few conclusions, it may nevertheless have far-reaching effects on the rest of the research.

This chapter is concerned with my own 'first days in the field' on a new research project. It considers the potential impact of early fieldwork and also discusses the ways in which past experiences and transient personal phenomena may influence what the observer sees and records.

ENTERING THE FIELD

The research project with which this chapter is concerned is a comparative study of policy on schooling for religious minorities. The three-year project has the aim of examining policy formulation and implementation within England and the Netherlands, looking at national, local and school level policy and practice. My previous research on sponsored grant-maintained schools led me to choose evangelical Christianity and Islam as the two minority religious groups to be studied (Walford, 1997, 1998b). In order to understand the details of policy, at the school level, the research involves conducting 'compressed ethnographies' (Walford, 1991b, p. 91) in several primary schools in each of the two countries. Here, over the three-year period of the research, the aim was to spend about three weeks in four schools in each country.

As my recent research had been concerned with policy at the legislative level, it was some considerable time since I had conducted any ethnographic work. In fact, the work for *City Technology College* (Walford and Miller, 1991) was the last real ethnographic study – and that was, of course, of a secondary school. I had never conducted an ethnography of a primary school, and my most recent visits to primary schools had been to conduct interviews with headteachers at Al-Furqan primary school in Birmingham (which had successfully applied to become a sponsored grant-maintained school) and the Maharishi School of the Age of Enlightenment, Ormskirk, Lancashire (which was rejected). At the latter I had been quickly shown round the school – children all in uniform, small groups, very polite – but such a tour could not even be regarded as 'instantaneous ethnography'.

So I decided that, before I started research in an evangelical Christian or Muslim school, it would be beneficial at least to spend a little time in a state-maintained primary school. I chose a multi-ethnic primary school in London primarily because I had easy access through a friend who taught at the school. In this case the choice of school was not important beyond that the school was 'good' as measured by Ofsted inspections. The school is a two-class entry primary school, and has relatively new buildings with good physical facilities and resources. It is spacious and light, and has a welcoming and safe architectural feel. It is well known as a 'good' school. It has a highly stable staff with a range of years of teaching experience. At the time of my initial approach to enter the school, my purpose was straightforward – it was simply to allow me to gain some insights into some of the activities of a multi-ethnic primary school. Entry to the school was easily arranged and two teachers whom I had not previously met gave their consent to allow me to be with them in their classrooms for one day each. I was not particularly concerned about what age group I observed, except that I did not want nursery or reception children. Years 3 and 5 suited my initial interests well.

By the time I actually entered the school, I realized that I should consider writing a paper about these initial days in the field. This was in accord with a recent article I had written on publishing research, where I had argued that 'My writing, and to a great extent the conduct of the research itself, is always structured around particular books and journal articles that I wish to write' (Walford, 1998c). If I was going to do this preliminary observation, it might just as well be useful in several ways. Conferences always act as a spur to writing and, although I had co-organized the annual Ethnography and Education conference for three years, I had not actually presented a paper at it for several. The forthcoming conference had a focus on gender issues, which I felt I might be able to say something about. My most obvious 'foreshadowed problems' (Malinowski, 1922, p. 8) for the two-day experience thus centred on gender issues. How would someone who had never observed in primary schools make sense of gender issues? How would the gender-related activities of this primary school compare with the many older descriptions that I had read? Would gender be identifiable as an important differentiator between children?

THE GENDER AGENDA

In selecting gender differentiation as a key area to observe, I needed to do little new homework. I had taught sociology of education for many years and had an extensive booklist on the subject of gender and education. Although my own writing on gender is limited, I had just completed co-editing a volume entitled *Children Learning in*

Context (Walford and Massey, 1998), which contained several ethnographic studies examining aspects of gender in primary and other schools. I knew what to 'expect' – or, at least, what sort of activities it would be worth commenting on.

The first days in the field are often seen as the most challenging and emotionally awkward. Meeting any new group of people in an environment which they already inhabit can be uncomfortable and embarrassing, but it can be particularly so where those being met are to be research 'subjects' and do not fully understand the nature of ethnographic research. Yet the first days of research are also often seen as particularly exciting, for so much of what is experienced and observed is new to the researcher. Indeed, the researcher is often overwhelmed by the amount of new information that it is necessary to take in. Bogdan and Taylor (1975) advise limiting observation periods at first to an hour or less, and spending a great deal of time writing fieldnotes. They remind us that 'Observations are only useful to the extent that they can be remembered and accurately recorded' (p. 42). In contrast, Geer (1964) recorded all her notes at the end of each full day. I followed the latter's example and dictated notes into a tape-recorder at the end of each day. There is an obvious problem here that the notes I made may have been coloured by some sort of 'generalized' impressions of the day, but there was little else I could do with such a short visit. The quotations in this chapter are from those dictated notes.

Given that I had gender as a focus for my observations, it was inevitable that many of the notes I made would relate to that issue. There was much to record. From the names on the coat-pegs (pairs of hooks, one above the other, each pair having same-sex names) to the boys' football in the playground which occupied nearly all of the main space, gender differentiation and stereotypical gender reinforcement was sadly very evident.

Perhaps the most obvious difference was in the way the children looked. The school has a uniform code which is strongly enforced. The boys' summer uniform sees them in dark short trousers, white shirt and tie. In winter, I was told, they must wear long trousers. In contrast, the girls have to wear a skirt with their white shirt and tie. Do boys' legs get cold in the winter and girls' legs not? And why do they have to be differentiated in this way? Are skirts (or short trousers) what the children would choose to wear?

Of course, one would not now expect to see the extent of crude gender differentiation that was found by such researchers as

Stanworth (1983), Evans (1988), Wolpe (1988), Delamont (1990) or Measor and Sikes (1992). I did not observe registers being called with the names of boys and girls separately listed, or see lines of children where they were divided into these two gender groups. Generations of teachers in training have read books on gender and schooling, and it might be hoped that younger teachers, at least, would not make simplistic assumptions or inadvertently reinforce gender stereotypes. Yet, even in these first two days, there were examples where slightly more sophisticated assumptions were being made. For example, physical education was taken by boys and girls together. In picking teams for rounders, boys were certainly not competing with girls, yet the teacher-set rules for choosing were that each of the two 'team leaders' had to pick first a boy then a girl in turn, such that the teams were nearly balanced in terms of the number of boys and girls. What sort of assumptions about sport and gender were operating here?

In the first class I observed, the children sat at tables of four. Each table had two boys and two girls, and they sat with each child of one sex diagonally positioned to the child of the same sex. The teacher explained: 'They are at an age when the boys say that they don't like being with the girls, but they really get on fine.' And, of course, they did. But the cost of this 'getting on' was that the children had little choice about where they sat, and the gender implications of the arrangement were obvious to all those involved. Stereotypical ideas about girls and boys led to a pattern of seating where the girls were seen as 'pacifying' the potentially disruptive activities of the boys.

Another obvious feature of the school is that it is staffed by women only. I had my lunch and coffee in the staffroom on both days, and the only other man I saw in there was a peripatetic music teacher who was in and out of the room within about one minute. His rapid exit suggested that he was taking his coffee mug with him to his own haven of safety. But perhaps my interpretation is simply my reaction to what, for me, was an unusual environment. To me, it was not male-unfriendly, but it was not male-friendly either.

I wished to offer a little gift to the staff for allowing me to observe in the school. I asked my friend who had negotiated access for me what would be appropriate. Without any hesitation she recommended cream cakes, which I duly bought. The gift was greatly appreciated. I bought more cakes than I expected would ever get eaten, yet they all quickly disappeared. What roles did we all fall into at that point? Would I have dared buy cream cakes at a secondary school and for men? And would they have been so obviously appreciated?

ANOTHER AGENDA?

While there were many occasions I recorded where gender issues were evident, it was not this issue that struck me as the most significant aspect of the school. To someone who had never observed within a primary school (and had not done so in secondary for many years) the oppressive nature of the school on all children was far more evident than the differential pressures on boys and girls.

The very first note on my tape for the first day was:

> I suppose the most important thing is the amount of control: just how long the teacher speaks and the very, very small amount of time the children speak.

I found it very difficult to describe the way I felt at the end of the first day, but the note reads:

> I noticed the way the children were treated. In many ways she is a very Christian woman, yet she seemed to me to be treating the children appallingly. It was the sarcasm, no, not sarcasm, the superiority. The way that shame was used to control the children. The 'when you have stopped speaking' type of voice; the way in which a girl can sit there with her hand in the air for a very long time. And she had been seen, but she was not allowed to speak. The way the children were treated in moving them around. It was 'James, sit here', 'move forward (on the mat)'. Not 'please', no 'would you like to?' – just plain orders. At one point a child was told off. I just did not know what he was doing wrong, and he got a shouting at. Then it was the 'I'm waiting for you' voice. I'm finding this very difficult to describe.

What shocked me was the way that the children were treated.

It may seem naive, but I had not expected to observe such oppression of individuality and of other people's rights. What exactly had these children done to be denied their rights and to be subjected to the will of one adult for such a substantial part of their lives? Why were they not treated as people with rights? Why were they expected to undertake whatever task the teacher chose without question?

> At one point they were learning a song, and the whole thing was done so slowly. The kids were waiting so much of the time. Waiting for quiet, waiting for one another, waiting for something to happen. They were expected to be quiet – and for the most part they were quiet – just sitting there doing nothing. They were grouped and herded. 'Now who is in group 1. Put up your hands group 1', 'Group 2 go through that door there.' And later, 'James, you're not singing. You're supposed to sing as well.'

Now, obviously, a class of 30 needs careful handling. If we believe that schooling is worthwhile, then it *is* important that the teacher is able to control the children and maintain order in the classroom. Yet, the way in which this was done still surprised me. The language use suggested that children were not to be treated as full human beings. Imagine using the following sentences in any conversation between adults. Each sentence (and many more like them) was said with 'appropriate' sarcasm, coldness or aloofness:

This is the last time I'll warn you.

James, come and sit over here.

I'm waiting for you

If you don't mind, Peter.

Table one, you may go. Table four ...

Sit with your pencils and pens down. Look at me.

What did I say? [*Silence.*] You weren't listening, were you? Now listen to what I say.

When you've finished that, go on to page 17.

Perhaps this sort of treatment might be tolerated if the children appeared to be learning something of substance within the lessons. But most of my memories of the first day are of trivial learning. The main learning was not about subject matter, but about obedience to authority (no matter how arbitrary) and living with boredom.

One girl was very annoyed with the whole thing. I went over to her and she said she was bored. And she obviously was bored – because it was very boring what she was doing. They were all being asked to do something that was very boring, with no challenge in it at all. And she had been up to the teacher and the teacher had said that her picture was not quite right, and she had come back. And she said, 'I don't know what she wants, I don't know what she wants', in an angry voice. I said, 'Why don't you try putting a pattern around it?' She said, 'No, it's not that, I don't know what she wants.' She genuinely did not have a clue what it was she was supposed to be doing. And neither did I.

Later in the day an older girl from another class came into the room. She had been sent to this class of younger children because she was 'acting as a child' in her own class. Once this had been explained to the teacher she told the class:

Now what do you think of a girl from year 6 being with us? She's been sent here because she can't behave. Now let us show her how she should behave.

In an aside to me the teacher said that it was important that the girl be shamed in front of the class. Humiliation was part of the process of control. When the girl left the class she was told, 'I hope I don't see you down here again.'

I was continually struck by the degree of control, obedience and power that was exerted by the teacher over the children. I noted:

There is no choice of what you do in the classroom. Where to sit, what to do, when to do it. The arbitrariness of the power of one person over thirty others. She acts to control the other thirty, what she says goes. They all have to colour, draw a picture, play the recorder, write their family trees, write an essay. They line up, they move when told, they sit down when told, they go to the toilet when allowed to. They wait in silence. Individuality is severely constrained.

Such a comment was highly evaluative, of course, and in many ways not the type of comment that is helpful in educational ethnography. But I found that I could not simply describe what I saw, I needed to speak it into the tape recorder in order partially to deal with the frustration and anger that I felt. To have not recorded my feelings about the day in this way would have been to omit some of the most important data that I generated in that first day.

I was very grateful that I moved from the first class on the second day. As I put in my dictated notes:

> Day 2. I suppose the most important thing is to note how important it is for the children's experience who the teacher happens to be. This second teacher didn't actually try to belittle the children – OK she did a little bit, occasionally there would be a little 'have you finished?' which meant – 'I'm talking, how dare you talk while I'm talking.' But the majority of comments were actually quite friendly comments, showing a lot of patience with the kids. She obviously valued them.
>
> The second day, at least they were treated reasonably. Not 'well', but 'reasonably'. And they had some fun. Quite a lot of fun. I feel that, if you are going to treat children badly, they should at least learn something. And I think the second day they were at least learning something.

I was bluntly reminded on this second day of the importance of the individual teacher to children in primary school. While they may meet other teachers for a small part of the week, for the vast majority of time, primary school children are with just one teacher. They are at the mercy of the particular person who happens to be paid to teach them. She will control a large slice of their waking lives for the year, and it is just luck as to which teacher is selected to act as their controller.

MULTIPLE AGENDAS?

There are two aspects of this account of 'first days in the field' that I feel are worth reflecting on further.

First, my notes about the differences between the first and the second day are stark. My notes on the first day were predominantly 'anti-school'. I interpreted the children's experiences as almost entirely negative – not only did they seem to be unstimulated and to learn very little during the day, they also had very little fun. They seemed to be cowed by an authority figure who did not even amuse them. In contrast, my notes on the second day were far more positive. I still had many negative comments, but I also had far more accounts of what I interpreted as positive activities and events. My concern is that I am unsure about the extent to which these differences are due to the teachers and how they conducted themselves on the particular days I observed them, or to changes in the way I observed and interpreted what it is to be a child and a teacher in that primary school. To what extent are the differences owing to my changing perception and interpretation of events?

Although I had never before observed in a primary school, I had read numerous ethnographically based accounts on the topic. I had read, for example, the series of studies by Woods and his colleagues (for example, Woods, 1995, 1998; Woods and Jeffrey, 1996). Although these studies intentionally focus on the creative and positive aspects of primary school experience, I knew that the authors would not do so to the extent of misrepresenting their own perceptions. Yet these authors did not seem to see teachers as people who crushed and humiliated children and who denied children their rights. Further, I knew I was observing in a 'good' primary school and, although the period of observation was near to the end of the term, there was no reason to suspect that the observation days were particularly extraordinary days. There was every reason to think that similar sorts of interactions between the teachers and the children would have occurred on many other days. Additionally, when I talked to these teachers during their breaktimes, they appeared to be warm, caring people who wanted the best for the children they taught. Why did I perceive the first day, in particular, in the way I did? And why did the activities of the second day seem 'better'?

In her guide to research, *Fieldwork in Educational Settings*, Delamont (1992, p. 99) gives an example where she was shocked by the way in which children with special disability needs were treated by teachers, and the way in which those children accepted the behaviour and designations of teachers. She argues that experienced teachers of children with learning difficulties would probably have found such treatment 'normal', and so, presumably, would the children. It may only be in the early days of fieldwork that a researcher is able to problematize the 'normal' and begin to ask questions about the ways in which the participants in any culture structure their behaviour, beliefs and meanings. The pressure on researchers to be accepted by those in a new culture is such that this period of 'culture shock' may be very brief. In Delamont's (1992, p. 97) terms, it is easy to sink into the 'warm sand'. There is a need to maximize the research insights that can be gained while the researcher is still 'alien'.

It may be that ethnography within schools is even more difficult than most educational ethnographers admit. While it is possible for the ethnographer of the New York Stock Exchange (Abolafia, 1998) or of sexual behaviour in public toilets (Humphries, 1970) to enter that world with very little previous knowledge, the vast majority of ethnographers of schooling have experienced at least twelve years within schools as students and many such ethnographers have experienced many more as teachers. This very long period of socialization into the culture of schools cannot easily be negated or the understandings of what is 'normal' in such cultures problematized. My feeling now is that at least some of the difference between the fieldnotes that I made on the first and second days was due to my rapid reacclimatization into a culture that I had lived through in my formative years. If the Jesuits are correct, the first few years of life are crucial. Perhaps, I slipped back into this culture very quickly and I began to see the treatment of children that I had noted so negatively on the first day as 'normal'.

Second, there is an alternative way of discussing my observations. I explained that my 'foreshadowed problem' for this research period had become that of gender. Yet it may have been that I had several foreshadowed problems, not all of which were explicitly formulated.

Way back in my youth I had initially become interested in the study of education as an academic subject through reading the clutch of Penguin Specials and Penguin Education paperbacks of the 1960s and early 1970s that provided a radical critique of schooling. I had read Paul Goodman, Paulo Freire, John Holt, Ivan Illich, A. S. Neill, Everett Reimer and many more. I had kept contact with similar work throughout my academic career, subscribing to such journals as *LibEd* and *Education Now*. In the few weeks before starting to observe I had quickly read David Gribble's latest book, *Real Education*, which describes a variety of different schools where children have a far greater degree of freedom than in conventional schools. Schools such as Summerhill, Dartington Hall School, Sudbury Valley School and the pre-1981 Countesthorpe Community College are described. One paragraph from the introduction had particularly struck me. Gribble (1998, p. 2) claims that most schools try to produce young people who will fit into society like cogs in machinery. In contrast, he argues that school-leavers need to be:

literate and numerate, of course, but also happy, considerate, honest, enthusiastic, tolerant, self-confident, well-informed, articulate, practical, co-operative, flexible, creative, individual, determined people who know what their talents and interests are, have enjoyed developing them and intend to make good use of them. They should be people who care for others because they have been cared for themselves.

Such people, Gribble believes, are more likely to be produced by the type of school he describes than by conventional schools.

To what extent did my recent reading of this book influence the way I perceived and interpreted within the fieldwork setting? Was the culture of the school so overpowering and so much a part of my socialization that I quickly neutralized the message of this and many other books? I do not know, but the fact that I do not know has many implications for ethnographers of schools. What is clear is that Geer (1964) is correct in arguing that, 'while early fieldwork reaches few conclusions, it may nevertheless have far-reaching effects on the rest of the research'.

—5—

Research role conflicts and compromises

It is now widely accepted that fieldwork roles in ethnography are not fixed, but gradually change and develop as a result of negotiations between the researcher and those who are the subjects of the research. The researcher does not simply choose an appropriate role and adhere to it throughout the project; nor is it possible to think in terms of a single role, no matter how dynamic, for a variety of roles must be adopted which will vary with the different individuals with whom the researcher interacts. There have been several attempts to analyse the development of field roles. Janes (1961), for example, describes five separate phases through which he perceives roles may pass: newcomer, provisional acceptance, categorical acceptance, personal acceptance and imminent migrant. Olenson and Whittaker (1967), on the other hand, emphasize the process of exchange between researcher and researched and discuss four phases through which they perceive the process to develop. One of the clearest examples of change within research roles is given by Burgess (1984a, p. 85), who uses the framework proposed by Janes to show the way his own role relationships with three school staff changed over the first six months of fieldwork at Bishop McGregor School.

This greater realism about research roles is a clear improvement on earlier typologies put forward by Gold (1958) and Junker (1960), which are still widely discussed in research methods textbooks even though they have long been the targets of criticism (see, for example, Collins, 1984; Hammersley and Atkinson, 1995). From my own fieldwork experience, however, the present literature still does not adequately describe the process of role definition, negotiation and renegotiation. In this chapter I wish to emphasize one simple factor: that the only fieldwork roles initially open to researchers are ones that are recognized and accepted by those with whom the researcher interacts. Those who are to be the subjects of research abhor uncertainty in the role definitions of others as 'nature abhors a vacuum', and will automatically assign a role to a researcher. Over a period of time it may be possible to 'educate' the subjects of research and develop new role possibilities, but the researcher initially is restricted in the choice of his or her roles by the knowledge, experiences and expectations of those to be studied. This can be a major limitation on what can be accomplished in ethnographic research.

In this chapter I move onwards from the first days in the field and describe a number of items related to research roles that I feel may be of interest to others conducting research. Throughout the chapter I use my ethnographic study of boys' public (private) schools as an example. I make it clear that, in that research, I took on a range of accommodative roles, roles which restricted what it was possible for me to do and observe. But I believed at the time that these were the only reasonable roles that it was possible for me to adopt, in the time limits of the research, if I was to remain at the schools.

SOME DETAILS OF THE RESEARCH

This chapter discusses ethnographic fieldwork conducted in 1981 and 1982 in two of the major British public schools. Four weeks in the summer of 1981 were spent in the first school and the whole of the summer term of 1982 was spent in the second. In both schools I aimed to be an open researcher. Staff and pupils knew that I was at the school for the specific purpose of writing a book about public schools. In the first school, I did no teaching, but in the second I taught two sets of lower form boys – six periods a week for the first half of term and three thereafter. During this time I lived in accommodation provided by the schools on the school sites. In both schools my research method was eclectic. I talked with boys, girls, masters, wives, secretaries, other staff and headmasters. I became involved with the various aspects of school and community life, including sports, visits, drinking at the local pub, dinner parties and other activities. I observed lessons, chapel, meals, sports and meetings of masters, parents and prefects. I also conducted eighty taped semi-structured interviews with academic staff.

At the end of the fieldwork I had two boxes of questionnaires, a drawer of tape-recorded interviews, about 800 pages of A4 notes, twenty hours of tape-recorded notes and comments, and a pile of documentation about two feet high. Only a small proportion of this material was directly used in publications! The main publications have been a full-length book on life in public schools (Walford, 1986a), two journal articles on girls in boys' schools and on reproduction of social class (Walford, 1983a, 1986b) and an article in a collected volume about the changing experiences of public schoolmasters (Walford, 1984).

CHECKING MY BACKGROUND

One of the first questions that teachers asked me was whether I had attended a public school as a boy. In fact, I had not, and had worked my way through the state-maintained system until I found myself taking a physics degree at the University of Kent at Canterbury. My first contact with the independent sector came when I was 23 and working for a doctorate at that same university. Even that long ago I found the grant rather too small to support a reasonable lifestyle, so when my supervisor told me that a local minor public school wanted someone to teach mathematics part-time for two terms, I willingly took on the task. I am sure that I learnt far more from those twenty-two 14- and 15-year-old 'bottom set' boys than they did from me, for my lessons were noisy and chaotic. I yelled at them and threatened them and they fired paper missiles back at me. Eventually we came to a compromise but I was more than grateful that the room I taught in was physically isolated from the rest of the teaching rooms and only accessible by an external stairway. Educational though the experience was to me, the school struck me as a strange institution, for I could never understand why it was that parents were prepared to pay a considerable amount of money for their boys to be taught by an incompetent and untrained part-timer, rather than send them to local authority schools which had better facilities and equipment and fully trained staff.

I intended to teach in 'normal' schools and a few months after hearing the not unexpectedly disastrous mathematics results of my twenty-two boys, I started a PGCE at Oxford University. As I had already had some experience of the independent sector and was also well qualified it seemed 'appropriate' to the department that I should do my teaching practice term in one of the local and prestigious public boarding schools. I should say that the same department (which is where I now work) would certainly not make such an assumption today. Yet I enjoyed the challenge of teaching highly able boys, and the experience led me to a deeper concern with the oddities of such schools.

By the end of that year I wanted to study for a higher degree in sociology and was fairly sure that I could get funding for two years. I needed a job to tide me over for two terms. A public boarding school, with its cheap accommodation supplied for teachers, good teaching conditions and ample facilities, seemed an obvious choice. I received confirmation of funding for my higher degree on the very day I started teaching at another of the major public boarding schools, so from the first day I knew that my permanent position was only a temporary one. The staff I worked with were up-to-date and enthusiastic, and gave me help when I requested it, but otherwise left me to teach in the way I felt best.

This background of my association with public schools was important for the development of the research project. It meant that after I had been appointed as lecturer in sociology of education at Aston University in 1979, and the time came for me to think about conducting new research, trying to understand the micro-world of the public school was an immediate first thought. I wanted to attempt an ethnographic study, and public boarding schools had many factors which made them specifically interesting. Perhaps the most important of these was the role that these schools have played in reproducing our inegalitarian society and educating the sons of the affluent to take their place in social, economic and political elites. The research on the culture of these schools was limited and out of date. There had been a flurry of research activity in the early 1960s which found its way into print later on in the decade. This included Wakeford's (1969) study of a school at which he had originally been a pupil and which was based on research conducted in 1962 and 1963. Weinberg (1967) based his work on a larger sample of schools, while Kalton (1966) surveyed statistically all schools in the Headmasters' Conference. The deluge of publications on boarding schools by Royston Lambert and his colleagues was based on extensive survey and observational work at about the same time (Lambert *et al.*, 1968, 1970, 1973; Lambert and Woolfe, 1968).

For girls' independent schools the data were a little more up to date. Sara Delamont's study of girls' public schools in Edinburgh was conducted in the early 1970s (Delamont, 1973, 1976a, b, 1984a, b), while Mallory Wober's account of girls' boarding schools, which was part of the Lambert research, was published in 1971. However, by the 1980s some twenty years had passed since the studies of boys' schools and, according to commentators from within the schools, much had changed in that time (Thorn, 1978; Rae, 1981).

I had a number of other 'foreshadowed problems' (Hammersley and Atkinson, 1995) beside that of documenting the lives of the various inhabitants of the schools and trying to see how this fitted with social reproduction. I had done some work on sexism in science textbooks (Walford, 1980b, 1981b) and I had become interested in aspects of gender reproduction as well as class reproduction. The fact that many of these public schools had recently admitted girls, usually only into the sixth form, gave rise to a whole host of questions about the changing role of these schools in the reproduction of gender.

A further major foreshadowed problem was the whole area of the links between the state-maintained and the private education sectors. I knew that a number of public schoolmasters had been very influential in curriculum development, especially in the sciences, mathematics, economics and classics. I was interested in the nature of school knowledge and the way that, where a selection of knowledge was made by public schoolteachers, it was likely to favour these pupils at the expense of pupils in local authority schools. I hoped to be able to interview teachers who had been involved in curriculum development, writing of textbooks and examination work and document curriculum changes which would show how 'objective' curriculum content actively favoured and embodied the assumptions of the ruling class and ruling gender.

I show, later in the chapter, that only some of these topic areas actually came to fruition, and that some were eased out as others took their place.

GAINING ACCESS

Initial access to independent schools has to be negotiated through the headteacher of the individual school but, as has been discussed in Chapters 2 and 3, gaining and maintaining access in ethnographic work is a process. Even when initial permission has been granted by the headteacher, negotiations must be conducted with all those involved over what the researcher is allowed to see or do. My 'credentials' as someone who had taught at a public boarding school in the past were vital at all stages of the negotiation process. Gaining access to conduct research in the two public schools was not easy, and I am fairly sure that anyone without some previous contact with the public school sector would have found initial access even more difficult.

It took a considerable time to gain permission to conduct research in the first school. My original intention was to spend time in three of the major public boarding schools. I wanted to study boarding schools because that would allow me to conduct a 'mini-community study' in what was virtually a 'total institution' (Goffman, 1961), and I wanted to study the most prestigious of the Headmasters' Conference schools because of their key roles in curriculum development and in the reproduction of social elites. I excluded such schools as Eton and Winchester because I was interested in the similarities of experience rather than differences, which left me with about thirty schools to choose from. It didn't seem to matter very much which I chose from these. In letters to headmasters I stressed that I was particularly interested in the public schools as an alternative to the state system and that I was gathering information to write a book. 'I wish to describe in detail the experiences of teaching, learning and living in a public school from the rather different points of view of the masters and the boys.' I stressed that I was 'interested in the similarities of experience rather than the differences, which would mean that it would not be my intention to identify the schools studied in any publication or to make any comparison between them'. The letter continued with an outline of my own academic and teaching history in which I mentioned by name the three schools in which I had taught and gave the names of four referees. I initially asked to visit the schools for a period of about six weeks, hoping that I would be able to extend this once actually there. I made no mention of the word 'sociology'. I had five refusals.

My interview with the headmaster of the first school to express interest lasted only twenty minutes, but I experienced it as being far longer and more nerve-racking than any of the interviews I had previously had for academic appointments. He was extremely sharp and shrewd and demanded precise answers to a range of questions about my purposes and methodology. I had envisaged presenting myself as an open ethnographer and thus had prepared only a fairly flimsy outline of the sort of areas in which I was interested – I intended, in true ethnographic style, to develop my research strategy once actually in the school. The headmaster, however, had a rather different view of how research should be conducted, where questions are tightly framed, questionnaires or interview schedules developed and representative samples drawn from populations. It quickly became obvious that the role of 'open ethnographic researcher' was one which he would not entertain. This was the first occasion when it became clear to me that possible research roles were structured by the definitions of others. At the time I had no intention of systematically interviewing a sample of boys, as it seemed unlikely to me that any particularly useful information could be gained from schoolboys by multiple one-off interviews of this type. Yet I found myself discussing random sampling, possible sample bias and interview schedules. The headmaster also spent time checking the question 'Are you one of us?', where my background of teaching in the schools was clearly of major importance. This was also the occasion of the first appearance of what I came to know as 'the ghost of Royston Lambert'. As I explain below, the ghost was to haunt me throughout the research.

By the end of the interview I had been forced to agree that six weeks (which I actually thought was far too short) was too long, and had compromised with a period of four weeks. I was to send him more details in writing of the topic areas I wished to cover in interviews with masters and boys, while he was to contact my academic and public school referees. The latter had been forced from me during the interview, and were clearly seen as more valid than any number of academic referees. Their references were evidently convincing, for an invitation to conduct the research soon followed.

It is worth spending time considering my problems of access because they raise a number of questions with regard to the responsibilities of researchers to the wider research community. My experience was in direct contrast to that of Delamont (1984a), who states that she had no problems whatever about obtaining access to research on girls' public schools. Part of the difference is undoubtedly due to the fact that I was asking to be accommodated by the school (which would be paid for, of course), while Delamont only wished to visit during the daytime, but I feel that 'the ghost of Royston Lambert' had a far greater debilitating effect. Royston Lambert started his research on boarding education while a Fellow of King's College, Cambridge, where he founded and directed the government-financed Research Unit into Boarding Education between 1964 and 1968. When Lambert moved to Devon in 1968 to become headmaster of the progressive Dartington Hall School, some of the research team moved with him to form the Dartington Research Unit. The original study was very wide-ranging, covering 66 boarding schools in England and Wales, for boys or coeducational. One in three of Headmasters' Conference (HMC) boarding schools were included. A sub-sample of seven schools (five of them HMC) were 'studied minutely during a period of observation and survey lasting in each at least a term or more'. In these schools the headmasters 'welcomed us into their communities, gave us unrestricted freedom in them, housed and fed us, entertained us and gave us unremitting help, information, material and guidance' (Lambert and Millham, 1968). The output of the two research units has been prodigious. Lambert (1975) lists six books, eight sections of books and sixteen pamphlets or articles which resulted from the research, but only one of these is really widely known. In 1968 Lambert and Millham published *The Hothouse Society*, which was described as a 'by-product' of the main research study. It was based on written comments by boys and girls at boarding schools provided in answer to questionnaires, in diaries and in other writings. The pupils' own words are used to describe the boredom and pettiness of life at the schools, their own cynicism and what they see as masters' hypocrisy. An underworld of bullying, drink, drugs and gambling is uncovered, followed by a chapter on 'problems' and a further one on 'sex in single sex schools', where a flourishing homosexual life is described in some schools. The book was a considerable public success, later being republished by Penguin, but the schools, quite understandably, were horrified.

For some masters this horror was compounded when the *First Report* of the Public Schools Commission, using Lambert's research, was to argue that the public boarding schools should make about half their boarding places available to 'children with special boarding needs', which would ensure that they became more academically comprehensive and less socially divisive. He who had seemed a supporter had turned traitor.

During my research and subsequently I have talked with many schoolmasters who had been closely involved with the Lambert research. Almost without exception they felt that he and the team had been dishonest and had tricked them. 'He came looking for trouble and found it', 'the boys fed him with exactly the sort of comments he wanted – and he lapped it up', 'the bad bits all came from one very run-down and antiquated school' were typical comments. They accused him of 'rigging the questions', being 'obsessively concerned with homosexual activity amongst the boys' and 'not giving a fair report', but only including 'all the sensational bits'. I am obviously in no position to judge whether these accusations are true; my point is that whenever one of the headmasters or schoolmasters had read this book, I had to fight against its effect in order to gain access or interviews. The negative effect of previous research had even become enshrined in HMC's official *Manual of Guidance* (1978), which notes: 'Experience shows that headmasters can be too trusting in regard to enquiries made by researchers and sociologists. Evidence obtained in so-called confidence may be used several years later, in ways totally different from those intimated at the time of original approach.' Faced with the 'ghost of Royston Lambert', I am quite sure that I would not have obtained the degree of access and help that I did without being able to point to my own previous experience of teaching in public boarding schools.

It is also worthy of note that, once into the system, it was very easy to be given permission to conduct research in other schools. The headmaster of the second school simply telephoned the headmaster of the first for a reference and let me loose for a whole term with hardly a question as to what I was going to be doing. I felt I had joined the 'old boy network' myself.

ETHNOGRAPHY IN PRACTICE

When doing fieldwork ethnographers construct a variety of different types of field notes. Burgess (1984a) uses the terms substantive, methodological and analytic field notes, while Hammersley and Atkinson (1995) describe ways of recording observational data, interviews and documents and recommend the development of a fieldwork journal to include notes on emerging ideas and theories, a running account of the conduct of the research and a record of the ethnographer's own personal feelings and experiences. The notes I made while in public schools are best described as substantive, methodological and reflexive. For the latter I used a small pocket tape recorder and the range of material included was from early formulations of theories to shouts of anger, agony and self-pity. At the end of any traumatic experience I would simply talk all my anxiety into the tape recorder, and I would recommend that every ethnographer do this simply for the therapeutic effect alone. That it is also a record of the experience of doing ethnography, which might be used in accounts such as this, is a bonus.

Numerous researchers have now written about the emotional and psychological stresses that are a part of doing ethnographic research. Johnson (1975), for example, tells us about his own physical pain and sickness, which were a constant accompaniment of fieldwork, and we now know that even the pathsetting anthropologist Malinowski (1967) experienced severe stress and anxiety during his fieldwork with the Trobriand Islanders. Junker (1960) sees one of the main problems as that of striking a balance between being a 'good friend' and a 'snooping stranger', for the 'subjects' of the research do not ask for research to be conducted on them. Researchers have to use whatever social skills they can muster to convince people that they are 'on their side' and can be treated as a friend. The researcher asks about personal plans, feelings and failures and, like a good friend, promises not to tell anyone else, but the relationship is not reciprocal. The researcher does not tell his or her secrets to those being interviewed, for the objective is not friendship at all but information – a cache of data that can be stored away and analysed later. Quite simply, the ethnographer *is* a 'snooping stranger' but one who has to conceal that identity behind a mask of friendship in order to gain information.

There have now been numerous personal accounts about ethnographic research in schools which have indicated similar anxieties. Hammersley (1984), for example, writes of stress, lone-liness and fear of personal inadequacy. My own experiences of doing research in public schools were, if anything, worse. Most researchers doing fieldwork in Britain do so on a part-time basis. Each morning they leave their homes and drive to the 'fieldwork site' knowing that whatever happens during the day they will be able to return at night to the warm security of their home, family and friends. In my case I lived at the schools and there was no escape from being 'the person who was writing a book about public schools'. While at the schools I ate most of my meals with staff in the communal facilities provided largely for unmarried masters and in the main research school I lived communally with about twelve unmarried masters. Even in the local pub it was inevitable that people connected with the school would be around. This made the research experience more like that of a community study than that of most school ethnographers (see Bell, 1977), but it was a community study being conducted by a single lonely individual rather than with a group who could share my ideas and pains. Moreover, the community was one where there was considerable submerged hostility to my presence.

At the end of the first week I returned to Birmingham for a day. On the train journey away from the school I wrote: 'I, even already, feel the continued turning stomach beginning to subside. I've had continuous sleepless nights, diarrhoea and churning stomach for all of the week.' It did get better as time went on and I became less fearful of being thought incompetent or making a mistake which could lead to my being thrown out. But I always felt anxious and worried about the next person I was going to interview or having to push my way into groups of pupils who often did not want me to be there. For most of the participants in the school I was and felt myself to be a 'snooping stranger', which was a role I did not enjoy.

I got most open hostility from pupils, who would usually, fairly early on in any discussion, ask a question something similar to 'Are you pro- or anti-public schools?' I tried to answer such questions as truthfully as I could, which necessitated unpacking the question to discuss the various aspects with which I was concerned. To pupils who had clear ideas about their own answers to these questions this seemed like an evasion and sometimes led to lively argument with the older pupils. The pupils were always polite and well mannered but, like most young people, tended to see problems in clear-cut terms, and were thus often suspicious of me. Most of the time at the schools it was possible almost to forget just how right-wing most of the pupils were, but there were many times when I was jolted into such a recognition. While observing one lesson, for example, one boy joked about the National Front being the right way to run the country. Not only did the teacher not make any comment, but neither did any of the other boys in the class. On another occasion I asked one pupil whom I knew quite well whether there was anyone who was left-wing in his House. The ferocity of 'no, certainly not' was stunning.

Hostility from staff was less open. I wrote in my fieldwork diary:

It is not that the people are not helpful – they are, and are as helpful as I could or should expect. But I feel that behind that mask of gentlemanliness there lurks a deep suspicion of educational research in general and of this sort of research in particular.

Many of the staff were far more critical and questioning about public schools than were the pupils, but they still wanted to know how the research was going to help them. They were fed up with innumerable MSc and MEd theses that tied up many teachers yet were never of any use to them, and demanded that I explain how my research might help others if not themselves. Public schoolmasters are busy people and an undercurrent that I felt and recorded in my fieldwork diary was:

A really annoying part of doing this sort of work is that everyone you meet believes that you have found yourself a really cushy job. (This includes other academics who have not done this sort of work.) A number of masters have been really fairly angry that someone should be able to 'come and have a nice holiday at the beginning of the summer' and at the same time take up their valuable time and stop them from working.

Researchers are not unaffected by such comments, and while I was quite clear that I had not found myself 'a cushy job', I realized that it was important to ensure that staff and pupils knew that I was actually keeping myself busy. Most ethnographic fieldwork techniques, which involve simply talking, observing and listening to people in pubs, common rooms, classrooms and homes, were simply not seen as work by others. The role of ethnographer was not one which masters were prepared to accept as legitimate. I thus undertook systematic interviewing with masters as much to show staff that I was doing something – collecting real, solid data – as for the data themselves. They expected me to take on their view of what a researcher was, and that was someone who interviewed and asked specific replicable questions rather than someone who, in Delamont's (1984a) terms, 'lurked' about the school, often with no clear function. The roles I adopted were not freely chosen, but the result of the expectations of others.

But only a few staff were actively hostile. Many of them were very open and helpful and some clearly enjoyed the experience of being interviewed. For others the interviews acted as something akin to therapy, as I fell into a 'good listener' role. Housemasters especially, it seemed to me, really appreciated the chance to talk about their experiences with someone who was knowledgeable about the school, yet outside it. I tried to interview housemasters in the evening so that I could have another chance of being in houses when all the boys were there and see just how involved the man was with the affairs of the house. They were usually very pleasant occasions with food being offered and gin and tonic flowing liberally, but they were still a strain for me because I had to ensure that I did not say too much about my own views, which could frequently be in opposition to those of the person I was interviewing, or about the views of other masters in the school.

Housemasters frequently asked me to draw comparisons between the way they conducted their house and the way other housemasters organized theirs, for they simply did not know. One of the peculiarities of the boarding house system is that each house is very isolated from the others. Housemasters will only very rarely enter the house of another housemaster and will never enter the boys' part of another house. Housemasters did not know the real extent of fagging, smoking and drinking, for example, in other houses. By the end of the research period I found myself in the unique position of having visited all the houses and having eaten in most. I had much 'guilty' knowledge that was of interest to others. I found the strain of being evasive and of simply continuously 'being nice' to everyone extremely exhausting.

In short, the roles that were available to me were not planned, but the only suitable roles that were available to me within the time limits of the research that would enable me to gather data. Just as Peshkin (1984) found in his fieldwork in a fundamentalist Christian community, the roles were all accommodative and the effect of maintaining these roles was exhaustion.

COMPROMISE IN FIELDWORK ROLES AND AREAS OF RESEARCH

Both of my periods of research in schools were fairly short, and I initially attempted to cover a wide range of foreshadowed problems. I recognize now that the range of problems was far too great to be satisfactorily covered in such a short time and that this meant that with many of the people I met I was unable to develop greatly the initial role in which they placed me. With pupils I was rarely able to negotiate any role beyond those of 'teacher', 'adult/ authority figure', 'snooping stranger', 'left-wing troublemaker' or whatever other role was initially cast for me. With the schoolmasters, on the other hand, I was interacting with them for a far longer period and with some I was able to move beyond their first assessments of my role.

This had a great effect on the final subject matter of the study. When I first started the research project I was much more interested in how the pupils experienced the school rather than the masters; I was interested in what the schoolmasters could tell me about curriculum development, but I did not feel that their own experiences would be particularly worthy of study. In the end, much of the book (Walford, 1986a) and one article (Walford, 1984) were concerned with masters, and the only publication about curriculum was a paper on a very peripheral area (Walford, 1985).

My interest in schoolmasters was forced upon me by the schoolmasters themselves and by the limited types of research role open to me. At the very first staff meeting I attended there was a discussion about how a large amount of money was to be spent. One master, whom I had not even spoken to before, passed a note to me which read, 'This is a v. political area of debate.' I had not expected a consensus world, but here was conflict near the surface begging to be uncovered. The pressures from senior staff in particular to push me into a research role with which they were accustomed ensured that I quickly started to conduct systematic interviews with a sample of staff. I found that a number of the younger masters, on interview, were prepared to accept the research role of critic and confidant. They were still suspicious of what I was doing, but welcomed the chance to talk to an outsider and wanted to ensure that what I wrote would not be a whitewash. They told me about problems of pay and housing, about 'the winter of discontent', about masters being eased out of their jobs and about the pressures from the school on wives and families. They wanted me to know, and I felt almost obliged to ensure that their voices were heard, as they were in the article on 'the changing professionalism of public schoolmasters' (Walford, 1984). In a similar way a considerable amount of space in the book (Walford, 1986a) was devoted to schoolmasters, including a chapter on housemasters.

Like Hammersley (1984), I found that doing ethnographic research on these teachers led me to modify my initial perspectives on them. I was originally not particularly well disposed to people who could devote their entire lives to children of the affluent (I justified my own periods teaching in public schools as part of a 'finding out' process and temporary). But the empathy that is a prime requisite for ethnographic work led me to modify my feelings. Hammersley (1984) describes the problems thus:

> I therefore found myself facing a severe dilemma, especially since empathy tends to lead to sympathy. The very process of gaining and maintaining access also pushed me in the direction of sympathy for the teachers; one cannot constantly present an image of agreement, friendliness and understanding without strong pressures towards such feelings.

Part of the eventual emphasis on teachers was also due to corresponding lack of data in other areas. I soon found, for example, that it would not be possible to write very much on curriculum development within public schools because, although I interviewed several textbook writers and others heavily involved, each case was idiosyncratic and thus would have been impossible to write about without identifying individuals involved and thus the research schools. My major problem, however, was that I had great difficulty in gaining useful information from pupils.

The headmaster of the first school wanted me to interview a random sample of boys. I saw no reasonable way of organizing this and thought at the time that it would probably lead to few useful data. The essence of ethnography, after all, I argued, is that information is gained over a period of time once trust has been established, rather than through interviews with strangers. I preferred to try a less structured approach, but in practice I found it very difficult to meet and talk with pupils except on a superficial level. Quite simply, there was no suitable role for me to adopt and no time to develop any. Some researchers have suggested that it is possible for adult observers to participate fully in the world of the school by taking on the role of the pupil (e.g. Spindler, 1974; Llewellyn, 1980), but I did not find this possible. I spent time 'following' pupils and sitting with pupils in lessons, but I always felt uneasy and aware that I was observing rather than participating. The junior common room appeared to offer a good place to meet older pupils, but the opening hours were so short that they were more interested in getting the maximum number of half pints into them than in talking with a weird adult who was pushing his way into their territory. I was automatically a 'weird adult' because no other adult roles were available to me in the junior common room. Any other adult in there was automatically in an authority role, which I wished to avoid. While only a few of the pupils were openly hostile, it was often made clear to me that they would rather I was elsewhere. Those who wished to talk with me were obviously unrepresentative.

I felt that the ethical problems of ethnography were also of greater concern when it came to pupils. None had given informed consent to be part of the study – I had simply forced my way into their lives with few of the common courtesies. Somehow exploiting what 'social graces' I had with other adults to encourage them to give me data seemed less offensive than doing the same with pupils. The guilt at 'ripping people off' for data was worse with pupils.

Younger boys were usually much more willing to talk and, like those in Burgess's (1983) school, saw the exercise as a chance for fame and wished to have their names in the resulting book. But there was still no role that I could conveniently fill. I was able to talk with boys at breaks and over lunch, but these were rushed affairs and I found I would spend more time explaining to boys what I was doing rather than asking them questions. The houses were the obvious places to gather such informal data, yet the only adult roles available are housemaster, assistant housemaster or tutor and matron, all of whom have clear authority positions over the boys. An adult cannot simply 'hang around' the house watching what is going on, listening and asking questions, any more than a researcher could do this in a private home. It is an invasion of privacy and perceived as such by pupils. Several housemasters allowed me access to their houses 'at any time I wanted', an invitation which I only accepted if the boys themselves seemed happy for me to be there, but in practice when one of the housemasters found me talking with the head of house and a prefect at 2.30 in the morning it was clear that I had overstayed my welcome. He acted coolly and calmly, but next day I found that the 'news' had swept through the staff.

I thought that it might be easier to make contact with pupils if I did some teaching in the second school. I hoped to take the role of teacher with a small number of pupils; I could then relax into 'friendly teacher' and then 'friend' role as the term progressed. I took on two groups for a total of six periods a week. However, I had to ensure that my role with the schoolmasters was that of 'competent teacher and researcher' rather than 'incompetent educationalist', so I had to ensure that I could keep order and cover the work. My 'rules of the game', which were meant to be fairly generous, kept the younger group completely docile for half a term. I had quite clearly terrified them without meaning to, and it was only when I stopped teaching them in the second half of term that I could become friendly with any of them. The older group saw through my imitation thunder more easily. I learned more from this group, but I am not convinced that all the extra work that I caused myself by wanting to teach (my physics was very rusty) was actually worthwhile in terms of additional data from pupils. It helped at first to establish myself with teachers into the 'fellow teacher' role, but when I gave up teaching three of my six periods because 'it was taking up too much of my time', I felt my reputation plummet, as it was clear to the staff that I would never be able to cope as a real teacher. In fact, I felt my 'teacher' role to be always in some doubt. The head of department initially treated me as a 'trainee teacher' and sat at the back of the lesson until he was convinced that I would not do the pupils too much harm. I felt he was also quite happy to take one class back after half-term.

The role of 'observer' is recognized within classrooms. Both teachers and pupils are reasonably happy with the idea that someone should come into the classroom to view either teaching or pupil behaviour. I found, however, that the role of observer is only acceptable within tightly defined circumstances. One weekend I simply wished to observe what was going on in the main quadrangle of the school. I sat in a corner, and almost everyone who passed either gave me a strange look or came over to ask me what I was doing. There was simply no acceptable role that I could take on which would allow me to sit and observe in the main quadrangle. Watching cricket, on the other hand, seemed designed to help me out. Although I have never been able to understand the game and dreaded people asking me questions about how it was going, the 'cricket fan' was a role that served me well.

Staff found assigning a role to me particularly difficult at times of social activity. I often used to go for a drink or two in one of the local pubs with some of the schoolmasters and, perhaps because I was there, the topic of conversation would often come round to the school. I was asked several times, 'Are you on duty or off duty?' Was I going to force them to be careful about what they said at every occasion when I was around? Surely I could compartmenta-lize my research role? Yet, of course, I could not do so, but had to force myself out of hiding in the comfort of my rooms to intrude once more upon their privacy.

In the second school, in near desperation for some sort of usable data from the pupils, I fell back on questionnaires and issued a short version of the one used by Lambert (Lambert *et al.*, 1970). There was no way I could issue it to sixth form pupils just at 'A' level time, so I compromised by giving it to the whole of the first and second years of the school (13–14-year-olds). It was much more informative than I had hoped and had the additional benefit of adding to many more informal discussions with the boys. I wish I had given it to them earlier in the term and to boys at the first school.

The dearth of information from pupils led to a de-emphasis on their experiences in the book. Other topics that replaced this were forced upon me during fieldwork. I was aware of the introduction of girls into former boys-only schools, and was interested in the ways in which this related to class and gender reproduction, but I had not given a thought to the experiences of female teachers in these schools. I was shaken out of my complacency when I read the list of staff in the first school which, under the heading 'masters', listed several Mrs and Miss names. What was life like for these female 'masters'? They were more than pleased to tell me, although much of the information could not be used in the end for fear of identifying individuals. Acker's (1980) article on 'women, the other academics' alerted me to the way that wives of academics can play a vital support role in their careers. It became obvious that a similar process was occurring in public schools and that wives had a vital role to play in 'assisting' housemasters in particular. I remember being annoyed when Janet Finch's excellent book *Married to the Job* was published in 1983 and showed how widespread the problem was – I had hoped I was on to something fairly new.

CONCLUSION

In this chapter I have tried to indicate some of the compromises that I felt forced to make during fieldwork and their effects on the final content of published work. I found that while some negotiation of roles was possible over a long period, the roles open to me were severely restricted by the expectations of those being researched. Moreover, throughout the time at the schools I felt obliged to present an 'overarching role' which was somewhat in conflict with my own feelings. As Spencer (1973), who studied West Point Military Academy, suggests, there is an implicit, if not explicit, assumption made that the researcher will not directly attempt to harm the institution. Royston Lambert and his colleagues had, to the minds of most of the schoolmasters I spoke to, betrayed the trust the schools had put in them and 'shown his true colours' only after leaving the schools. Throughout my research I felt that an unspoken gentlemen's agreement had been assumed on the part of most of the staff in the schools. I also felt myself cast in the role of 'sympathetic researcher' – perhaps not wholeheartedly in favour, but moderate rather than left-wing or anything worse. Once again those being researched forced me to adopt a role which was shaped by their expectations. If I had not been prepared to take on such a role I would have neither obtained nor maintained access or legitimacy.

The ethical problems of such role-taking are considerable, for the line between personal restraint in putting forward one's own ideas and deliberate deception is a fine one. In my writing on public schools I have attempted to describe and analyse those schools in as fair, balanced and honest a way as possible. While ends cannot justify means, I hope that headmasters, staff and pupils will not feel that I have betrayed their trust in what I have written. I dread becoming another 'ghost' for future academic researchers to have to fight against, for public schools are far too important to be left unresearched in the future, and need to be open to researchers with a wide range of attitudes towards them.

— 6

Interviews

I well remember my thirteenth birthday. One of the presents that I was given was a new portable tape recorder. It was a reel-to-reel machine, powered by six large batteries and was about 30 × 15 × 10 cm (not, of course, that we would have used those foreign measurements back in 1962). Each tape lasted 15 minutes on each side, and it had to be threaded carefully through the recording head mechanism and fitted into an unused reel before it could be used. The machine also had a large microphone about 20 cm high with a lead that plugged into the side. It was cumbersome and awkward to use. Its mono, and decidedly 'low-fidelity', reproduction meant that there was little point in trying to record music.

But to me it was a joy. It was portable, which meant that I could now record the voices of my friends and our conversations outside the home. The family's massive, heavy reel-to-reel tape recorder – perhaps 50 × 40 × 25 cm – had meant that I could only record our conversations by inviting my friends to my home. Now I could take my machine with me.

The cassette was invented soon after and my 'portable' became a joke. The cassette recorder changed the way we listened to music and, more importantly in the context of this book, it changed the way we do qualitative research.

THE SEDUCTIVE TAPE RECORDER

The cassette tape recorder was first put into production in the mid-1960s. Expensive at first, it was soon to become the most convenient way of listening to music on the move. Young people, in particular, ignored the worries of doctors about possible damage to their ears, and the Sony Walkman, introduced as late as 1979, became a generational status symbol. But the influence of the cassette recorder was far wider than this. Researchers in the social sciences, and also in social history, quickly saw the potential of the new machines. Social historians recognized that it was now far easier to collect oral records of past events. The generation of those who had been involved in and survived the First World War was beginning to decline due to natural deaths, and oral history and life history developed rapidly in local social history. It was not that oral history was entirely new. Some had been done in the past, but the cassette recorder made the process much easier and opened it to local social history groups. The work of Thompson (1978) was central to this early historical work, which grew rapidly, especially into studies of women's experiences (e.g. Roberts, 1984; Sarsby, 1988). Similar developments occurred in sociology, where the work of such researchers as Plummer (1983) and Bertaux (1980) was crucial.

Up to the end of the 1960s sociology of education in Britain had been dominated by the highly statistical, survey-based, political arithmetic tradition. The publication of Michael Young's (1971) edited *Knowledge and Control* is often thought of as marking the start of the rise of more qualitative research methods in sociology of education. This is not actually correct, for Jackson and Marsden (1962), for example, had used qualitative interviews long before in their study of the experiences of 88 working-class grammar school children. But *Knowledge and Control* was one of the first books to include reports that reproduced tape-recorded speech and to present this as *evidence*. The very well known chapter by Keddie (1971) reproduced transcripts of tape-recordings of what people had said both in naturally occurring classroom talk and in interviews. Long quotations from the transcripts were presented as an essential part of the descriptive claims made in the chapter. The influence of this particular study was considerable, because this form of classroom-based research was seen as highly appropriate and relevant for the many teachers without degrees who were expected to join the newly established Open University. The School of Education at the Open University developed several courses, especially *School and Society* (Open University, 1972), which encouraged the spread and growth of studies based on observation and interviews in classrooms, and where classroom discourse was a central focus.

Overall, *Knowledge and Control* and the initial education courses of the Open University presented a new, critical sociology of education that 'raised questions' rather than 'answered questions' and which had the nature of school knowledge as its central concern. It was dominated by a belief in the efficacy of qualitative methods, and was thus seen as a challenge to the quantitative political arithmetic tradition. But the 'paradigm war' that flared during the 1970s perhaps had the strange effect of encouraging qualitative researchers to provide 'harder' soft data. Tape-recording allowed an element of the 'scientific' paradigm of research to be emulated. Tape-recorded conversations were seen as being a highly reliable record that could be presented as evidence in academic work. The fact that someone had said whatever was quoted was seemingly irrefutable – the 'hard' evidence was available for others to check.

I would argue that the cassette tape recorder changed the nature of sociology of education. Some researchers followed the model established in social history and sociology and conducted oral life histories of teachers. The books and articles by Goodson and Ball (1985), Sikes *et al.* (1985) and Woods (1985) are good examples of this movement. But the tape recorder quickly became the major piece of equipment used in most qualitative educational research. Researchers were seduced by what it could do, and the use of tape became the orthodoxy without any full recognition of any deleterious effects that this might have on qualitative and ethnographic research.

The change can be illustrated through my early qualitative research studies. My first piece of educational research was concerned with postgraduate natural science research students and their role in the research output of university departments (Walford, 1980a, 1981a). In 1977–8, I spent about a month at each of two of the leading experimental physics research departments and interviewed a sample of 26 academics and 39 research students. These were not tape-recorded, even though the first half of the research had been conducted as part of a higher degree. At that time it was still thought sufficient to interview using a schedule and write the replies on the schedule as the interview proceeded. The 'methodological appendix' to the dissertation simply states:

> During the interview it was only possible to make brief notes of the conversations. These notes were amplified as soon as possible after the interview, usually the same evening, the process of amplification nearly always taking longer than the interview itself. (Walford, 1978, p. 104).

At the time it was perfectly acceptable for the published papers derived from that research to contain 'quotations' from research students and academics that were based upon these amplified notes of conversations. Several such quotations are presented, but they are contained within a broader description derived from many such interviews and observation.

However, by the time I conducted my second major study of the private boarding schools in 1981, tape-recording of interviews was simply 'the way it was done'. There was hardly a question to ask. The only difficulty was that some respondents might be reluctant to be tape-recorded and had to be persuaded that this was acceptable. In that research I conducted 80 taped semi-structured interviews with academic staff as well as observing lessons, chapel, meals, sports and meetings of masters, parents and prefects. I also used self-completion questionnaires with about 200 of the younger boys. My methods were thus mixed, but on re-examining the book I am struck by the number of quotes that are used in the various reports (Walford, 1984, 1986b). The chapter on 'the changing professionalism of public school teachers', in particular, has many long quotes from the various masters that I interviewed. This time they are taken from transcriptions of tape-recorded interviews. They are presented as if they are 'hard' evidence that cannot be contradicted.

However, traditionally in ethnography, interviews are only one of several ways of generating data. This problem of partial and inaccurate information generated in interviews, which is discussed in the next section, is at least partially dealt with through the process of triangulation. While there are severe doubts about whether triangulation is theoretically possible (see Massey, 1999), generating data through several different methods does at least give the possibility of eliminating gross errors. What is concerning, however, is that there are so many qualitative studies where interviews are the sole method by which data are generated. Why is it that so many reports of qualitative research are dominated by transcriptions of the spoken word? Does this concentration on the spoken word – usually spoken in non-naturally occurring situations – actually distort understanding of the cultures that researchers seek to describe?

I try to read regularly ethnographic studies of a variety of organizations, and accounts of the research processes involved. I was recently impressed by an account by Abolafia (1998) of how he conducted a study of the New York Stock Exchange. He explains how an initial contact at a business school cocktail party, where his previous research on futures markets and bond markets was discussed, led to an invitation on to the floor of the Stock Exchange. The author became a guest of this highly influential man on the floor for several months, observing from his post. A trader who served on the Board of Trustees became aware of his presence, objected to it and brought it to the attention of the Board. However, the result was that they voted to allow the research to continue, and provided a permanent floor pass and a large office. As Abolafia (1998, p. 80) states, 'I was "in" or as one anthropologist described it, the natives had built me a hut.' He then goes on to state, 'With this degree of access my fieldnotes soon supplanted interviews as the major source of data.'

This last sentence is fascinating, and challenges much current qualitative research. It reminds us that most research is actually more interested in what people do than what they say they do. In the case of classroom research, 'what they do' may well include spoken language, but it is spoken language in the particular context of ongoing naturally occurring classroom activity. Abolafia's last sentence reminds us that descriptions based on observation should be central to most accounts, and that what people say when they are interviewed should be treated with extreme care.

I find Hammersley's (1991) framework for the evaluation of ethnographic research studies very insightful. In it he argues the need for clarity in the relationship between the focus of the study and the research case, and between the major claims made about the case and the conclusions drawn about the research focus. He shows clearly the need for precision in the claims made about any case, and recognizes that descriptive claims must be at the base of any higher order claims relating to explanation or, later, evaluation or prescription. In other words, ethnography is based upon descriptive claims. Yet reading the academic journals it becomes evident that many research reports increasingly use the data generated in interviews as the sole, or major, source for such descriptions. Rather than describing what they have observed and noted through participant observation, they present the accounts generated by others in interviews. The descriptive claims are thus based on what people say in interviews rather than what they actually do or say in naturally occurring circumstances.

This was far from always the case. The classic studies of Hargreaves (1967) and Lacey (1970), for example, used a wide variety of sources to support their descriptive claims. They were happy to use a wide variety of documents and notes of their observations to build a picture of the schools in which they conducted their research. They could then make explanatory claims about, for example, differentiation and polarization firmly based on their descriptions. While there are still some excellent cases of similar qualitative and ethnographic methods being followed, there are also many where interviews are overused – even where it is clear that an extensive period of fieldwork in an organization has been conducted.

I believe that this change may be also linked to changing technology. The ethnographer's traditional tools have been 'pencil and paper', and the record of the research was simply the pages and pages of fieldnotes made during the fieldwork. I fear that fieldnotes have become less important to many ethnographers and that most researchers simply do not write as much as ethnographers once did. This was starkly suggested to me recently in Denmark when I talked to an academic about his work. As he talked he used his hands to illustrate and emphasize. He spoke of 'writing' and his hands imitated typing words on a keyboard. I recognized that this is indeed what we now all do, and what we mean when we say that we 'write'. But most of us would find it very difficult to do such 'writing' at the back of a classroom. Using a laptop computer is potentially too offputting to the teachers and students, and there is the continued problem of low battery capacity with even the smallest laptop. It seems to me that it may be that researchers do not use fieldnotes in their descriptive accounts because they no longer write adequate fieldnotes. And they no longer 'write' fieldnotes because the use of a 'pencil and paper' is such an unusual sustained activity for nearly all of us. The change in the way that most of us write has made the activity of writing fieldnotes one that, at this most elementary level, forces us beyond what we do in everyday life.

One possibility here is to use the tape recorder to record fieldnotes as well as interview. In most of my ethnographic studies I have used a tape recorder to record fieldnotes as well as a notebook. I have found that in some places a notebook is perfectly acceptable and it can be used to record either fairly detailed descriptions or just keywords so that fuller notes can be made later. But in other circumstances I have used a tape recorder to generate fieldnotes. As discussed in Chapter 5, at the end of my private boarding schools research I had two boxes of questionnaires, a drawer of tape-recorded interviews, about 800 pages of A4 notes, twenty hours of tape-recorded notes and comments, and a pile of documentation about two feet high. The tape-recorded notes and comments were additional fieldnotes talked into a tape recorder at the end of most days. These were often very different in form from the A4 notes I wrote. Those notes, being written, had a clear structure of sentences and paragraphs. As I explain in Chapter 11, I recognized that these notes might form the basis of particular descriptions that I might eventually use verbatim in books and articles, so the words were chosen with some care. They included some diagrams and tables, but most were written in an explicit way so that they could be understood by me and others beyond their original writing. This was not always true with the tape-recorded notes. Speaking into a tape recorder is faster and less constrained than writing. I used this method to record my feelings and hunches as well as descriptions of events. Some of it was pure catharsis when I had a bad day; other parts were far more positive. Listening to these tapes again reminds me of the agonies and joys of the process, but the tapes also allow me to remember aspects of the experience that I would have otherwise forgotten. There are descriptions of events and contexts that allowed me to interpret and reinterpret other forms of generated data.

My choice of different ways in which to record fieldnotes may not be the same that others will make, but there is a clear need for fieldnotes in any qualitative research. I believe that we need to train researchers in this old-fashioned skill so that more descriptive claims can be based upon them, for the problems with interviews as a basis for such claims are manifold.

HOW VALID ARE INTERVIEWS?

Radio 4 was talking to itself in the background and I overheard: 'I think that once we all used to communicate by telepathy and we only invented language in order to lie.' I have no idea who said it, or in what context, but it struck me as a more useful assumption for researchers than the unexamined and unsustainable one that we should expect people to tell the truth.

Let us examine the nature of the interview. It is, by all accounts, an unusual affair in that the socially accepted rules of conversation and reciprocity between people are suspended. One person takes the lead and asks a series of questions of the other. The other has agreed that this is to be a special form of conversation and is prepared for his or her views to be continuously questioned without the usual ability to be able to return the question. The topics to be covered are under the control of the 'interviewer', and the 'interviewee' is expected to have opinions or information on each of the questions asked. Moreover, what the interviewee says is taken to have lasting importance – it is recorded for future analysis. This is not a transitory conversation, but one that is invested with significance.

Moreover, every person who is interviewed carries his or her own construction of what 'an interview' actually is. Most have sat through hundreds of interviews of the television. These might be 'talk show' interviews where the 'host' gradually encourages the 'guests' to tell interesting, and often slightly risqué or scandalous, stories about themselves or their friends and acquaintances. Potential interviewees have often explained to me that 'they have nothing interesting to say', perhaps thinking that their own lives and opinions do not match those of the 'stars' they see on television. Alternatively, potential interviewees may think of interviews on political or news programmes, where Jeremy Paxman continually badgers them to give an answer to a question, and to clarify exactly what they mean. In such interviews the exact words used by politicians are dissected and may appear later in newspaper articles. Neither of these images is likely to help academic qualitative researchers. But neither is the more academic image of the person with the clipboard lifelessly working through a seemingly unending list of unrelated questions. The interviews that some have been through for a mortgage application, or for social security benefit, or to gain employment or entry into schools or higher education are also unlikely to be helpful. In short, everyone has an idea of what an interview is, but few of these conceptualizations coincide with the relationship that most qualitative researchers would wish to establish.

In passing, it is worth noting that problems can develop from interviewees having 'inappropriate' ideas of what to expect in research interviews. Two of the most difficult interviews I have ever conducted were separate interviews with nuns who were headteachers of schools. Both were, in their different ways, inspiring people, but they acted as if they had little idea of what a research interview might entail. Both of these interviews were conducted as part of a study where I had no previous contact with the headteachers. Both had a great deal of experience of interviewing others – in particular prospective parents and teachers – and neither would allow me to take the lead in the interview. Both had their own tale to tell, and this was what I was going to hear no matter what I wanted. I was questioned by them as well, perhaps more than they by me. Their position was such that almost everyone they met listened to what they had to say, and I was cast in this same role. Eventually, both interviews took over two and a half hours, and what they had to tell me was important, but I was also able to wear my way through this initial situation, and eventually ask specific questions to which I wanted answers. But I first had almost to 'teach' them the role I expected them to occupy.

Of course, most qualitative researchers and ethnographers will make efforts to reduce the pressure that interviewees may feel. They will try to explain the nature of the interview and, it is hoped, the interview is only conducted once some previous relationship has been established. An unthreatening location will be chosen, and the interviewer will be prepared to respond to some of the questions that the interviewee wants to ask. The word 'interview' may not be used at all, and the process might be seen as more of a 'guided conversation', but people are not fooled. One person takes away a tape-recording of the interview and will dissect it later, while the other has told perhaps a little more than he or she intended.

As suggested above, there is a strong irony in the way that so much modern qualitative research relies on tape-recorded interviews as a main data source, for qualitative research and, in particular, ethnographic naturalistic research grew in part in reaction to the positivistic and experimental research that once held sway. Experimental methods were castigated as setting up unreal situations such that the results could not be expected to be valid. Ethnography, on the other hand, was thought to bring greater validity as the everyday activities being investigated would be disturbed as little as possible. Yet, within this ethnography, many researchers (including myself) construct these very strange and artificial situations called 'interviews', and we often use the results of these situations as the core of our writing.

This uncertainty about the validity of interviews is far from new. Quantitative survey interviewers have long been well aware of the possible effects that the interviewer might have on what interviewees say. The time of day or year, the weather and external events have all been shown to have an effect, as have the appearance, gender, ethnicity, clothing, accent, tone and other variables associated directly with the interviewer. Their 'solution' is either to standardize as many of these variables as possible or to have a range of each and hope that the differences cancel out with a sufficiently high number of interviews. Both of these are rarely done with qualitative interviewing – and indeed both 'solutions' are highly suspect. However, the problems are deeper than this.

We know that interviewers and interviewees co-construct the interview and the replies to questions are produced for that particular occasion and circumstance. Interviewees will select their words with care (as in other formal occasions) and will moderate what they have to say to the particular circumstances. If we put to one side the epistemological question of whether of not there is any ultimate 'reality' to be communicated, interviewees may have incomplete knowledge and faulty memory. They will always have subjective perceptions, which will be related to their own past experiences and current conditions. At best, interviewees will only give what they are prepared to reveal about their subjective perceptions of events and opinions. These perceptions and opinions will change over time, and according to circumstance. They may be at some considerable distance from any 'reality' as others might see it.

Interviewees may also lie. A recent article by Sikes (2000) discusses two instances where interviewees who had been reasonably well known to the interviewer had been subsequently found to have lied to them. In the first example, Sikes had conducted a life history project that focused on the impact of parenthood on teachers' professional perceptions, values and practices. She later found that one of the subjects of the research had been having an affair which had led to an abortion, at the same time as talking at length in the interviews of the importance of his family life. In the second example, another researcher had sought information from male teachers of young children about their experiences and views on physical contact with their pupils. One of these men was later found to have been committing indecent assaults on children at the time of the interview.

Sykes writes that she was 'astounded' at the discovery, while the other researcher was reported as having been 'horrified and appalled to realise how effectively she had been conned'. Did they really expect these men to tell them in interview that the first was having an affair and the second assaulting children? People in situations like these will obviously lie, and the researcher should not assume that the 'whole truth' is being given. To me, it seems much more reasonable to expect people to lie about anything and everything that is of importance to them. Interviewees have little to gain from telling an interviewer their innermost secrets. Indeed, I would be most suspicious of anyone who 'revealed' aspects of their own lives that appeared to reflect badly on them. What might their purpose be in doing so?

One of the most stimulating writers on this area is Douglas (1976), whose book proposes that researchers need to move beyond the traditional cooperative paradigm and recognize the underlying conflictual nature of society. In his typical colourful language Douglas argues that:

> In its most extreme form ... the cooperative paradigm of society assumed it is possible to ask members what is going on and they will tell. Yet everyone knows when he [*sic*] thinks about it that only the naive, the innocent, the dupe takes this position all the time in everyday life. Rather, all competent adults are assumed to know that there are at least four major problems lying in the way of getting at social reality by asking people what is going on and that these problems must be dealt with if one is to avoid being taken in, duped, deceived, used, put on, fooled, suckered, made a patsy, left holding the bag, fronted and so on. (Douglas, 1976, p. 57)

He then describes these four problems – misinformation, evasion, lies and fronts – and indicates ways of trying to avoid their effects. He follows this with a detailed exposition of the problems of taken-for-granted meanings problematic meanings and self-deception. In places, the book reads more like a guide to becoming a spy than one designed for academic researchers, and ethical questions are not always at the forefront of his suggested strategies, but the overall point is well made. What people tell us in interviews is often not to be trusted.

Telling explicit lies is only part of the problem. A recent article by Convery (1999) raises many questions about the nature of the life stories that have been collected by various researchers. By presenting a form of his own life history as a teacher, he exposes the variety of narrative strategies that he has used to present an individuality that is morally consistent. He states: 'in offering to reveal the truth of my experiences, I unconsciously took the opportunity to reconstruct a desirable, or preferred identity'. He continues:

> this is a normal activity; all individuals construct identities both by engaging in activities and by finding stories to tell about themselves ... lack of achievement in the actual activities can be compensated for by subsequent accounts of those activities, and the retrospective narrative has the attraction of

fixing a meaning to one's actions, thus ensuring a certain interpretation. (Convery, 1999, p. 139)

It can be argued that identity is created rather than revealed through narrative. Lives are not inherently coherent. We do not have control over our lives. They are the result of chance and circumstance as much as our own activities and plans. The unexpected happens; the expected does not. We act as if we will live forever (or, at least, for a long time yet), but we may be dead tomorrow. In this uncertainty we all try to make sense of our own worlds, and the interview is one occasion when we try to do so in a semi-public forum. We try to present a reasonably rational image of our own uncertainty.

In the case of teachers' life histories, Convery argues that taking these accounts as being 'true' can be highly damaging. This is not just a matter of our 'knowledge' being incorrect; in Denzin's (1989, p. 83) words, 'If we foster the illusion that we understand when we do not, or that we have found meaningful coherent lives where none exist, then we engage in a cultural practice that is just as repressive as the most repressive of political regimes.'

THE FETISH OF TRANSCRIPTION

In spite of their many difficulties, there are some obvious reasons why the interview is so greatly used in qualitative research. Clearly, interviews allow the researcher to generate a great deal of data relatively quickly. Interviewing allows people to express their views about a wide range of issues, and to wait for such information to be generated in naturally occurring situations would be very time consuming. Further, some information might not be generated in naturally occurring situations no matter how long the researcher waits. The interview gives the chance for particular questions to be asked that cannot be asked in any other situation. While we must ask questions about the validity of information generated in situations that are thus unique, this does seem to be a reasonable use for the interview as long as the results are treated with sufficient scepticism.

But there are less obvious reasons for the use of interviews as well. In my research on physics research students and on private boarding schools I felt obliged to start to interview even though I did not really wish to do so. In both cases I had intended to conduct interviews but, ideally, I wanted to observe what was going on for several weeks before doing so. This was simply not possible, for the image of the researcher that was held by most of the members of both groups was that of a 'questioner'. They expected me to conduct interviews and their concerns about my presence started to subside only once I started to interview. Interviews are thus, I believe, often forced on to the researcher. But the force does not only come from outside.

Researchers who wish to observe and use unobtrusive means of generating data are sometimes seduced by the tape-recorded interview. Participant observation can be a very frustrating experience where it seems that 'the action' is always somewhere else. It takes a great deal of patience to sit and wait for the data to be generated. In contrast, doing an interview gives immediate rewards. The interview has been completed; a tape-recording has been made. These can be counted, and progress in the research measured. The numbering of tapes is an important part of this psychological seduction. In reality we know that, if anything, it is the quality of the interviews that counts, not their quantity. Yet I know that I felt more content when I had 'finished' ten or twenty tapes. They were 'hard' data in the soft, uncomfortably insecure and always uncertain world of qualitative research. I know that many other researchers, perhaps especially doctoral students, have similar feelings.

A further feature that I believe adds to our over-dependence on interviews is the fetish that most of us have about transcribing every tape-recording. There can be no firm rules about transcription. The nature of the transcription, or whether it is sensible to transcribe at all, depends on the focus of the research and the exact research questions that need to be answered. If a study focuses on discourse, then it is reasonable to assume that fairly full transcriptions are necessary, and may include special symbols to indicate particular features of the speech. But in many cases the need for detailed transcription, or even any transcription at all, is more open to question.

Let me put on record that I have rarely fully transcribed more than a few interviews for any of my research studies. First, this is a matter of time and energy. Estimates vary, and depend on the nature of the transcription, but a ratio of five hours for every hour of tape seems to be the minimum. Many people take far longer than this – especially if they are not skilled typists. I find it extremely dull and literally mind-numbing work. While some say that transcribing makes the researcher engage with the data, I find that this simply does not happen with me. My concern is with the next word or phrase rather than what is actually being said, so transcription adds little to my understanding of the content.

But my second reason for usually not transcribing is that it has rarely been necessary. Instead, I listen to the whole of each tape using a tape player with a counter. As I listen, I note on a sheet of paper the topics of conversation and the changes of focus against the number on the tape counter. Then I go through again and transcribe those parts of the tape that I feel are most relevant to the research questions that I wish to answer. If my questions change, the original tape is still there, and I can find the relevant parts of each tape from my notes and transcribe the appropriate parts. So far, I have never destroyed any tape-recorded interview. I still have hundreds of cassettes stored away, numbered and coded, just in case I ever want to go back to them. I have one idea, for example, that it would be good to go back to the public school teachers I interviewed in 1981 to see how their views have changed. One of the questions I asked was 'Where do you see yourself in 15 years' time?' It would be fascinating to find out.

A third reason for not transcribing is that I think it is often actually better to conduct the analysis using the original tape-recordings rather than the transcripts. The tape-recording itself is *not* an accurate record of a conversation. At the practical level, there may be technical problems with words simply not being picked up by the microphone, or the background noise may drown out the conversation. (I have never understood why the ear is able to filter out background music at the time of recording, yet is unable to do so when listening to a recording. I have had several recordings made completely useless by background noise that I had failed even to notice at the time.) But at a deeper level, a tape-recording only records the audio part of the conversation. It is often necessary to be able to see what is going on to interpret the words. The physical context in which the interview takes place and the complex body language between the participants are all lost. The tape transcription takes us one further step away from the original event. The pace, accent, accentuation, tone and melody of the speech are all lost – even the most thorough transcription cannot capture them all. The conversation is reduced to symbols on a page. Sometimes, in academic papers I read a quotation and do not understand why it has been selected as evidence for a particular point the author wishes to make. My guess is that the author still remembers how the words were said and the context in which they were said, such that they have a specific meaning that makes sense. The reader, however, has none of this background memory and is unable to interpret the written words in the same way. But on other occasions it may also be that the researcher interprets the words on the page without remembering the original context. Going back to the recording may help to remind the researcher of the hint of sarcasm with which words were spoken, or the fact that a particular phrase was said just after an interruption, or that it was said rapidly, quietly or with emphasis.

This leads to a related reason for not transcribing, which is that the transcription can give the impression of permanence to something that is inherently transitory. As Graddol (1994) observes:

> Tape-recording has the effect of turning an ephemeral spoken event into a relatively stable object. A tape-recording of speech shares with other kinds of text certain key features. It can be edited, copied, and recontextualised: that is replayed in different contexts (and to a different audience) to the one in which the words were originally uttered.

The transcription takes this one stage further, so that the original event becomes data to be entered into a qualitative analysis package and segments become examples drawn from the data bank at the touch of a key. In short, the transcript encourages the possibility of the spoken word being taken too seriously. The phrase that someone happened to have used on a hot Monday afternoon following a double mathematics class gets wrenched out of its context and presented as if it represented the 'truth' about one person's views or understandings. Using the tape-recordings rather than transcripts will not remove this possibility, but it may allow the researcher to remember the complexity of the human condition and the context of construction of particular discourses.

CONCLUSION

Does this mean that researchers should abandon the interview altogether? I do not think so. I still believe that interviews can provide important data, and that it is often worthwhile conducting them. At the very least, they can inform us of what the person interviewed is prepared to say about a topic in the social context, time and place of that particular interview. We need to recognize that what is said will be co-constructed in that interview, and will be limited by perception, memory, evasions, self-deception and more on the part of both interviewee and interviewer, but that it can still have value.

It also needs to be recognized that the effects of the problems of interviews are likely to be related to the nature of the topics under consideration. The nature of information generated about events with which the interviewee has no direct investment is likely to be different from that about personal lifestyle decisions and other areas which have a greater potential impact. We need to be cautious in interpreting the words produced in interview, and should try to generate further data about the same topics in a variety of different ways.

However, I do believe that much research would benefit from greater time being spent in observing the activities of others and recording these observations in fieldnotes, and less time being spent in trying to construct 'hard' data from ephemeral conversations. I have empathy with Barley (in Elsbach, 2000, p. 67), who, in writing about his experiences of researching work in organizations, states:

> I really became an ethnographer who focuses on behaviors. So if you look closely at my work, I'm always talking as much about what people do as what they say, and often my work focuses more on what people do than what they say. And when they say things, I'm interested in how they say things and under what situations. So I don't use much interview data. If I'm in a situation long enough, I don't need to interview anybody.

My research into Dutch religious schools has meant that I have now sat in many classrooms where I am unable to understand the words that are used by the teachers and students. I do not understand Dutch, so I have had to observe what is going on in the schools without focusing on the meanings of words. This has had advantages as well as disadvantages. There have been many times when I strongly wished I had understood the words – occasions of laughter, for example – but there have also been many times when I have been pleased that I have not known. One great advantage is that it has not been possible for me to fall into 'student' mode in lessons and simply listen to the teacher's lesson. Since I am rarely interested in the content of the curriculum, what the teacher is saying is usually irrelevant to my aims. Instead, I am forced to observe interaction between people in its many forms rather than just the oral. I am sure that this has made me notice far more of the two- and three-dimensional visual data than I otherwise would have (Emmison and Smith, 2000). I am more aware of body language, the use of certain images and the way in which spatial factors influence and structure interaction than I have ever been. I am able to focus more on what all those in the classroom are doing rather than what just a few (often just one or two) are saying. I still use interviews, but with greater care.

—7

Researching yourself

INTRODUCTION

All research is researching yourself.

This chapter explores some of the many ways in which all research might be said to be 'researching yourself'. First, it needs to be acknowledged that all research has a subjective element. This is especially so in qualitative research, where the researcher is the main research instrument, but it is also true in more quantitative research and even in natural science. All research involves the researcher in making decisions about the choice of topic and how the research is to proceed. These decisions always involve individual choices, and often evolve from previous personal experiences and commitments.

In the first part of this chapter I discuss some of the effects of personal circumstance on three of my early research projects. I emphasize the ways in which these projects might be said to be 'researching myself'. In the second part, I contrast the ways in which these projects were conceived and conducted with those of some other researchers (often called action researchers), where the ongoing activities of the researcher are the focus.

THE PERSONAL IN RESEARCH PROJECTS

There have been many changes to higher education in the last two decades. In Britain, one of these changes was the removal of academic tenure that was part of the 1988 Education Reform Act. For the Conservative government this was simply a matter of increasing the 'flexibility' of this particular labour market by removing the security of tenure that established academics in the 'old' universities held as part of their contract with their Royal

Chartered institutions. Opposition from academics was framed in terms of 'academic freedom', for tenure gave them the right to research, think and write about any academic subjects they wished. They could not be dismissed for having unorthodox views or for disagreeing with those with power in their departments. As long as they were active in their teaching and research they could not be removed from office.

This particular battle was strongly debated in the House of Lords at the time, but the academics lost, and tenure was removed for all new academics or if the academic changed his or her post through promotion or otherwise. The result has not yet been as harsh as might be expected; those academics with continuing appointments still retain their privileged position of being able to choose their research topics. The degree of autonomy is certainly less than it once was, but there are few heads of department who would try to force someone into a research project with which he or she did not wish to be involved. This is not true, of course, for the expanding force of temporary research workers or lecturers. Their autonomy of action is severely constrained as continuing employment requires that they move from project to project as required by others.

My career has been such that I moved into a tenured academic post quite early and I have always been in a position to be able to choose my own research topics. I have never made any bids to the DfEE or other government departments to conduct research which they felt needed to be done, nor have I tried to tailor my research to any government's perceived needs. One reason for what might be seen as my lack of responsiveness is my training as a sociologist, where I learnt that my role was to question assumptions and to be careful not to 'take questions' that were set by others, but to 'make questions' that were critical of the status quo. I believe that university academics must retain their role as independent critics. But if research topics are not to be set by others, then they must be set by the individual researcher. This frequently means 'researching yourself'.

Postgraduate research – in two senses
Current research interests are always the result of complex interactions between various prior interests and accidents of personal histories. In my case, the desire to read a sociology degree and to undertake educational research at all were the result of a complex interweave of circumstance and opportunity, but the

choice of my first research topic is more simply explained. I completed a doctorate in neutron scattering physics just before starting my MPhil in sociology. That two-year, mainly coursework, degree at Oxford required the completion of a research-based dissertation of about 35,000 words. What was I interested in trying to understand sociologically? My own experience!

In the dissertation (Walford, 1978, p. 95) I stated:

> Current intellectual interests are of necessity the product of past intellectual interests and accidents of biography. The work presented here is no exception to this general rule. Before starting this research I spent three years working for an undergraduate degree at one of the New universities, followed by a further four years postgraduate work for the doctorate. The importance of this socialization and certification process must be strongly emphasized at every stage in the development of this project.
>
> My initial interest in the importance and problems of postgraduate scientists within universities, for example, developed from my own experiences, and the problem of blocked career opportunities for research fellows and lecturers within physics first became evident to me when I started thinking about my own possible future career.

My first sociological research study was thus on the experiences of postgraduate research students in an experimental physics department in a leading university. At that time there was very little research that examined the nature of scientific research activity or the experiences of academics and postgraduates involved in such activities. The project was thus on the borders between the sociology of science and the sociology of the postgraduate student experience. To some extent, I had a mission in wishing to conduct the research, for I felt that postgraduates in the natural sciences played a very important and undervalued part in the research output of departments. It seemed to me that much of the 'slog work' of experimental research was actually done by research students, largely under the direction of research fellows and tenured academics. Few of the tenured academics had the time, or perhaps the inclination, to conduct many experiments themselves, so they established research groups in which postgraduates had a major role. To me, it seemed that postgraduates were being used as underpaid research assistants. The certification in the form of a doctorate was an additional part of the pay, but one that was (even at that time) increasingly less 'cashable' into a future academic job.

The desire to understand my own predicament was linked to particular economic factors that were then about to affect the flow of postgraduate research students. From October 1977 (under a Labour government) there was a substantial increase in postgraduate university fees for both home and overseas students. The expectation was that the total numbers of postgraduate students would drop by 10–20 per cent as a direct result. This was coupled with a decrease in the number of studentships available from the then Science Research Council. It seemed to me that the resulting cuts would have a severely detrimental effect on the scientific output of university science departments, yet the discussions at the time were all couched in terms of the costs of training as if the students themselves made no contribution to research output. I wanted to conduct the research both to understand better my own experience and to make what I perceived to be the importance of postgraduate research to research output more public. It was thus in part an example of advocacy research – if only weakly.

For the thesis itself, I observed and interviewed in one department. A second department was added following the completion of the thesis, when there was a chance that I might extend the work into a second doctorate. The final publications were based on interviews and observation – interviews being somewhat forced on me through the necessity to be readily accepted by the department and the limited time I had available. In the light of what I have said in Chapter 6, on re-reading, I was pleased to see how sceptical I was about interviews even over twenty years ago. In the dissertation (Walford, 1978, pp. 99, 101) I wrote:

> From the conception of the project it was anticipated that I would need to have a fairly formal role within the department to justify my presence and become accepted. I initially attempted to present myself in the role of a 'traditional sociologists' with a list of questions to be answered, with the hope that I would be able to relax this role and enter into a more informal semi-participant observational strategy as I became more accepted.
>
> After a couple of weeks I recognised that it was not going to be possible to build any genuinely observational situations

within the complete department. If I wished to obtain information about the whole of the department then I would have to rely mainly on information from interviews supplemented by a small amount of informal contact and observation at tea and coffee times and in the evening. The initial hope that I would be able to relax my 'sociological' role and use observational methods began to look very unlikely – in fact, it is difficult to know how it could possibly have been successful in such a short time given that much research work is a solitary occupation or, at most, the work of two or three people working together at one time. Quite obviously, it is very difficult to observe what goes on within such small groups as people generally do not like being watched. Even if some people had allowed me to observe them, I realized that there were still considerable problems. For example, in such a solitary situation my presence would, undoubtedly, have considerably changed everyday interaction and behaviour. Another problem was that much of the work done by postgraduates is very repetitive, such that little information could have been gained in the short time available.

The published material from the research was based upon the two departments (Walford, 1983b). It described the nature of research activity in physics and the role that postgraduates had in research output, but it did not simply elaborate on what I thought I knew from my own experience as a research student. Talking with a variety of academics and being with them on some informal occasions led me to see the postgraduate research process from their points of view as well as those of the postgraduates. Moreover, I saw the vital importance of research groups and their relative size in the experience that postgraduates went through. One of my unexpected findings was that the differences between the roles of postgraduates were as important as their similarities. While some students became part of a team working on a set of problems, others were isolated workers with only slight contact with their supervisor. I also found that the possible effect of a reduction in the number of research students was not clear. For small groups, the postgraduates seemed to be essential. I found several cases where academics had simply ceased any experimental activity when their last postgraduate student had completed. They could only 'get going again' once a new student arrived. In contrast, for large research groups, where there were research fellows, the presence of postgraduates probably led to an overall decrease in productivity in the short-time. Fewer postgraduates in larger groups would free postdoctoral fellows to do more themselves. This finding was totally unexpected by me. By concentrating on the short-term outputs, my research had actually shown what I did not want to find. I had expected that in most cases a clear short-term benefit to research would be found, but I found that in some cases such a benefit was far from clear. It was only by considering the longer-term benefits of training students who might then become research fellows that having research students could be justified. A slight reduction in the number of research students might even be helpful to the research output of departments.

In the end I first published papers on why students started doctorates (Walford, 1980a) and on the relationship between student and supervisor (Walford, 1981a), before I published, rather late, a developed version of the whole dissertation (Walford, 1983b). I was slowed down by hopes of publishing it as a book, which never materialized.

Understanding public schools
I have discussed the choice of my second major research project in Chapter 5. There I explained that I had not attended a public school as a boy. My first contact with the independent sector came when I was 23 and working for a doctorate in physics. I taught, or tried to teach, mathematics to a group of 14- and 15-year-old 'bottom set' boys. During my PGCE year I again taught at a major boys' boarding school, and then I taught physics for two terms in another. In all these cases I had found the experience disconcerting. There were many things that I did not understand about these schools and about why people worked in them or sent their children to them. I wanted to find out more.

My chance came following my appointment as lecturer in sociology of education at Aston University in 1979. I decided to attempt an ethnographic study of public boarding schools. There were very many 'good reasons' for arguing that there was a need for such a study, and I have outlined some of them in Chapter 5, but the personal reason of trying to understand a part of my past was also crucial. This was another example where I was to some extent 'researching myself'. While I certainly wanted to understand more about the role that these schools have played in reproducing our inegalitarian society and the way they educated the sons of the affluent to take their place in social, economic and political elites, I also wanted to understand my own reaction to teaching in some of them.

I spent four weeks in the summer of 1981 in the first school and the whole of the summer term of 1982 was spent in the second. In both schools I aimed to be an open researcher. Staff and pupils knew that I was at the school for the specific purpose of writing a book about public schools. In the first school I did no teaching, but in the second I taught two sets of lower form boys – six periods a week for the first half of term and three thereafter. During this time I lived in accommodation provided by the schools on the school sites. In both schools my research method was eclectic. I talked with boys, girls, masters, wives, secretaries, other staff and headmasters. I became involved with the various aspects of school and community life, including sports, visits, drinking at the local pub, dinner parties and other activities. I observed lessons, chapel, meals, sports and meetings of masters, parents and prefects. I also conducted eighty taped semi-structured interviews with academic staff. The main publications were a full-length book on life in public schools (Walford, 1986a), two journal articles on girls in boys' schools and on reproduction of social class (Walford, 1983b, 1986b), and an article in a collected volume about the changing experiences of public schoolmasters (Walford, 1984).

In order to conduct the research I needed some funding from the department. I already had a sabbatical that gave me the time away from teaching, but I needed some funding for accommodation and travel. I discussed this with my head of department and he advised me against doing research in this area. He thought that it would be seen as a diversion away from the mainstream of sociology of education and that my reputation would suffer as a result. He also pointed out that researchers tend to become associated with the type of institution they research and that being known for having an interest in private schools, even under the Conservatives, would not necessarily be helpful. What is worthy of note is that, even though he thought I was making a mistake, he granted me the right to take my own decision. Once he was sure that I really wished to do this ethnography, he supported the work financially, practically and with enthusiasm. I recognized then the privileged position that I was in.

When the work had been done, as with the research student study, some of my findings surprised me. I found myself having far greater empathy with the teaching staff than I ever though I would have. I was fascinated by the way the schools were adapting to change. I was also made aware of the way that female staff were treated and the decidedly odd way in which girls were included, yet excluded, within the schools. This was another case where I was researching part of my history, yet I was centrally concerned to generate data that would allow me to describe the nature of these schools as they were at the time of the research. In my next major research project I was involved continuously with the situation that I was describing. The institution that I was researching was my employer.

Understanding change in a university

The University of Aston in Birmingham came into being in 1966 as a result of the Robbins Committee's recommendation that the ten colleges of advanced technology (CATs) should become universities. By 1980 Aston had become a university with over 5,500 students studying engineering, science and technology, but also business studies, social sciences and modern languages. It had a thriving Department of Educational Enquiry which I joined in 1979. The university had gradually shed its CAT role as a major provider of part-time courses and had become much more like other British universities. By the time I arrived it had about 540 academic staff and taught 34 separate single honours BSc degrees alongside a large combined honours scheme. It also had 20 different MSc and MBA courses and gave MPhil and PhD research degrees.

In July 1981 the University Grants Committee (UGC), which at that time acted as a channel for government funding to the universities, announced its allocation of financial support for each of the universities for the following three years. Aston was informed that it was to lose more that a third of its funding and that it would have to reduce its student numbers by more than a fifth within three years. The announcement marked the beginning of a long and often bitter internal political struggle as the university accommodated to these demands and reorganized itself such that by 1985 it was in a stronger position to face the anticipated problems of the late 1980s and early 1990s. By the end of 1985 more than half the academic staff of 1981 had left and not a single new permanent academic staff member had been appointed. Many courses had been cut and over half the departments within the university had either closed or merged with others. Yet at the same time the university spent over £5 million on physical restructuring and campus development, established a rapidly expanding science park with venture capital, ensured that the average 'quality' of student in terms of A level entry grades was higher than the national average of all universities in every subject and developed a unique Extension Education Centre based on tutored video instruction.

The book that I wrote (Walford, 1987e) was an account of some of the major changes that occurred up to 1985, and an attempt to understand the management process in action during this time in terms of a political theoretical model. In some ways the book could be seen as the end product of an extended period of participant observation. The department to which I was appointed in 1979 closed in 1983, and I moved first to a Department of Sociology and Social History and then to the Social and Technology Policy Group within the Management Centre, as that department was itself dismembered. Later still this group became part of the Strategic Management and Policy Studies Division of the Business School. In spite of being closely affected by these changes, I did not set out to present a strongly partisan view of events, or try to defend or attack various decisions that were made both inside and outside the university. My natural inclination has always been that of an observer rather than protagonist, and even though the results of being 'at the sharp end' of political decisions were personally painful and at times even traumatic, I never played any significant role in the unfolding internal political process.

In an attempt to ensure that the account was not merely a reflection of my own situation, evidence was largely drawn from a considerable collection of documentary sources that were gathered as the events unfolded. This included committee meeting minutes, newspaper articles, internal memoranda, letters, fly sheets, advertisements and news sheets. One of my colleagues was heavily involved in Association of University Teachers activities during the period, and he also provided much documentary material. Informal interviews were also held with about twenty of the university's academic and administrative staff specifically to gain a variety of views and to check accounts. These interviews were not tape-recorded, partly because most of those involved were not prepared to be identified and anonymity could not be guaranteed. The first draft of the book was read by eight people, six from within the university, including the Vice Chancellor and the Registrar. There were many corrections of specific errors, but there was no attempt at censorship. The Vice Chancellor, however, did not wish to be acknowledged in the book for his help.

This research was thus a form of participant observation where I, as researcher, was employed by the organization I was writing about. However, it differed from most of the classic studies of this type (for example, Dalton, 1959) in that I still wished to be employed in that same institution after the research was published. It is difficult to describe the pressure which all the staff at Aston were under at that time. The Vice Chancellor used the opportunity provided by the dramatic reduction in funds to restructure the whole university. This meant that many staff simply had to go – through 'mobility packages', 'enhanced mobility packages' or compulsory redundancy. Theoretically all tenured Aston academics benefited from very strong tenure in their contracts, as the former CAT had been strongly unionized at the time the Royal Charter was drawn up. The University Council, however, made it clear that it was prepared to test the strength of these tenure clauses if it became necessary to make academics compulsorily redundant because of financial need. This threat was clearly present throughout the negotiations on 'voluntary redundancy' and a high court case was called off just days before it was due to be held because the final academics 'volunteered' to leave.

The Aston case was thus significant at the national level as well as the local. It was the first university to go to high court, and many other university councils were waiting for the result to see if they could make similar moves to remove staff. At the personal level, it was obvious that my department was going to close and, as a relatively new academic with a limited research record, my chances of obtaining another academic job were small at this time of staff reduction throughout the system. I simply had to stay or get out of academic life. The fight to save the department and individual jobs went on from 1981 to 1983. In 1981 my Department of Educational Enquiry had 16 staff with an average age of 35; in 1986 only four academic staff remained. Collecting the documents and discussing the situation with others was thus in part a cathartic activity, but I was also very interested at an academic level in the way that 'change management' was occurring around me. The final book examined the process in terms of various models that helped to explain the process, and it emphasized the political model where other models, such as 'collegiality' or the 'bureaucratic model', were used politically by those in power at appropriate times. This meant that the role of the Vice Chancellor was central to my account.

I thought that the account that I gave of the Vice Chancellor's role as a central power-broker and decision-maker did not, at the very least, paint him in the most desirable light. But I wanted to publish. I felt that if academic freedom meant anything, it had to mean that I was free to write about my own university, and the ways in which the Council and Vice Chancellor had acted. I had checked my sources, I felt that the account was fair. I was ready for a fight and, strangely, I felt that a fight would make my own position more secure. Even in 1986 there were still background threats of compulsory redundancies, and my own position (teaching sociology in a university where the Vice Chancellor had clearly told me that he was not going to have sociology in 'his' university) was far from secure. I felt that no university could risk the potential scandal of sacking an employee who had written a critical academic book about it. When I sent the Vice Chancellor a copy of the manuscript I expected to be summoned to his office and told to modify it greatly. In fact, this did not happen. He made generally favourable comments, and I later found that he had bought several copies of the book to give to members of the University Council. Clearly, my own understanding of what was happening was limited. This was, after all, the way of the future.

RESEARCHING YOURSELF: GETTING IN ON THE ACTION

In all three projects outlined above I have made it clear that personal issues were central in the choice of research topic and in the issues that were confronted during the research. In the first two, the research was conducted some time after I had actually been in a similar situation to that which I was researching. In those cases I conducted the research as an overt researcher, with all those involved knowing about my research role. In the third case, I was still employed by the university when I researched and wrote about it, and few knew that I was conducting research at all. I never asked permission of anyone to conduct the research, but some of my colleagues were aware of the study and were helpful in obtaining particular documents and in interviews. This last case is closest to a form of research practice that has been encouraged among teachers and has expanded greatly in the past ten years: action research.

The title 'action research' is now often used to describe activities carried out by teachers and other educational professionals where they examine practice in classrooms – often their own classrooms. In Britain it has become associated, in particular, with the work of McNiff (1988, 1993), Whitehead (1989) and Lomax (1990), and has become something of an evangelical 'movement' designed to change the nature of educational research such that it becomes an 'integral part of the work of teachers in schools rather than an activity carried out on schools by outsiders' (Hammersley, 1993). The teacher-as-researcher is far from a new idea, for such a movement was active in the 1950s in the USA, where Corey (1949) argued that teachers should conduct research to improve their own practice. At that time, however, it was also closely associated with the quantitative and 'scientific' methods of Lewin (1948) and others.

While Lewin is still given ritual reference in action research texts (for example, McNiff, 1988), the modern conception has emerged largely independently from the American model or from earlier British forms of action research. The classic action research work of Halsey (1972) on educational priority areas, for example, or that of Kelly (1985) and Whyte (1987) on encouraging girls to enter science subjects in schools has been forgotten and replaced by references to the work of researchers at CARE at the University of East Anglia. The Centre for Applied Research in Education will always be associated with the work of Stenhouse and the Schools Council Humanities Curriculum Project. This curriculum development project led Stenhouse to develop his ideas on the role of research in the development of teacher professionalism and to the improvement of teaching. Stenhouse believed that teachers should systematically question their own teaching, have the commitment and skills necessary to study their own teaching, be concerned to question and test theory in practice, and be ready to allow other to observe their teaching and be open to their comments (Stenhouse, 1975). The key idea here is that the professionalism of teachers should not be based upon external knowledge, but on ideas tested through their own action through continual invention and reflection. Other writers associated with CARE (such as Carr and Kemmis, 1986) have taken these ideas further and argue for a form of action research which is critical and emancipatory – one that builds towards a rational, just and democratic society. It has to be said, however, that such books have much to say about the importance of the emancipation of teachers and very little to say about students. They fail to recognize the conflictual nature of schooling, and the fact that schools are caught in a web of often mutually contradictory demands from parents, employers, the state, children and the teachers themselves. There is even, of course, conflict within each of these categories.

The difficulty in being critical about this form of action research is that the activities themselves are frequently highly desirable. An important aspect of being a teacher is reflection on the process of teaching itself. It should be expected that teachers will evaluate their own work on an ongoing basis, and when they develop new strategies for teaching they should be particularly careful to assess the effects. Such activities are to be welcomed and the more structured the self-reflection becomes the better are likely to be the results. In some ways, this is the production of new knowledge. But it is a form of new knowledge that is highly specific to its context and its generator. It may well show that a specific researcher-teacher had great success with a particular method of teaching algebra, but a teacher researching herself is unable to determine the extent to which the effect was due to the method, her enthusiasm for the method, her rapport with the students or a host of other potential variables. Of course, the exact cause of the effect does not greatly matter in the context of the single classroom in which the action research was carried out – success is success. But it does matter if this structured self-reflection is to be disseminated to other teachers and the 'causes' of the change are to be identified (or perhaps misidentified). Researching yourself simply does not work at the micro-level, for no teacher is able to generate sufficiently objective data about her own ongoing activities that can be generalized to other classroom contexts.

The action research movement has criticized conventional academic research on teachers, classrooms and schools as (as summarized by Hammersley, 1993, p. 215) largely irrelevant to the practical concerns of teachers, often invalid because it is separated from the objects it claims to understand, undemocratic in that it allows the views of outside educational researchers to define the reality of teachers and amounting to a process of exploitation. Hammersley himself has rebutted these criticisms and still sees an important place for traditional academic research, but his voice has been heard only by some.

Criticism of educational research has come not only from teachers, but also from within academia itself. Questions about the quality and relevance of educational research have recently been at the centre of a prolonged, public and sometimes acrimonious debate. This debate is far from being isolated to Britain, as it was two major reports from CERI (Centre for Educational Research and Information) and from Australia that originally sparked the concern (CERI, 1995; Australian Research Council, 1992; see Rudduck, 1998). These reports led the British Economic and Social Research Council to commission two reports that reviewed 'the position of research into education in the United Kingdom with a view to increasing the Council's knowledge of the particular problems facing educational research and its development over the next decade' (ESRC, 1993), and considered the educational organization and management of research (Ranson, 1995a; see also Gray, 1998; Ranson, 1998).

A further 'strategic review of educational research' was commissioned by the Leverhulme Trust and conducted by David Hargreaves and Michael Beveridge (1995), and a sustained critique of educational research was launched in 1996 by David Hargreaves in a much publicized speech given at the annual Teacher Training Agency conference. In that lecture he argued that much educational research was irrelevant to the needs of teachers and policy-makers. He called for an end to:

> second-rate educational research which does not make a serious contribution to fundamental theory or knowledge; which is irrelevant to practice; which is uncoordinated with any preceding or follow-up research; and which clutters up academic journals that virtually nobody reads. (Hargreaves, 1996, p. 7)

This contribution was influential and much debated (Hammersley, 1997). The intervention was indirectly responsible for two further highly critical and contentious studies of the educational research literature (Hillage *et al.*, 1998; Tooley and Darby, 1998) which have themselves been the subject of considerable criticism. But the result of this critique and debate is that the Labour government has been led to emphasize the need for educational research to have relevance for teachers, policy-makers and others involved in educational practice. This has become linked to the call for teaching to be a 'research-based profession' (Davies, 1999) and to increasing pressure from government and other research funders for researchers to justify their activities in more directly instrumental ways. Putting to one side the fact that there is a clear need for at least some research that does not have instrumental objectives, the call for a 'researcher-based profession' has encouraged many to believe that action research is the answer.

There has been confusion about the nature of the research on which a 'research-based profession' can be built. While the Department of Education and Employment has established a Centre for Evidence Informed Policy and Practice in Education at the Institute of Education, University of London, the Teacher Training Agency took a rather different path. The Centre will build its version of an 'evidence-based profession' on extensive and critical literature reviews of research evidence. Each piece of research will be evaluated, with special care being taken to assess the quality of the research methodology used. For example, randomized trials, of which there are few in education, will be given particular weight in coming to conclusions about particular research areas. Teacher-based action research would be unlikely to rate highly in such evaluations.

In contrast, the Teacher Training Agency (TTA) was far more influenced by the teacher-as-researcher and action research movement, and took a 'research-based profession' to mean that teachers should themselves conduct research. In 1996 it launched a Teacher Research Grant Pilot Scheme and invited teachers to bid for grants to help them conduct small-scale research projects on aspects of classroom practice. In all, 231 bids were submitted and the Agency gave an average of about £2,000 to 27 of these. The reports from 25 of these studies were evaluated by Foster (1999) in terms of their clarity, validity and relevance. There was a variety of styles of research reported but five of the studies did not appear to be research at all in that they did not appear to seek to produce knowledge. The remaining reports included action research as well as more conventional methodologies. Foster was careful to admit the difficulties of any evaluation, yet he found many problems. He states:

> A lot of the reports made bold descriptive and evaluative claims – and, in some cases, evaluative and prescriptive ones – which would have been very difficult to establish even aside from the limited resources at the teacher-researchers' disposal and the circumstances in which they were working. And, in a few cases, the teacher-researchers appeared unable to distance themselves from their preconceived views about effective practice, and their findings and evidence seemed shaped to support these views. (Foster, 1999, p. 395)

He recognizes that similar problems can be found in the published academic research, but the TTA intended that these reports would be made widely available to other teachers. It seems to me that the problems identified here stem from the fact that research is far more difficult to do well than most people appreciate. It demands a great deal of time and energy and a range of specific skills that have to be learned and practised. If knowledge is to be cumulative, at least in some small way, it also requires knowledge and critical assessment of the vast amount of literature of teaching, learning and education. My belief is that teaching is itself a complicated and exhausting enough job, without adding the expectation that teachers should be involved in research. Even if time and resources were made available to serving teachers, the ability to distance oneself from the struggles of the everyday experience of the classroom is far from easy.

In Kurt Lewin's form of action research there was collaboration between teachers and external researchers. This was also true for the work of Kelly and Whyte on girls in science and in Halsey's work on education priority areas. In these projects it was recognized that different people have different skills and opportunities to develop and use them. Through cooperation, this division of labour does not lead to exploitation, irrelevance or invalidity but to a gradual building of a greater knowledge of teaching and schools.

Political commitment

This chapter considers the relationship between political commitment and research objectivity in the City Technology College
research conducted between 1987 and 1990. The results of the
research have been published in book form (Walford and Miller,
1991) and in a series of articles (e.g. Walford, 1991b, d). In order to
understand the particular issues, it is first necessary to outline the
wider political context in which the research was conducted.

THE WIDER POLITICAL CONTEXT

The creation of a 'pilot' network of City Technology Colleges was
announced in October 1986 by Kenneth Baker, then Secretary of
State for Education and Science. These new secondary schools were
a first step towards the greater diversity of types of school that was
a prominent feature of the 1988 Education Reform Act. But
increasing diversity was just one aspect of their purpose. A second
feature was the desire to encourage what was seen as greater
technological and business relevance in schools. The intention was
that the CTCs would offer a curriculum strong in technology,
science and business studies, and attract children who were
particularly interested in these areas. A third feature of the idea
was that substantial financial and other inputs would be made to
the CTCs by industry and commerce. This was clearly intended to
encourage a privatization process within education where the state
would be seen as just one of several possible funders of education.
A further important feature of the CTCs was that they were part of
an open attack on local education authorities (especially those
controlled by Labour), for they were to be established in inner-city
areas without any consultation with the relevant LEAs. The CTCs
were designed to deal with perceived educational problems in the
'loony left' boroughs by creating a new form of government-
funded, yet officially independent, school run by educational trusts.

The ethnographic study of two of the major Headmasters' Conference boarding schools that I had conducted in the early 1980s had developed in the 1990s beyond this initial interest in private education to include work on the more political aspects (e.g. Walford, 1987a, b, 1988a; Robson and Walford, 1988). In particular, I was beginning to see the similarities between many of the changes in education and the privatization that was occurring in many other areas of the public sector (Walford, 1988b, 1990). My immediate reaction to the CTC announcement was to see this as a further example of openly encouraging a process of privatization within education, where new well funded private schools would compete with local maintained schools for students. I was extremely hostile towards the whole idea of CTCs, fearing that it was part of an attempt to build a more inegalitarian educational system and to reintroduce selection by the back door.

In February 1987 it was announced that the first college was to be in Conservative-controlled Solihull, just a few miles from Aston University. That Solihull was first was fortuitous for, in addition to my longstanding interest in private schools, I had also published an article on an earlier unsuccessful attempt to reintroduce selective education in Solihull (Walford and Jones, 1986). The conjunction of interests and potential accessibility made it almost inevitable that I should try to conduct research on the first CTC.

I consulted with a colleague at Aston, Henry Miller, and we decided that we would approach the Economic and Social Research Council to fund a three-year project to look at the national, local and college effects of the CTC policy. A somewhat similar research strategy had been used by Tony Edwards and Geoff Whitty in their ESRC funded study of the Assisted Places Scheme, so I wrote to them to see whether we could use their successful application for that research as a model for our own. It turned out that they already had the same idea as us, and were in the process of applying to the ESRC for funding for research on CTCs. We recognized that they had a far greater chance of obtaining funding than us, so the final proposal to the ESRC from Tony Edwards and Geoff Whitty included Henry Miller and myself as 'consultants' to their project. The intention was that we would conduct the Kingshurst case study, looking at the two LEAs involved, the local secondary schools in the CTC catchment area and the CTC itself. We planned to write a short, mainly descriptive, book about Kingshurst as rapidly as we could, as well as feeding our data into the national study.

My initial interests were thus linked to my continuing research on private schools and privatization. I was against the idea of selection of children for particular well funded schools, whether by IQ tests or by motivation and aptitude, simply because I feared the effect of such selection on rejected pupils and other nearby schools. But I was genuinely interested to know what a CTC would be like – how it might differ from other schools, what the curriculum and teaching would be like, what the backgrounds of teachers and pupils would be, how pupils' experiences in a CTC would differ from those of pupils in other schools. It was an example of the simple 'nosiness' of the sociologist about how organizations structure themselves, and how these different structures affect the lives of those within them. I expected that there would be an interesting story to tell about the CTC, which many would wish to read.

But the study was also not intended to be an evaluation of the college. It would have been presumptuous to suppose that an adequate evaluation could have been conducted in the short time that I had available to me to conduct the research, and also somewhat ridiculous, as the CTC was still at such an early stage of development. We also had no desire to produce what we expected would be a glowing report on how the college was developing. Our expectations were that superior funding and facilities, coupled with highly selected staff and pupils, would almost automatically lead to a positive learning environment, but we did not wish to act as a free advertising agency for the college.

A POLITICAL MOTIVATION

While our interest in undertaking the research might, in part, be explained in terms of the 'nosiness' of the sociologist about organizations, we did not approach the research with a neutral stance about the CTC concept. We were firmly against the idea of selection of children for particular schools, especially where the schools involved were designed to be better funded and resourced than nearby schools. We were also against the privatization of the educational system that the CTCs implied. We embarked upon a form of policy evaluation, yet we already had our own ideas about that policy.

Our research was, then, in large part, politically motivated. We believed the topic to be worth our research time and effort because of its political importance. The CTCs had been announced during the Conservative Party Annual Conference which preceded the 1987 general election. They were surrounded by politics, and represented the first stage of the increased diversity of schools that was the centrepiece of Conservative education policy as outlined in their manifesto for the election. Our objective was not to try to influence those involved in the college itself, nor was it to try to influence conservative policy-makers at a high level (we had long since given up any ideas that they might be open to logical argument!). However, one of our primary objectives was to try to have some small direct and indirect influence on the way the national electorate voted in the next general election.

This centrality of the topic to the Conservative Party education programme not only led us to tackle the research, but also structured the research timetable. To a large extent we 'cut the cloth' to fit the time available within a political context. Thus, following the pattern of previous Conservative governments, it was reasonable to expect that there would be another election during 1991. We hoped to make some small impact on the result of this election. We hoped to be able to show that the CTC programme had severe problems and was acting to the detriment of many children. Rather than being part of a scheme to 'raise educational standards', we hoped to be able to show, they were doing the opposite. We recognized that, if we wanted to make any slight impact on the result of the election that we expected in 1991, we would have to work very fast on the research. We would also need to present our results in such a way that they would be picked up by the press and might be of use to the Labour opposition. We decided that a book would probably have the greatest impact and, towards the end of 1988, Henry Miller and I sent a proposal to Open University Press. We received a contract in March 1989 for a book of 55,000 to 70,000 words to be delivered to them by 1 April 1990 at the latest. This was a rather optimistic deadline for, at the time of signing the contract, we had still not managed to negotiate access to the CTC itself. As explained in Chapter 2, it was actually the possession of a contract that finally helped to secure access.

PARTISANSHIP AND NEUTRALITY IN RESEARCH

On reading the preceding paragraphs many of those on the political right (and not only those on the right) would, no doubt, argue that such political motivation automatically invalidates any results of the research. How can partisanship on such a scale be compatible with social science research?

My belief is that such partisanship *is* compatible with social science research. Indeed, the motivation for conducting all research is linked to subjective political evaluations of what is important and unimportant. At the same time I believe that it is still possible (and desirable) to fight for some form of neutrality in the way in which research studies are conducted.

This idea is far from new. Weber's idea of value neutrality, for example, has a very similar emphasis. As Hammersley (1992, p. 104) points out:

> For Weber, the phenomena investigated by the social scientist are *defined* in terms of practical values. There is no question of those phenomena being value free in some absolute sense. At the same time, he argues that once defined these phenomena should be investigated in a way that (as far as possible) suspends practical value judgements in the attempt to discover the truth about them.

In looking at these potential dilemmas, I find an early discussion by Alison Kelly (1978) particularly useful. Kelly's article considers the question of what constitutes feminist research. She argues that feminist research cannot be defined simply as research which supports the aims of feminism, as that would imply that the results of research are known in advance. This is unacceptable, as the essence of research is that it sets out to explore the unknown. But she agrees with Myrdal (1969, p. 9) that: 'There is an inescapable *a priori* element in all scientific work. Questions have to be asked before answers can be given. The questions are all expressions of our interest in the world: they are at bottom valuations.' The motivations of the researchers are thus an important element in whether or not a particular piece of research should be regarded as feminist. In part, it is feminist if the reason for doing the research is feminist. But Kelly feels that this alone is an inadequate criterion, and goes on to reformulate the question 'What is feminist research?' in terms of 'At what points does feminism enter the research process?'

Kelly's model of social research is based largely on her own quantitative international comparative studies of girls' and boys' achievement in school science. But there is no particular reason why her basic framework of understanding cannot equally well be applied to more qualitative social research, and to all forms of overtly committed research.

In her analysis, Kelly divides the research process into three rather crude stages:

1. Choosing the research topic and formulating hypotheses.
2. Carrying out the research and obtaining the results.
3. Interpreting the results.

She argues that a feminist commitment enters the research in the first and the third stages, but that researchers should seek to avoid any political or social commitment during the second stage. In particular, she rejects the idea that objectivity and rationality are masculine traits, and that there is a 'masculine bias' embedded in traditional social science methodology. She sees feminist research (and by implication all committed research) as being a catholic activity, embracing a wide range of methodologies, and accepting the results that are produced once the questions have been formulated and the appropriate methods selected. Commitment can enter the process again at the stage of interpretation, after the results have been produced, but not to the extent that unfavourable results are suppressed.

I recognize that this view of feminism has been strongly contested. Stanley and Wise (1983, p. 22), for example, reject Kelly's threefold division of the research process and her view that particular research methods should not be identified with specific commitments (see also Stanley, 1990), but I hope to show in this chapter that the threefold classification does have some utility. Its strength is that it forces the researcher to face her or his own subjectivity and commitment, to make these clear and open, and to try to ensure that the 'middle stage' of the research is as free from them as possible. Good research should include a 'search for subjectivity' (Peshkin, 1991, p. 285) which will enable the degree of objectivity of the 'middle stage' to be enhanced. This 'objectivity' is not an absolute, but is part of a process or, as Phillips (1989, p. 23) argues, ' "Objectivity" seems to be a label that we apply to inquiries that meet certain procedural standards, but objectivity does not *guarantee* that the results of inquiries have any certainty.'

The book *City Technology College* covers a variety of different interlinked topics concerned with the college and its relationships with other nearby schools. It thus may be seen as a series of research questions and research results and analyses. In the next two sections I show how Kelly's framework can be applied to some examples from this research.

THE CLOSURE OF SIMON DIGBY SCHOOL

The research covered a wide variety of different interlinked topics concerned with the college and its relationships with other nearby schools – there were thus a series of research questions and research results. This first example from the study is largely quantitative, and the research process can thus be discussed fairly straightforwardly in terms of Kelly's threefold scheme. The research question that we set out to answer was 'Could the establishment of the City Technology College, Kingshurst be identified as the reason for the closure of a nearby local authority school, Simon Digby School?'

To most local teachers, parents and politicians the answer to such a question was unambiguously 'yes' – it seemed almost too obvious to question. The whole catchment area of the CTC, which extended into East Birmingham and North Solihull, had rapidly declining secondary school rolls. Over the years, several schools in the area had been closed to adjust the accommodation available to the decreasing numbers of pupils. One of the schools to close was the old 11–16 Kingshurst Comprehensive School, which ceased to admit students in September 1984. The decision to close Kingshurst School was made mainly on the basis of low pupil numbers in relation to places available in the building, its geographical position in relation to other schools and the fact that it was housed in inferior quality buildings compared with neighbouring secondary schools.

In spite of this and other recent school closures and the continuing falling rolls in the region, the government was so desperate to get agreement on at least one CTC before the 1987 general election that it decided to give Hanson Trust substantial financial backing in order to establish Kingshust CTC in North Solihull. Solihull had the convenience of being close to Birmingham, yet being controlled by a Conservative council anxious to reintroduce selective education. The unfortunate fact that the only premises available were of poor quality could be solved by throwing sufficient money at them. The substantial rebuilding programme was under way as the last cohort of pupils in the former Kingshurst Comprehensive were in their last year, and the new CTC opened in the September immediately following the final closure of the school in July 1988.

When, about a month later, Solihull LEA announced that it was entering into a period of consultation over the closure of Simon Digby School it seemed obvious that the reopening of the Kingshurst site had caused an alternative school to be closed instead. It seemed that a clear case of careful LEA planning had been overturned by the introduction of an expensive CTC, and that here was good ammunition for arguing against CTCs. The question we asked – 'Could the establishment of the City Technology College, Kingshurst be identified as the reason for the closure of a nearby local authority school, Simon Digby School?' – was selected because we thought that we already knew the answer and believed that the answer would show some of the problems of the overall policy.

However, when we actually examined the data (Walford and Miller, 1991, pp. 135–8), we found that the situation was not so simple. The analysis showed (much to our dismay) that it was highly likely that Simon Digby School would have closed whether or not the CTC had been established. In the data collection and analysis stage of the research we attempted to be as objective as we could. We collected all the data to which we had access and interpreted the data in a way which we felt any fair researcher would agree with. The unfortunate part from our politically committed viewpoint was that our findings did not show what we hoped – they actually weakened the arguments being used by local Labour politicians and trade unionists.

In spite of this finding, we decided that we had to include these results in the book. In fact, it was hardly a decision at all, for it was felt that suppression of results was not only undesirable, but ethically wrong. Kelly's middle stage of research, in practice, implies the duty to publish results which do not agree with personal commitments. However, Kelly argues that commitment can again enter at the third stage of research – interpreting the results. In this example of the closure of Simon Digby School our own commitment shows through in the interpretation that we give to the results. For example, we discuss the variety of possible definitions of space in secondary schools, and argue for the advantages of a generous definition. Further, we consider the wider question of Simon Digby's attempt to become grant-maintained. We argue that the particular conjunction of historic events at that time made it likely that Simon Digby would be forced to close whether or not a CTC was in the area, but that the changed circumstances of just a year or two later would have made the presence of the CTC a significant factor in whether Simon Digby would have closed. We argued (now, I believe, wrongly) that the threat of Simon Digby opting out would have led Solihull to have not scheduled it for closure if the CTC had not existed, but that the CTC's numbers would have forced them to do so. In the end our interpretation led us to a more general conclusion that although the CTC could not be identified as the cause of the closure of Simon Digby, this was a result of special circumstances.

FIELDNOTES AND INTERPRETATIONS

It is relatively easy to apply Kelly's understanding of how commitment enters research to quantitative examples such as the one above. With ethnographic work, however, the 'three stages' of research are less well defined – they overlap, and the process has a more cyclical nature. Yet I would wish to argue that it is again useful to separate out particular aspects of the process and to attempt to conduct that stage of the research in as objective a way as possible. I would not wish to deny in any way the fact that subjectivity is embodied within ethnographic work, but I would argue that good ethnography should have an element of research method where objectivity is sought – even if never achieved.

Four of the chapters in *City Technology College* are derived from my short period of observation and interviewing within the CTC Kingshurst. The formal interviews were mainly conducted towards the end of my stay. The initial period was spent simply trying to understand what being in the CTC was like for staff and pupils. In the usual ethnographic fashion I tried to follow selected staff and pupils through their day. In the classrooms I usually found myself a seat as out of the way as possible and simply watched. I took very few notes in the classrooms, but recollected at length using a tape recorder at the end of each day. I tried to describe what I had seen in each of the lessons, noting anything which struck me as being routine, unusual or of special interest. I also noted my conversations with staff and students, and my feelings about how the research was going. Description, hunches, problems and even tentative hypotheses were all jumbled on to the innumerable tapes.

I present below extracts from the tape I made resulting from my first day at the CTC. I have selected this particular tape because I believe it indicates the assumptions that I had about what the CTC would be like before starting the research, and the way in which those assumptions were quickly challenged. This tape should thus be analysed in the search for subjectivity, such that the processes of gathering data on the various topics covered can aspire to be more objective. It is another example of the importance of the 'first days in the field' discussed in Chapter 4. Looking back on the tape now, I am surprised by the number of topics that occurred in this first tape which became topics that I investigated further. I have indicated in Chapter 2 that I was closely 'managed' during the first days of my stay, so it is even more surprising that so many areas of interest should have occurred so quickly. All these comments come from the first three-quarters of an hour of tape.

(1)   Second of October [1989] Good Morning America. One of those days when you just don't know why on earth you're here. You're still tired because you're away from home again, and you wonder what on earth you are letting yourself in for. You know it's going to be a real strain of a day.

(2)   Second of October. It's now about six o'clock in the evening, and I'm in the Nelson Building bar drinking a well deserved gin and tonic ...

(3)   It is strange how 'normal' the school is in some senses ...

(4)   And there was a lot of wasted time. I mean, most of the kids were totally unoccupied most of the time. They were occupied for just that five or ten minutes in which they were involved in the videoing. The rest of the time they were sitting round doing nothing. Looking, smiling, laughing, as appropriate, but not doing anything con-structive at all. And when we replayed the videos there were a few comments about how you might do it better, but it did seem a total waste of time, really. It seemed that the video had been used, OK, to make an end product, and that was good, I suppose, because it made them take it seriously, but I didn't see the point of the video, really.

(5)   One of the interesting things is that the atmosphere is rather nice. When things went wrong the kids certainly didn't laugh, it was that they wanted things to go well. I noticed one girl in another lesson who stooped down and picked up something that had been dropped on the floor – a piece of equipment, because she thought that was

appropriate. Just putting it on a desk out of the way so that it wouldn't get damaged.

(6)   The kids are *very* working-class kids. Very working class. The Brum accents, the friendly Brummies, the 'chummy Brummie' as one of the girls said in her 'selling' speech about her friend. They seem very lively and chirpy, but you also wonder what they are going to be like in a few years time. At the moment they are 11, 12, some 'coming on 13' as they made it known. And they are very controllable at the moment, and very nice too, but then most kids are at that age. I just wonder – at another point I was in the registering period for the afternoon, and one boy had come in white trousers, no tie, a rather strange shirt, and he got told off for that – totally non-school uniform basically – but I just wondered how it was going to last, you know, in the next few years.

(7)   In the lessons there was a lot of talk. Friendly talk, casual talk, very nice talk, very relaxed atmosphere, but I wasn't actually sure that much was happening in that English lesson at all.

(8)   Assembly was *very* formal. Children lined up outside the entrance to the hall, and filed in to their seats. Staff either sat or stood round the outside. Valerie Bragg was at the back, standing as the kids came in, and left it to the coordinator for post-16, who was standing at the front. It was very quiet, some music was being played on the piano. When everyone was in, the children were asked to stand – they had been all sitting on seats – and Valerie Bragg walked from the back, down the central aisle, to the front ...

(9)   And then she had a timetabled free period, which was a meeting of those four people who teach English. ... It was quite a fascinating meeting altogether. There was an indication that they kept fairly strictly to a syllabus. ... There was stuff about PSE as well. There had been a working party evidently, and it had been decided what sort of things should go into PSE, and [one of the teachers] was adamant that they were seeing it in terms of content and, of course, it is process that is much more important. And they had been sent a little letter asking

them to tick when they were going to do certain things, which she thought was ridiculous. And she had been to Valerie Bragg and said this was ridiculous – because that's not what PSE is about, and Valerie Bragg had seemed to agree with her, and they were going to develop a rather different system. It was interesting how it was obviously Valerie Bragg who they went to for anything – she made decisions about that, and it seemed no one else really. It was a matter of 'if Valerie Bragg agrees with me, then we'll do something else', and if she doesn't then we'll just throw it in the bin. She is a very independent principal.

(10) Sat through a two hours biology lesson with him, on flowers and sexual reproduction, which was *long* and fairly tedious. Basically what they did was, in those two hours, look at a diagram first of a flower, explaining what the flower was all about, then looked at a real flower, dismembered it, stuck bits into their books and labelled them, wrote a section, paragraph on each part. Then, moving from there, they watched a video for about 20 minutes I suppose, in a group, and then clustered round a microscope which had a camera on it which allowed you to see what you would see. There was quite a lot of technology used there, nice to have the camera there and so on ... but I wasn't clear that the technology was really very vital. In fact, they were using microscopes in three different laboratories at the same time – one of the problems of following the same syllabus by everyone – you tend to want to do exactly the same things at the same time, so you had boys coming in at the very beginning of the lesson and borrowing four microscopes, which left them with two – which, of course, wasn't enough to use in the lesson. So the kids didn't have any real practical work at all with microscopes – all they did was see what he had done on the one microscope with the camera on it. ... He finished about 20 minutes early, and allowed them to start what was really homework, and we dragged on to four o'clock. ... It wasn't a very exciting lesson.

(11) One thing I noticed all the way through was that there was a lot of sexism in it. He used, expressions like 'big,

strong lad'. There were expressions like, well, all the way through, the boys and girls were entirely separate – in two separate groups, in all the lessons. And there was play on that in several cases. In the English there was play on boyfriends and girlfriends, and reinforcing gender stereotypes in that way. Reinforcing the idea that the natural thing for a girl was to be married, I'm sure that same sort of comment would not be made by a boy. Comments about 'pretty' girls and so on. But, of course, they are very working-class kids. It's the sort of, they live in a very sexist environment. It would seem to them very odd if the teachers pulled them up for sexual stereotypes.

(12) Security is also impressive – there isn't any! Computer bits and pieces floating all over the place. And when I left, there was in fact a staff meeting at four o'clock ... and all the staff were gravitating towards the room ... and all the computer equipment was left out all over the place. And there was a lot of stuff around which, in other schools, might have been more lockable. It's fascinating the balance between what a normal comprehensive school would be like and what a public school would be like. ... This is more like what a public school would be like, where of course, security would also be incredibly lax. ... It has a very comfortable feel and you don't feel there are any problems about stealing and so on.

(13) In the lesson where they were 'selling' their friends they said what they liked and disliked. Actually all they liked, in fact. And what their favourite subjects were. The favourite subjects were English and drama often, and a couple of the girls and, I think a boy, made a very special point of saying that they didn't like science at all – which is fascinating.

(14) It's interesting the idea of being a CTC. It isn't really in some senses, because there's lots of other things going on. For example, the little girl who showed me round at first was playing a lot of instruments, in the orchestra and so on. And there's also lots of other things going on – sport is important, and drama is important as well.

(15) It's interesting that my feeling about the CTC is not one of excitement. I thought it would be. I though that there

would be a feeling of 'wow'. But at the moment there really isn't at all. ... I'm just not wildly excited about it at the moment.

(16) I've remembered the library. It really is very poorly equipped, which means that there are hardly any books in it at all – so few in fact that the books are placed on the shelves face forward to make it look as if there are more books. ... It is actually interesting that there isn't *that* much equipment around. There are the computers, of course, but not really that many computers even.

I would emphasize that these notes were simply talked into a tape recorder at the end of the first day. They record my first impressions, some of which I now feel were unfair. They clearly show my own subjectivity of response to a new situation. Most obviously, the first extract (1), which was made while I was still in bed and worrying about the day ahead, and the second extract (2), which was made in the bar where I debriefed, were typical of the rather self-pitying (but very therapeutic) personal responses that I recorded about my feelings. But many of the other extracts show my subjectivity in other ways. Extracts (4), (7) and (10) imply that I have an idea of teaching and learning which stresses children being 'on task' for as much of the time as possible. Extracts (4) and (10) also show a scepticism about the possible overuse or misuse of sophisticated technology in teaching. The doubts expressed in extract (6) seem to indicate a rather prejudiced view about accents, working-class children and schooling. Extract (11) shows an interest in sexism, and (12) has a comparison with public schools, both of which link, in part, to my previous academic work.

Reviewing these notes that I made after that first day, it is clear to me that they were *my* notes. No other researcher would have talked these notes into a tape recorder. They would have selected a different range of topics, and discussed them in diverse ways. They would have perceived the English and biology lessons in their own unique ways, and remembered a different range of actions that occurred during the day. Yet I believe it is still possible to see Kelly's threefold research process in these notes and in the subsequent research work. I also believe that there is a stage where the aim should be (and was) objectivity.

Social class

Extract (6) shows that my unstated assumption was that the CTC would select many more middle-class children than it did. I knew that the catchment area was officially supposed to be as 'inner city' as possible, but I hardly knew the actual area at all before I went there. More than a year earlier I had visited the site and had wandered round some of the nearby streets. It had seemed a mixed area, with some very poor housing, but also with some pockets of high quality housing. On the first day of my research period I was clearly still influenced by the middle-class associations of the Solihull location, and the belief that the CTC was likely to select a disproportionate number of middle-class children. My unstated hypothesis was that a disproportionate number of middle-class children would benefit. As the extract shows, this initial hypothesis had to be questioned on the very first day, but it rapidly reformulated itself into a more general one which asked about the social class backgrounds *and* other characteristics of the selected children. The hypothesis was widened because I recognized that social class alone was unlikely to provide any ammunition which could be used against the CTC policy. Thus, when pupils were later interviewed and answered questionnaires, there was an extended section which tried to examine the whole process of choice of the CTC and selection by the CTC. The 'hypothesis' was thus committed to trying to find weakness and unfairnesses in the selection procedure, but in the actual data collection processes the aim was to be as objective as possible.

Quantitative data were eventually collected on the social class distribution of the children selected by the college, and this was compared with the social class composition of the area. The samples of children who completed the questionnaire and who were interviewed were selected to be as representative as possible of the pupil populations. The questions were asked in such a way as to give the children a chance to say what they believed to be the case. Clarifications of any possible ambiguities were asked for. Thus, for example, it would have been to my political advantage to have allowed children's description of their father's work as 'manager' to stand uncontested, but the search for objectivity led me to question further and to try to assign children to particular class locations as fairly as possible.

Children were also given time to talk about the selection process, and the analysis was conducted in such a way that all comments were considered and classified. Uncertainties were sometimes classified twice. There is, of course, still subjectivity in the allocation of answers and comments to particular categories and in the choice and definition of categories. But the aim was that any 'reasonable person' would have come to an analysis as close as possible to the one conducted.

The third stage of research, the interpretation, allows subjectivity to enter once again. It became clear that, overall, the CTC was selecting very few children from social classes I and II. It would have been possible to have presented the data in a way that suggested that the CTC was that selecting children who were reasonably representative of the social class distribution of the catchment area. This information is made available in the book, and indeed we make it clear that the middle class had not made significant inroads to the CTC, as some commentators (e.g. Simon, 1988; Morrell, 1989; Walford, 1990) had suggested. However, the book also notes that there were differences between the social class distributions of the first and second intakes – there were more social class I and II in the second intake – and implies that there may be a trend towards more middle-classness that should be watched. The presentation of the social class distributions in two separate tables was designed to make a political point which researchers with other commitments would have avoided.

Sexism and sex-stereotyping
Extract (11) is just one of very many comments that I talked into my tape recorder about sexism and sex-stereotyping within the college. It was something that I did not expect. If anything, my unstated hypothesis was that there would be great attempts to avoid sexism and sex-stereotyping because of the need to encourage girls in science and technology. I saw the fact that a female principal had been appointed as significant, and believed that this area would be one where the best of good practice was evident. It wasn't. Children, teachers and, in this case, visiting industrialists and others brought their existing sexist assumptions into the college. Girls were praised for being pretty, boys were encouraged to be strong, classroom and social activities unintentionally (or sometimes intentionally) reinforced gender inequalities. In my tape-recorded notes I have several powerful examples of such language and activities, yet in the end I did not discuss this topic in the book at all. There were two reasons for the omission. The first was an ethical issue, in that it was very difficult to conceal who were the individual people involved. Most examples involved particular

subject teachers and the subject would have had to have been identified in any examples. As, at that time, there were low numbers of teachers for each subject, my examples would have identified individual teachers to the principal and to other teachers. I did not feel justified in doing this. Before gaining access, it had seemed to me that there was some public 'right to know' what the CTC was doing (Barnes, 1979; Pring, 1984). But I recognized that such a right was not absolute, and that it had to be conditional on not causing 'too much' harm to individuals involved. Although it was very important, I did not feel that what I had found about the extent of sexism justified the possible damage to the private lives of those involved which publication might bring.

The second reason for not discussing the area was that to do so would have implied a hypothesis which included a comparison that I could not make. It was only worth discussing if I could show that the level of sexism was 'better' or 'worse' than in other comparable schools. Even if I did not make this comparison explicitly, it was one that others would make. The search for objectivity here showed that it would have been dishonest to have written about sexism in the CTC without having any knowledge of the extent of sexism and sex-stereotyping in other schools in the area. Politically, of course, it might have been very useful to have 'exposed' the college on this aspect of its work, but it might actually have been a very positive atmosphere compared with that in other local schools.

Technology
Extracts (4), (10), (14) and (16) refer in different ways to technology and facilities. They indicate I had held a whole host of unarticulated assumptions about the CTC's technological nature and abundance of facilities which were rapidly challenged. The lack of books in the library simply shocked me. That so many of the children seemed to enthuse over what I saw as 'non-technological' areas such as drama and music, and some actively disliked science, struck me as decidedly odd. These initial impressions and challenges to my assumptions led to more formulated hypotheses about the extent to which the CTC could really be seen to emphasize technology, and also to question once more the selection process.

This initial surprise led to a more thorough examination of the nature of the curriculum than might otherwise have been the case. It led to a range of tentative research questions, and I began to look in a systematic way at the use of technology in the teaching I observed. In the book, a table is given (Table 4.1) of the periods allocated to each subject area, and this is discussed in some detail. It would be a dull and uninteresting table if it were not for the fact that it illustrates just how little technology appeared on the formal curriculum at that time. The data were collected and analysed in as objective a way as possible, yet the discussion emphasizes the lack of technology, and goes on to discuss the ways in which the curriculum is both familiar and unfamiliar. The discussion is an expression of a subjective commitment to show that the CTC policy was not working in the way the government might wish.

This commitment also shows itself in the desire to explore in more depth the importance of technological interest and aptitude in the selection process. It was stated in the initial CTC booklet (DES, 1986) that 'A prime consideration in the selection of pupils will be whether they are likely to benefit from what the CTC offers', yet even on this first day it seemed that some of the children actively disliked the scientific aspects, which I saw as being central to most views of what a CTC was supposed to offer. A research question developed which asked 'How important was the pupils' interest in technology in their decision to apply?' In order to answer it a specific question was included in the questionnaires and interview schedules used with the representative samples of children. The result was that few of the children saw the technological aspects of the CTC as being of prime importance in their own decision to apply for the CTC. By using systematic techniques, the research method tried to encompass objectivity, yet the decision to publish this information in a separate paper (Walford, 1991f) once again shows subjectivity and commitment. The information about the role of technology in the choice of the CTC was included within a paper that discussed the importance of children themselves in the decision-making process. It made points which might be usable in any attack on the government's increased commitment to parental choice, and also argued that the CTC idea did not seem to be a particularly efficient or effective way of dealing with perceived problems in technological education. This paper was published before the book – just in case a general election was called earlier than expected.

CONCLUSION

In this chapter I hope to have shown that the ideas of commitment and objectivity are not incompatible. I have given several examples from the work on the City Technology College Kingshurst where I believe Kelly's three 'stages' of research model is helpful in examining where commitment and the search for objectivity should come in research.

However, the story does not end there. *City Technology College* was published in June 1991, as it turned out, well before the 1992 general election. Aston Business School held a 'press conference and meet the authors' for the book in association with Open University Press. Our information office invited press and other interested people, and we also invited people. Valerie Bragg also attended to answer questions, and was advertised on the invitations. The only reporter who actually came was from the *Financial Times* and probably fancied a trip to Birmingham. He gave us a 'balanced' 70 column centimetres (including a picture of the CTC) under the title 'In a class of its own'. While none of its reporters came to the launch, the *Times Educational Supplement* gave us 38 column centimetres (including another picture of the CTC) under the headline 'Inner city CTC plan a "costly failure" '. Lawrence Denholm from the CTC Trust gave us more publicity with a 64 column centimetre letter of complaint (including an even larger picture of the CTC!). Two months later the *TES* gave us a further 30 column centimetres in the form of an academic review. The only other publicity that the book received (that I know of) was a 20 column centimetre review in *ISIS News*, the magazine of the Independent Schools Information Service. None of the local newspapers carried the story at all.

In all, the book sank with hardly a ripple. It might have swayed one or two votes in the general election at most. Such an end to a politically committed research study raises questions. It might be possible to aim for objectivity within a committed research project, but is it desirable? Does it just mean that the political commitment gets lost? I look at my shelf of pamphlets from the Educational Research Trust, the Hillgate Group, the Adam Smith Institute, the Centre for Policy Studies, the Campaign for Real Education, the Institute of Economic Affairs. I see the slim volumes, each based on equally thin research, each openly committed, each usually with a side or two of 'Summary and recommendations' which reporters can easily use to construct a story. These are what get into the newspapers and are discussed on television, and these are what probably have a considerable indirect influence on voters.

Whenever there is commitment to particular policies and politics there is a temptation for academic researchers to move beyond the data. However, in spite of these doubts about the potential influence of academic research, without objectivity as a goal, social research becomes indistinguishable from journalism or political polemic. I believe such a development would be highly undesirable and that academics have the responsibility to ensure that they seek objectivity within a framework of commitment.

—9—

Ethics

This chapter discusses several ethical issues I have had to deal with in research. The main examples are drawn from the research project concerned with the campaign to obtain state funding for private evangelical Christian schools, but the ethical problems of publication are illustrated by examples drawn from the City Technology College project.

THE DEVELOPMENT OF THE RESEARCH PROJECT

My original interest in the new Christian schools developed from my longstanding research focus on the private sector. I began to recognize that there was great diversity within the private sector and that very little research had been conducted on the smaller and more idiosyncratic schools. I attended some meetings of various groupings of small private schools and began to visit a few, but my interest intensified as a result of attempts in the House of Lords to amend the 1987 Education Bill such that 'opting-in' was included as well as 'opting-out'. The amendments had little chance of success and were duly rejected, but they generated considerable publicity. It was evident that many of those involved would continue with their campaign.

I decided that I would attempt to follow the campaign and also find out more about the 'new Christian schools', which are a group of small private schools which share an ideology of biblically based evangelical Christianity that seeks to relate the message of the Bible to all aspects of present day life. These schools have usually been set up by parents or a church group to deal with a growing dissatisfaction with what is seen as the increased secularism of the great majority of schools – including the religious voluntary schools already within the state system. The schools aim to provide a distinctive Christian approach to every part of school life and the curriculum and, in most cases, parents have a continuing role in the management and organization of the schools (Deakin, 1989; O'Keeffe, 1992). In general, these schools are not well provided for in terms of physical facilities: fees are modest, with teaching staff often on low salaries. They do not serve the 'traditional' private school market and are often in a financially precarious position.

Once I had decided to investigate the schools and the campaign, the research project passed through several stages. At first it was very much a 'background' project while I conducted and published research on a rather different form of private school – the City Technology Colleges (Walford, 1991b; Walford and Miller, 1991). However, I collected newspaper cuttings, visited a few schools, attended some meetings (including a three day meeting of the schools), conducted some interviews and published an early article based on this work (Walford, 1991e). But intensive activity did not really start until I obtained a small two-year grant from the Nuffield Foundation in early 1992. Following the award of this grant, further schools were visited, headteachers, principals, politicians, officials and academics involved with the pressure group were interviewed and a further crop of meetings attended. A questionnaire survey of the schools was also conducted which eventually drew a response rate of 83 per cent (Poyntz and Walford, 1994). Further articles have now been published (Walford, 1994a, b).

This high response rate to the questionnaire is indicative of the level of support that I received from the schools. Access to schools was always granted, and all the headteachers asked agreed to be interviewed. The Director of the Christian Schools Campaign and those most closely concerned with the campaign were particularly helpful throughout the research, being prepared to give access to documentary data as well as to respond to long interview sessions. There are several possible reasons for this level of support. The first is simply that, being Christians, they felt some obligation to help others where they could. The second probable reason for helping me with the research was that they wanted publicity. If a group is trying to campaign for change, almost any publicity is seen as potentially beneficial. This poses obvious problems of possible 'incorporation' of the researcher.

The Christian Schools Campaign was able to achieve consider-able success by working together with other groups campaigning for funding of their own schools and by closely associating with several powerful and prominent individuals on the political New Right. While there is no necessary overall ideological agreement with those on the New Right, the aims of the Christian Schools Campaign coincided with the right's wider project of encouraging a greater diversity of schools and a more market orientation towards schooling (Sexton 1987). As a result, the Christian Schools Campaign was able to ensure legislative changes in the 1993 Education Act which enabled these Christian schools to apply to become a new form of state-funded grant-maintained school.

THE ETHICS OF THE INTERVIEW

All research brings ethical decisions, but these decisions are particularly difficult if the researcher has political, ideological or religious views that are in opposition to those being studied (Klatch, 1988). One of the most difficult decisions to be made by interviewers is the degree to which their own views should be explained to interviewees. To what extent is it right to allow others to believe that you agree with them?

When I visited schools and interviewed headteachers and principals, they were welcoming and helpful but, quite understandably, wanted to know something about me. I could, of course, explain my research interest in terms of my previous work on private schools and a parallel concern with educational policy-making. But this was not really what most wanted to know – they wanted to know whether I was a Christian. The easy (and correct) answer to the question is 'yes', and at first I simply stated this. However, my own Christianity is a very liberal version. To those involved with the new Christian schools the sort of liberal interpretation of Christianity that I hold is definitely *not* Christian, and many would see it as potentially more dangerous than atheism.

Where I did just reply in the positive to the question of my own belief, I found the resulting interview both difficult and embarrassing, for the interviewee believed that we shared a whole ideological view that we did not. I gathered good data, but at some cost to my own self-respect. I decided that in future interviews I would be more honest and explain that my interpretation of Christianity might be some distance from their own. In some cases this led to severe suspicion of my motives, and corresponding reticence, while in others the interviewee clearly did not fully comprehend my explanation of 'liberal Christian' or, at least, forgot what I had said once the interviews progressed. As I did not generally challenge anything that was said, interviewees appeared to believe that I was in agreement with them. This was far from always true, as I found some of their literalist interpretations of the Bible simply perverse and simplistic. Neutrality caused me some severe ethical doubts.

In general, while I did not always agree with my interviewees, I found them to be congenial, thoughtful and reasonable people. But a few were not. A very few had extreme views that I found abhorrent. The following extract gives an example. It is noticeable that, in this case, I have not simply allowed the interviewee to state his own views unchallenged, but the challenges are still very weak indeed.

GW   Are there any bits of the National Curriculum that you are unhappy with?

A   No.

GW   You're happy with the whole thing?

A   Well except for the idea, I mean, I would be unhappy with the lunacy of AIDS idea, because AIDS is basically a homosexual disease ...

GW   Mainly, and it depends where you are actually.

A   ... and it is doing a very effective job of ridding the population of undesirables. But, it is basically, according to the statistics, and I've got them, it is basically homosexual. Out of 600, 6000 ...

GW   In this country, that may be true, but not in ...

A   In the States, it's drug related. In Africa, it is basically a non-existent disease in many places, but the statistics have been grossly distorted because they find western countries will give them money.

GW   Some of that may be true ...

A   It *is* true, but the ignorant West doesn't want to know that. ... And you take the figures as they really are, and not as the Trust, what is it the Higgins Trust, wanted to put over, it's a woofters disease. If you're a woolly woofter, you get what you deserve. And that's the end of it, as far as I'm concerned. I know in America, intravenous drug users and sharing needles has caused it. I just feel that politically they are not telling society the truth, because they don't want to. They don't want to face up to it, because they don't. ... I would never employ a homosexual to teach at my school. I do not believe it's a lifestyle that is alternative – I believe it's evil, intrinsically.

This man was actually a minister of a church that supported a school. He also showed what I thought was a horrific attitude towards women and used the term 'welfare state' almost as a swear word. At one point he launched into a tirade against socialist and communist teachers. According to him, most teachers were socialists and communists – that was the trouble. 'They teach the kids that there is no point in working because there are no jobs. In one junior school the teachers told them that there was no point in working because there were no jobs for them anyway.'

At this last point, I agreed with him that this would not be an appropriate thing to say. Technically, I only agreed with what I truly agreed with, but he probably interpreted this as meaning that I was against socialists and communists, and that I agreed that 'most teachers' were such, and that this was the problem.

I left that interview with some very 'good data', but with great anger at myself and at the irreconcilable difficulties that interviewing sets up. The interview had been a long one, and had been very informative about divisions between schools themselves and within the campaign. I obtained information that I had not been able to obtain elsewhere. To have challenged his views would simply have brought the interview to an abrupt close, yet my lack of challenge meant that he probably had the feeling that a university academic specializing in education policy studies actually agreed with his crude bigoted views.

OBSERVING MEETINGS

During the research, at the invitation of the Director of the Christian Schools Campaign, I attended several meetings where strategy was being discussed and information shared between interested groups. The Director obviously had some apprehension about this, for I had been clear with her about my overall political position, so I agreed with her that I would not use any information gained through interviews or meetings to act politically against the campaign. This was a self-imposed agreement more than a negotiated one, but it certainly made my sometimes ambiguous position easier to deal with. After all, here was an academic who had written passionately against privatization in education (Walford, 1990) and who had been critical of the increased diversity of schools inherent in the City Technology College initiative (Walford and Miller, 1991), actually at a meeting where the wording of an amendment to an Education Bill was being discussed which was designed to encourage further diversity (this amendment failed). Among those present at that particular meeting was Stuart Sexton (see below), who clearly did not link me with anything I had written.

One particularly interesting series of meetings was the 'Educational Issues Group' held irregularly in the House of Lords under the auspices of Baroness Cox. At the beginning of each meeting Baroness Cox would remind the 60 or so people gathered that the meeting was not an official meeting of any kind, and that the House of Lords was the location merely 'because of its convenient geographical position'. But the location was clearly more than of passing convenience. It allowed busy politicians to spend some time at meetings and gave a spurious authority to the proceedings. The meetings were officially not party political and open to anyone interested in educational issues, but the method of announcing the date of the next meeting (through the post to those on a list) meant that the vast majority of those present appeared to be supporters of the New Right. The meetings were designed to 'share information about matters of common interest' and the format was that various speakers who were active in various pressure groups would, in turn, explain their recent activities to the meeting. Few questions were asked, and only very rarely was there any open disagreement. The assumption was that everyone there was of 'like mind' about the problems of education and possible remedies.

I attended only five meetings, but others present included John Marks (who was secretary for the meeting), Stuart Sexton, Nick Seaton (Campaign for Real Education), Martin Turner, Fred Naylor, Professor Anthony O'Hear, Professor Antony Flew, Katie Ivens, Jennifer Chew (English Curriculum Association), Anthony Freeman and Chris McGovern (History Curriculum Association). This is very like a roll call of the educational New Right during the early 1990s, and a group with whom I had little affinity.

Baroness Cox (formerly Caroline Cox), for example, was a key figure in the New Right. She was made Baroness in 1982, and from 1983 to 1985 was Director of the Centre for Policy Studies. She is a committed Christian and has also been a key member of several small but influential right-wing educational groups, including the Academic Council for Peace and Freedom, the Educational Research Trust, the National Council for Academic Standards (NCAS) and the Parental Alliance for Choice in Education (PACE) (Griggs, 1989). She was a contributor to one of the early Black Papers (Cox *et al.*, 1977) and to the Hillgate Group's two influential pamphlets, *Whose Schools?* (1986) and *The Reform of British Education*

(1987). Along with John Marks, she is firmly in favour of selective schooling (Marks *et al.*, 1983; Cox and Marks, 1988).

Stuart Sexton also had a key position in the New Right. He was policy adviser to two past Conservative Secretaries of State for Education and Science (Mark Carlisle and Keith Joseph), and was the guiding hand behind the controversial Assisted Places Scheme and later a leading proponent of City Technology Colleges. He has been a key figure in the Institute of Economic Affairs and Director of its Education Unit. Over the years Sexton (1987, 1992) has made clear his desire for a fully privatized educational system, preferably financed through vouchers which can be 'topped up' by parents. In 1987 he set out his 'step-by-step approach to the eventual introduction of a "market system", a system truly based upon the supremacy of parental choice, the supremacy of purchasing power' (Sexton, 1987, p. 11). His ultimate plan is to have per capita funding from the state, which would be the minimum sum to be spent on each child's education. Schools would be allowed to make additional charges to cover any extra provision beyond the basic level of schooling. Sexton further envisages that, eventually, the proportion of taxpayers' money spent on education will reduce from its present level as parents pay more and more for the schooling of their own children.

With the regular attendance of such key people at these meetings, I found them extremely informative. They provided me with a host of background material that I would have been unable to obtain in any other way. Because the assumption was that everyone was 'of like mind', a wide range of comments were freely made by the participants which indicated their beliefs, long-term aims and ideologies. As most people present did not speak, I shall never know if there were other 'spies' present at these meetings. They were certainly not as evident as Klatch (1988, p. 80) found in her study of American New Right women.

At the meetings, I simply sat near the back and took notes, but it was not always easy to remain quiet. I often wanted to shout out that the information a speaker was giving was simply incorrect, or that the interpretation or argument was specious. After one irregular attender who was sitting nearby gave some information about forthcoming changes in higher education, I felt compelled to tell him that his was the only speech of the day with which I had agreed. He, and others, looked aghast.

In October 1992 the National Commission on Education published my briefing paper on 'selection for secondary schools'

(Walford, 1992), which was widely circulated and reported in the national press. These Briefing Papers were only 3,000 words and were designed to summarize research in particular areas. I included a very brief comment on some work by Caroline Cox and John Marks. I received a letter from John Marks informing me that he thought that my summary misrepresented their findings and that I should circulate a correction to all those who had received the paper. I sincerely believed that the summary was a reasonable one given the space limitations and wrote back in that vein. I heard nothing more, but also, and perhaps coincidentally, I never received any more invitations to attend the 'Educational Issues Group'. I also became ultra-careful about what I wrote concerning the powerful.

This little incident illuminates several important points. First, the powerful have the ability to exclude researchers – in this case simply by limiting the supply of information about future meetings. Further, of course, any of the members of this network could have made it very difficult for me to have obtained access to the whole group of similar people. Exclusion by one could easily lead to exclusion by all. Second, although the visibility of academic work should not be overestimated, publishing comment that is perceived to be critical may inhibit future access and cooperation. Third, in many cases, research about those with power necessitates naming those people. As they are in powerful positions and have made significant contributions to particular policies, they are widely known and it is usually impossible to conceal their identities. It is not only what was said that is important, but who said it. However, if academic reports are to name individuals there is always the potential problem of perceived libel and, being powerful people, the possibility of libel writs has to be taken very seriously. This means that self-censorship becomes an ever present problem. If there is any doubt at all about a comment or interpretation, the researcher of the powerful may tend to omit discussion of it in any publications.

WHOSE SIDE ARE YOU ON?

Howard Becker (1967) has exhorted us to be clear about 'whose side we are on'. But, in this case, at first, I simply did not know whose side I was on. I could see that those campaigning for state support for these new Christian schools had a good case. There was something deeply unjust about the Church of England and Roman

Catholic churches being able to have their schools funded by the state, yet Muslims and new Christians being forced to pay for their own private schools if they wished their children to be taught as they wished. However, I was also aware that the New Right's support for these schools was an indication that a growth in the diversity of schools would suit their long-term aims and could be instrumental in leading to greater inequity throughout the whole educational system.

When I first started visiting schools and interviewing headteachers and others I did not have a clear understanding of how the campaign might be seen as a piece in the New Right's jigsaw. At first, my interest focused on an unusual group of private schools more than the campaign that was linked to it. I thus was unable to tell interviewees what viewpoint I might take in any subsequent publications. This might be conceived as a form of 'objectivity', but it is doubtful whether the interviewees actually believed my indecision, and it certainly made interviewing more difficult. Many of those involved with the schools saw state support as a simple question of 'righteousness', and argued that they were currently 'paying twice' for the education of their children. They often did not consider the wider issues of what the changes might mean to the whole of the education system as being their concern. As they saw the question of state funding as a relatively simple one, and clearly expected me to have already come to a conclusion on the issue, they became suspicious if I said that the issue was more complicated than they seemed to feel.

Once I had begun to uncover the extent of the links to and involvement of key actors in the New Right, I became clearer about where my support should be given. My visits to schools also had an effect as I became concerned about the potential effects on children of the extreme views being voiced in a few of the schools. The interview quoted and discussed above, for example, made me recognize that there was a need, in some cases, for the state to protect children from the ideas of their parents. As a result, I became convinced that a compromise was needed where faith-based schools should be supported, but only within a strong framework of local education authority (or similar) control which would enforce minimum standards and ensure equity between schools.

As the research progressed I became concerned about the extent to which those linked to the campaign might not be fully aware of the ideas of those on the New Right with whom they were working.

It became clear from my research in the schools that many of those involved would not wish to be associated with any plans for an inequitable educational system. Indeed, the schools themselves often have fee policies which attempt to redress inequalities by charging according to financial means. Many of the schools try to offer open access, irrespective of ability to pay, and their curriculum is one which emphasizes the Christian virtues of sharing and caring for others. They are not natural allies of the New Right, but had become enmeshed within this wider political programme, as a result of their own individualistic desires to obtain funding for their own schools.

This does not mean that those involved were naive, or that they were being 'used' by the right. They saw it as a matter of God's law and justice that parents should have control over the education of their own children. They pointed to other countries, such as Denmark and the Netherlands, where it is relatively easy for groups to establish their own state-supported schools. But it was clear that those involved had not read Sexton's ideas about privatization, or fully understood the right's vision for the future. Should I provide a 'reader' of relevant extracts, or a booklist?

I decided that I should at least tell some of those involved about particular books that I thought they might wish to read, but I did not provide any books myself. Strangely, it was Dale Spender's *Man Made Language* (1980) that probably had the most effect on the campaign, for the female Director of the Campaign resigned in 1992 – in part due to problems over 'women in positions of authority in the Church'. She moved to another campaigning organization instead (Christian Action Research and Education, CARE), and the final campaigning on the 1993 Education Act was done from there.

PROBLEMS OF PUBLICATION

Researching named institutions brings particular problems of publication that are somewhat easier to avoid where the identity of the research site is concealed. I had particular problems with the City Technology College project. As the research progressed I began to recognize a number of difficulties of conducting research in the CTC that I had not thought through earlier. At the time I was there, only 27 teachers were spread across all the subject areas. Many fellow educationists, teachers, politicians, parents and others would be fascinated by an account of the effectiveness of various teaching styles and strategies within each of these subject areas.

How much technology was used in various subject lessons? How was it used? How did students respond? These were very important questions, but ones that I increasingly recognized I could not fully answer in print. The problem was that with only two or three people teaching each subject, it was impossible to write about individual lessons without identifying the teacher. Had it been possible to restrict the possibility of identification only to those directly involved within the college, it might have been possible to write about specific lessons, but even this would have been ethically dubious. I certainly did not see my role as that of inspector reporting back on teaching to the principal and others. Some sociologists have delayed the publication of their books until it was judged that disclosure could not do any harm to those involved. For example, Burgess (1983, 1985d, 1987) published his often critical study of a comprehensive school ten years after that research had been conducted, in part because he feared that the head might use information available in the accounts against the staff involved. In the case of the CTC, if the study was to have an impact and be widely read, there was no possibility of delaying publication. More importantly, because the college was named, any identification of individuals could be made by those outside as well as inside. The fact that staff have continuing careers which might be affected by inappropriate and unverifiable comment made it unthinkable that I should discuss lessons in any but the broadest terms. That I might wish to stress positive aspects of particular lessons rather than negative features does not fundamentally alter the situation. In the end, I did not feel it appropriate to include in the book anything other than a few 'cameos' of partially reconstructed lessons which were intended to give a general indication of the culture of the college.

Ethical problems surrounding the publication of research have been quite widely discussed in the literature (see, for example, Becker, 1964; Burgess, 1989). As discussed in Chapter 5, I had encountered similar problems with my previous research on public schools, where an initial interest in the influence of private school teachers on National Curriculum development had to be shelved as the data could not be published without identifying individuals. In the case of the CTC, the problems of possible identification of staff also led to self-censorship of whole areas of interest, some of which were of major importance. For example, one topic area where this self-censorship was at work was that of gender and sexism. One of the requirements of the CTC plan was to provide a balance of provision for boys and girls, and the City Technology College Kingshurst takes this objective seriously. As in many aware schools, all lessons are taught in mixed sex groups, including PE and CDT. There are attempts to balance the gender mix of student chosen 'enrichments', which include a range of sporting, cultural and physical activities. Some girls play five-a-side football alongside boys, while a few boys take part in aerobics. There was an equal opportunities working party dealing specifically with gender issues in the college.

Yet, as in all other schools, this does not mean that sexism and sex-stereotyping have been overcome. Children, teachers and, in this case, visiting industrialists and others bring their existing sexist assumptions into the college. Girls are praised for being pretty, boys are encouraged to be strong, classroom and social activities unintentionally (or sometimes intentionally) reinforce gender inequalities. In my tape recorded notes made at the end of each day I have several powerful examples of such language and activities, yet I was unable to report them in detail as they would identify individual people. My concern with this issue does not mean that the CTC is particularly bad – I am sure that gender issues are taken far more seriously there than in the majority of schools – but gender equality is one criterion by which the success of the CTC will be evaluated. If too many of the girls eventually choose to become highly skilled word-processing secretaries, then the college will surely have failed. Yet this whole issue is hardly touched upon in the research reports, because individual teachers might have been identifiable. Now, some ten years later when staff have moved on to other positions, it has become possible for me to write about these issues. Chapter 8 of this volume contains some discussion of sexism within the CTC that was not included in the original published paper (Walford, 1994e).

The fact that the institution was named makes the ethical problem clear. There has to be a balance between the 'good' that might be done through publication and the 'bad' that might be done to individuals or institutions through publication. But the problem still exists where the institution is not named in publications. If a research project is based on a single secondary school, even where the name is not widely known, those involved in the school are well aware that it is their school that is being discussed. The headteacher in the school may well know who was observed and be able to identify individual teachers. In practice, those who may be able to do the most harm to teachers (or to students) are those who are within the school, and it is often very difficult to hide identities where the research has been tightly focused. What to publish and what to conceal is a problem that all ethnographers have to live with.

— 10

On analysis and theory

There is far too much mystique about theory. For reasons that are not fully apparent to me, social science and, in particular, sociology valorizes its theoreticians far more greatly than those who engage in the whole process of generating data and sorting out what it might mean. Yet while theorists are parasitic upon empirical researchers, those engaged in empirical research are actually forced to be theorists as well. For whether it is recognized or not, generating new data is always a theoretically driven activity, it is just that in some cases the theory remains unexamined when it should be subjected to scrutiny. The analysis of data and the use of theory are not 'add-ons' to the work of empirical research, but a necessary accompaniment to the entire process.

I thus find it odd when students sometimes come to ask me, 'How do I analyse my data?' or 'What theory can I use?' They have generated data in a particular way without recognizing their theoretical assumptions about the issues they are concerned with, and now see 'analysis' and the application of 'theory' as a separate task that needs to be done before 'writing' can occur. In this chapter I seek to show that the reality is both more complex and more simple, but that it is also possible to utilise particular forms of theory late in the day.

THE NATURE OF THEORY

One of the difficulties that pervades social science and educational research is the lack of agreement about the meanings of words. The same word can be used by different authors to indicate various concepts, methods or phenomena, while a particular concept, method or phenomenon can be described by a variety of words. The concept of theory often causes problems, and I will attempt no definitive discussion here, but there are clearly different types of theory that need to be recognized. At one extreme are 'grand theories' such as Marxism, functionalism, feminism or symbolic interactionism. These present a general way of interpreting the world; a framework within which various studies of diverse phenomena can be situated. It is always necessary for researchers to examine their own 'grand theories' about how the world operates, and to recognize that this will have influenced the way the data were constructed and the interpretation that the researcher may give to them. At another extreme are the micro-level testable propositions that attempt to attribute causality to particular phenomenon. The most certain way of trying to link cause and effect is through the controlled experiment, which is unusual, although not impossible, in ethnographic and qualitative research. Seeking to attribute causality to particular actions where there are no controls is a common error in much published qualitative research.

The type of theory that I wish to discuss here lies between these two extremes and is what might be called 'middle-range theory', where a set of concepts is used to define, describe and suggest possible explanations for some phenomenon or activities. While these middle-range theories may stand by themselves, they do often also try to make links both to grand theory and to micro-level theory. I see this sort of theory as being linked to models.

To me, model-building is a straightforward was of explaining what is occurring when we use and develop middle-range theory. Models are essentially simplifications of complex realities. By focusing on one particular aspect of the complexity, within strict time and space constraints, it is possible to construct a way of looking at that aspect which allows a story to be told. Concentrating on a different aspect of the complexity might have brought forth the development of a totally different and even seemingly contradictory model, and it is possible that other researchers could have developed equally intelligible, but different, models even though they were focusing on the same particular aspect.

An example from the natural sciences should help to clarify this point. For many centuries argument raged over whether light was 'really' composed of waves or particles. Both of these possibilities must be seen as models of what is an exceedingly complex reality, but models which have great utility. In considering the problems of diffraction of light, for example, a wave model is in many cases a perfectly adequate model to describe what occurs and what is likely to happen in similar new situations. It allows us to understand simply this particular aspect of the behaviour of light. The model, however, is totally inadequate when it comes to trying to understand the photoelectric effect. Here the particle model of light has far greater utility, but it, in turn, is unable to give any insight into diffraction. It is not that one model is 'correct' and the other 'incorrect', or that they are both 'correct' or 'incorrect'; they both are extremely useful in aiding our understanding of a complicated phenomenon within a particular context. By not considering the contexts within which the model does not hold, each model is able to simplify what would otherwise be incomprehensible.

The example of light is a useful one in discussing the nature of models because, somewhat unusually in science, the two seemingly contradictory models were able to be synthesized within a new model – quantum mechanics. But the nature of this new model is not different from that of the two original models – it is not 'correct' or 'incorrect' – it is merely a useful simplification of a complex reality which can be used in a wider variety of circumstances. It is worth noting that for practically all everyday aspects of the phenomenon of light the original wave or particle models are more than adequate, and it is only in the consideration of very special cases that the quantum mechanical model offers greater understanding.

Models are thus human constructs and in the social sciences and education, where situations are studied where it is not possible to 'hold constant' the various extraneous variables, the process of model-building is less clear cut than in the natural sciences. As Becher and Kogan (1980) argue:

> Representations of reality in the social sciences may have certain features in common with striking caricatures, telling metaphors or good interpretations of a play or musical score. They highlight particular aspects of the whole, at the expense of others; but do so in such a way as to enhance understanding rather than distort reality.

One way of thinking about theory is that it acts to simplify, to restrict the focus such that a story can be told – a story that links with other stories that have used similar theories and a story that builds upon those theories. This does not mean, of course, that the data can be forced to fit any theory. Systematic work with the data needs to be conducted throughout the data analysis to ensure that all data are covered by the theory and that, where there are oddities, these are investigated in full. It is not my intention to discuss these more 'mechanical' methods that are used within all analysis. It is obviously necessary to make sure that the data generated during fieldwork are systematically examined. All explanatory or prescriptive claims made about the case or cases must be based upon descriptive claims first, and these must be drawn from the data. In the rest of this chapter I give some examples of the ways in which I have used theory in my previous work.

BERNSTEIN'S CODES

In several of my papers I have used some of the concepts developed by Basil Bernstein. This is in spite of the fact that I have never found Bernstein's work easy to understand. I believe that his later work, in particular, has become unnecessarily complex and thus less worthwhile in theoretical terms. The beauty of his original formulations of the concepts of classification and framing and integrated and collection code was that they simplified a complex reality rather than added to it. My own understanding of the utility of models is that they enable broad statements to be made, which may well not hold in every instance, but which allow a deeper understanding of the overall phenomenon and allow new insight to be generated. It was in this spirit that I first used Bernstein's concepts in a paper on research students (Walford, 1981a). That paper was concerned with trying to understand problems of research supervision, which was at that time beginning to become a research area in itself. In order to understand how I 'played' with the concepts by stretching them considerably, it is first necessary to outline the original formulations.

The relevant part of Bernstein's early work is that relating to the form and structure of the curriculum. The concepts of classification and framing were first introduced in a much quoted article (Bernstein, 1971) where two educational knowledge codes are discussed, differing according to the underlying principles which shape curriculum, pedagogy and evaluation. A curriculum of a *collection* type is characterized by strongly bounded knowledge areas with little linkage between them. The learner is required to collect a group of favoured contents in order to satisfy some criteria of evaluation. On the other hand, an *integrated* curriculum emphasizes the interdependence of various areas of knowledge and attempts to transcend traditional boundaries. Bernstein argues that any structure for the transmission of knowledge will symbolically reproduce the distribution of power in society, and introduces the concept of *classification* to clarify this relationship.

> Where classification is strong, contents are well insulated from each other by strong boundaries. Where classification is weak, there is reduced insulation between contents, for the boundaries between contents are weak or blurred. *Classification thus refers to the degree of boundary maintenance between contents.* (Bernstein, 1971, p. 89; original emphasis)

The concept of *frame* was introduced to refer to the strength of the boundary between what may be transmitted and what may not be transmitted in the pedagogic relationship. It indicates 'the degree of control teacher and pupil possess over the section, organization, pacing and timing of knowledge transmitted and received in the pedagogical relationship'. The strength of framing thus refers to the range of options available to teacher and taught in the control of what is transmitted and received. Thus,

> From the perspective of this analysis, the basic structure of the message system, curriculum is given by variations in the strength of classification, and the basic structure of the message system, pedagogy is given by variations in the strengths of frames. (Bernstein, 1971, p. 89)

The usefulness of the concepts can best be seen in Bernstein's own early articles. In *Class and Pedagogies: Visible and Invisible* (Bernstein, 1973) they are used to uncover the relationship between social class and educational advantage in progressive pre-school and infant school classrooms. He shows that the invisible pedagogy which is at the base of progressive methods is inherently advantageous to pupils from new middle-class families, while children from working-class homes are at a disadvantage. Another important article is 'Aspects of the relations between education and production' (1977), which looks at the continuities and discontinuities between education and work. Here, the earlier definitions of classifications and framing are broadened; they 'have become more abstract and the link between power and classification and framing and control has become more explicit'. Bernstein argues against a simple correspondence theory of education which assumes that dispositions valued in the school are identical with dispositions required by the workplace, and uses these developed concepts to argue that classification and framing in schools does not always mesh with the classification and framing required in the workplace. My particular research had nothing whatever to do with the relation between schooling and the workplace. Instead it tried to challenge ideas about the importance of identifying somewhat simplistic student and supervisor roles, and making sure that these roles were known and acknowledged by all. My research with postgraduate research students in experimental physics had made me realize that difficulties between students and supervisors were more complex than this and that relationships between them might differ greatly from those in the arts or social sciences. The nature of experimental physics was such that most students were not able to construct their own research project, but joined a group of lecturers, research fellows and other students working together within a topic area. The structure of the group is fluid, and the members work on a series on interlinking projects within a fairly tightly defined research area. Of course, eventually the student has to make an *individual* contribution to research, and understanding this tension between the needs of the individual and those of the group is crucial.

It was some years after I had generated the data, while I was teaching Bernstein's work to a group of MSc students, that I realized that I might be able to use something like his framework to illuminate what was happening between students and supervisors. Finding exactly the developments to the concepts that were necessary was an enjoyable and playful task. Eventually I reinterpreted the concepts such that classification became an indication of how closely specified the individual student's research project was, and how clearly differentiated it was from the work of other people in the research group. The concept of framing then became the degree of control that the supervisor or student possessed over the selection, organization, pacing and timing of the research project, or broadly the production of new knowledge. It became obvious that the degree of classification and framing of the research project must change during the period of the research project. I then went on to use the data to illustrate how dissatisfactions about research supervision often stemmed from disagreements about the strength of classification and framing. I argued that satisfactory supervision depended upon initial agreement and future negotiated changes in classification and framing. In this case I stretched the concepts of classification and framing and decoupled them from their relationship in Bernstein's work with social class. The second time I used the concepts, they were still fully coupled, but stretched in a different way.

In the work on boys' public boarding schools (Walford, 1986b) there was an important question that needed to be answered about how the schools played a role in the maintenance of the dominance of the ruling class in Britain. In Bernstein's own work, he uses the example of less able working-class pupils who (if they are to be employed at all) are likely to occupy unskilled or lowly skilled manual jobs. The most clear example might be production line assembly work. These jobs are ones where the ability to follow instructions within an organized hierarchy of command is valued, and where initiative, individuality, creativity and criticism are discouraged. In short, they are usually jobs where both classification and framing are high. There is high insulation between those who control the production process and those who execute production, and between the various tasks and grades of production personnel. Tasks are simple, repetitive and tightly defined. The pacing, organization and timing of the production process is strictly controlled by people other than those actually doing the work. This is the exact opposite of the type of ruling-class occupation that the public school boys were expected to enter. If there was to be continuity between the experiences of these boys in school and in work, then the curriculum should be weakly classified and framed.

Yet my research presented me with a contradiction that took me some time to understand. These boys were in schools where classification and framing were both strong. Their work was dominated by the collection code of public examinations, and the pedagogy was such that the teacher had almost complete control over all that occurred in the classroom. They were usually taking between eight and twelve separate academic subjects. The teaching throughout was rigidly timetabled, with each different subject being taught by specialist academic staff. There was no integration whatsoever between subjects. At first sight, it seemed that, far from the schools acting smoothly as agents of reproduction of the workforce, they were acting as interruptors and producing a clear discontinuity in the system. While strong classification and framing in public schools clearly gave a high chance of entry to higher education, there appeared to be a considerable discontinuity between the strength of classification and framing in schooling and the strength required in the higher education institutions and the high status and ruling-class occupations for which these pupils hoped they were destined. The archetypal professional occupation is weakly classified and framed. The professional is expected to be creative and forward looking, to initiate and control rather than be controlled. The nature and extent of occupational responsibilities are not firmly bounded, but expand as new initiatives are taken. The division between 'work' and 'play' is porous, as professional commitments overlap with family responsibilities, professional colleagues merge with personal friends and work from the office overflows into the home study. The professional does not work set hours but works until the particular projects with which he or she is concerned are completed to satisfaction. Organization, pacing and timing of the work are set by the professional rather than any superior. It would be difficult to conceive of anything more different from the strongly classified and framed formal curriculum of public schools!

At the time I was conducting the research I was still teaching Bernstein's work to both undergraduates and postgraduates. Initially, it seemed to me that the theory did not work. The data I was generating did not show the continuity that I expected, yet there was little reason for suspecting that those who were entering prestigious occupations from the public schools were later failing in these positions. It took me a long period of working with the data to recognize that my problem was simply that I was defining 'curriculum' too narrowly. In boarding schools the school curriculum must be seen to be far wider than merely timetabled lessons and even formal 'extra-curricular' activities, such as sport, music and the arts, for the influence of the school extends deep into areas which elsewhere would be not business of the school and in the private domain. For the boarding school pupil life is lived completely within the school's influence for the whole of the term. Official regulations thus extend to cover all activities of pupils, from the time a pupil must be out of bed and into breakfast until the time that lights must be out in the dormitories. There are regulations as to where pupils may or may not be at all times of the day, what they may wear and how they should behave. But, although the rules may be many, this part of the total school curriculum is essentially weakly classified and framed. Individual rules and restrictions are open to negotiation between masters and pupils and, as it is simply not possible to lay down rules for every eventuality, schools rely on a general overarching rule such as 'You are expected to show common sense, good discipline and good manners at all times', with all its possible ambiguity and space for different interpretations.

Within the houses pupils have considerable autonomy of action for, as long as they do the required timetable activities, they are free to spend the rest of the time much as they wish. Masters will generally only interfere in social activities if they are perceived to go beyond the general rule of 'common sense, good discipline and good manners' which can never be explicitly defined. Yet, while these expectations are poorly defined and diffuse, pupils recognize that they are of major importance and know that masters expect an 'appropriate' level of keenness, enthusiasm, responsibility, behaviour and so on from them throughout the entire time they are at school. A far wider range of the pupils' attributes and activities are seen as legitimate objects of evaluation and scrutiny, and judgements of success or failure are based on a multiplicity of dimensions. This was the weak classification and framing that Bernstein's theory predicted, yet to find it I had to stretch the original concepts to include the whole of school life.

POLITICAL MODELS OF MANAGEMENT

While I have often made use of explicit theoretical models in my work, I have rarely found that the concepts or the models themselves directly fit the data that I have generated. In the process of working through the data, I usually find that I have to modify the concepts and theories such that they become more useful for my particular case. Of course I hope that, in doing so, others may also find my developments more useful for their particular cases.

In my work on the management of change at Aston University I outlined several models that had traditionally been used to understand how change occurred. These included those that stressed rationality and consensus, those that stressed ambiguity of goals and processes, and those that stressed politics and micropolitical activity. But when I examined the data that I was generating I found that none of these models was fully helpful. I thus moved on to look at models that tried to combine elements of two of more of these models, but in the rapidly changing circumstances of universities in the 1980s I expected that a model based on conflict and political activity would have greater utility than one based on consensus. Yet my data showed many calls for consensus and for collegiality. Academics insisted that collegiality should be preserved and that decisions should be based upon rational arguments; they drew upon the models of management and change in a normative way rather than implying that this was the best model for what was actually happening.

In seeking to develop a model that would help to explain the data that I had, I thus started by taking Baldridge's (1971) political model, which itself had been developed to understand university management at a time of rapid change. It argued that, in times of growing external constraint, political activity gains prominence and must be seen as a normal part of management. Various groups and individuals have their own interests and goals and will act, both collectively and individually, if they see their interests attacked. Some, for example, may wish to ensure that their subject area is protected, that their research group is well funded or that a particular course is maintained, while others will simply wish to be left to follow their own research or even to do as little as possible. However, two of the six assumptions of Baldridge's model did not fit. His model assumed that inactivity was the normal state for all people in the institution, and that there was fluid participation of individual people in the policy-making process according to their interests. The data that I had generated suggested that these two assumptions did not hold, as there were some, especially among the senior management team, whose presence was not fluid but stable and who were able to call upon greater resources to influence decisions. Their lack of fluidity compared with others gave them greater power.

This then led to a greater concern with the nature of power and the ways in which power might be exercised. I found Lukes informative for his understanding of the way in which power did not always have to be exercised in conditions of conflict: 'To put the matter sharply, A may exercise power over B by getting him to do what he does not want to do, but he also exercises power over him by influencing, shaping or determining his very wants' (Lukes, 1974, p. 23). The most effective and insidious use of power is to prevent conflicts arising in the first place, by shaping the perceptions, cognition and preferences of others in such a way that they accept their role 'either because they can see or imagine no alternative to it, or because they see it as natural and unchangeable, or because they value it as divinely ordained and beneficial'. I included this insight into the model and the book then illustrated the ways in which those with power in the university had used these various strategies to try to ensure that their own views on what was desirable came to fruition.

There was one further twist. In searching the data it became obvious that the models of organization and management that could be used in the analysis were actually being used in the process as instruments of power. The models were being drawn upon selectively by various groups and individuals to increase their influence. Thus the Association of University Teachers drew greatly upon a model of collegiality. Those in the senior management team usually drew more on a rational bureaucratic model of decision-making, but they also drew on that collegial model when it suited their ends. The models of management were thus used as political resources within the university not for increasing understanding but as implied desirable norms. This further element was also incorporated within the model, but then I stopped. I began to fear that the model would soon become too complex to be useful.

FRANCHISED SCHOOLING

One important feature of the use of theory in the above examples is that existing theories were drawn upon and developed in the light of the data generated in the particular case study. The selection of the theory drawn upon was never completely obvious from the case itself, but was the result of considering a variety of different possible theories. One way of thinking about this is that the theories were selected because they allowed a simplification of the complexity to be achieved such that a story could be told. In the cases above there are some broad links between the theories selected and the nature of the cases. They were all theories that had been developed in other educational research studies, and it was reasonable to assume that they might have some utility in structuring and explaining these new cases. However, this is far from always true. Some theories are developed to explain very different types of phenomena from education.

In my study of sponsored grant-maintained schools I published a paper that described how the policy had been implemented by the Conservative government from 1993 to 1996 (Walford, 1997). I had a great deal of descriptive material on the various schools that had tried to become sponsored grant-maintained. Some of these had been successful and others not. Although the number of cases was small, I looked for patterns in the type of school that had been supported and those that had failed to find support. But I wanted to describe the nature of how the policy as a whole had been developed. I was reading an academic sociology journal when I came across an idea that was totally disconnected from education but which I thought might generate insights.

Although there had been a fair number of initial enquiries from potential sponsors and existing private schools, very few of these enquiries had developed into firm proposals. Most potential sponsors had presumably found the constraints and demands made on them too great for them to accept, and had not be able and/or prepared to proceed. In practice, the FAS and DfEE operated the scheme in a very tightly constrained way. It seemed to me that these constraints were such that, rather than encouraging diversity, the scheme was very similar to an industrial or service sector franchise operation (Felstead, 1993). Put simply, sponsors were given the franchise to operate a school in a particular area if their plan fitted with the FAS's overall strategy and they could show that they would attract sufficient children whom they could teach effectively in a financially efficient way.

The idea of franchising is far from new, but the past decades have seen a rapid growth in franchising in very many manufacturing and service industries. The practice is particularly prevalent in catering, hotels, cleaning services and retailing, and many household names such as Dunkin' Donuts, Burger King, Weigh and Save, and Ryman are actually individual businesses where a franchisee has paid a substantial sum to use the trade name, materials and processes of the franchiser. One definition is:

> Franchising is a contractual bond of interest in which an organization, the franchiser, which has developed a pattern or formula for the manufacture and/or sale of a product or service, extends to other firms, the franchisees, the right to carry on the business, subject to a number of restrictions and controls. (Quoted in Housden, 1984, pp. 31–2)

There are numerous different types of arrangement, but one particular broad type of franchise is the business format franchise, which is described by Felstead (1993, p. 47) as 'Under this system, the franchisee not only sells the franchiser's product and/or service, but does so in accordance with a set of precisely laid-down procedures or "format".'

It is most commonly used in retailing, but I found striking the similarity of this type with the new grant-maintained schools. For these schools the product or service is 'schooling'. They have to provide 'schooling' of a set type defined by the National

Curriculum, and do so for a set number of days per year. The private schools that had become grant-maintained had to extend the length of their school terms, as the 'opening hours' required are longer than those to which the schools previous adhered. They must adhere to statutory requirements for admissions, health and safety, equal opportunities, constitution and government. Set funding levels per student mean that they are required to pay staff salaries that may be less than before. They are accountable to the franchise holder (the government) through regular Ofsted inspections. The premises have to be of a certain set standard, and the service levels are fixed. Most importantly, sponsors have to provide substantial financial start-up costs, and have the energy and enthusiasm to establish the business and make it successful. Moreover, the larger the proportion of the capital costs that the sponsors can provide, the more likely they are to obtain the franchise. If they can provide continuing recurrent financial support, so much the better.

The idea was a simple one, but to see if it worked I had to read several books on franchising in various sectors and then search through my data to see the extent to which this new model fitted. As always in these cases, one looks for exceptions as well and those confirmatory examples, but I found none. Up to that point, the scheme could be well described as a franchise.

CONCLUSION

In this chapter I have tried to suggest that theory is a vital part of any analysis. 'Pure' description is not possible as data are generated with theories present whether they be acknowledged or not. Further, any account needs a structure and theory necessarily plays a part in this structure.

I have given some examples of how particular theories have been used and modified in my own work, such that they restrict the focus of investigation so that a story can be told. Complexity is reduced through the use of models. But it is perfectly possible that more than one theory can be usefully applied to explicate elements of the same data. One model may be used in a particular piece of writing and another used elsewhere. Fundamentally, research is only completed once publication has been achieved and theories aid that process by allowing simplification and linkage to other areas of interest. There is nothing magical about theory.

Publication

INTRODUCTION

In his classic study of life in a psychiatric hospital, Rosenhan (1973) describes the way that covert sociologists who took notes within the hospital setting were fully accepted as patients by the medical staff. The researchers' constant note-taking of every activity that occurred was taken as sure proof that they were insane! Such 'compulsive writing activity' could only be a sign that these pseudo-patients were really as mad as the rest of the inmates.

Now Rosenhan, of course, believed that the sociologists were sane and were only taking part in the rational activity called sociology, but I have my doubts. There *is* something insane about the way qualitative sociologists spend so much time writing. They write before they start generating data in the field, they write profuse fieldnotes while they are undertaking the research and, finally, they write endless articles and books about their findings and (increasingly) the process of doing research. In most cases very few people will read any of this writing. If this is sanity, then how does it differ from madness?

In this chapter I write about my own 'compulsive writing activity' linked to my research on the political processes that influenced legislation on sponsored grant-maintained schools. My focus is on that writing activity concerned directly with publication, but this cannot be separated from the earlier forms of writing both prior to and during the 'data construction' phase of the research. For me, 'writing' and 'publishing' are not distinct activities that occur at the end of the research period, they are continuously present in the design and practice of the research. The compulsive need to write and publish helps to structure what is done in the field, and the decisions made at all stages of the research.

The chapter starts with a consideration of the structure and constraints of the academic publication market place and the way in which these influence the publication process. This is followed by a description of how particular articles and books linked to the Christian schools project were eventually published and the form in which this occurred. Some general points are drawn in conclusion.

My objective in this chapter is to demystify some aspects of the academic publication process, such that new writers in particular will have a more realistic view of how publication occurs. In doing this I will also draw from my own experience of editing a major educational research journal. I hope that readers of research will also benefit from a greater understanding of how academic research articles and books come to be selected for publication and are structured by forces far beyond the purely academic. However, unlike several recent books (for example, Derricourt, 1996; Eggleston and Klein, 1997; Thyer, 1994), my aim is not to provide helpful hints about 'how to get published' for new academics, but to give a personal account of some aspects of my relationship to the process of writing and publication.

THE ACADEMIC PUBLISHING MARKET PLACE

The vast majority of academic books and journal articles are produced because someone believes that there is money to be made by doing so. With very few exceptions, book and journal publishers operate within a highly competitive market place where the single most important criterion for publication is the likelihood of short- to medium-term profitability.

There has been considerable recent research into the economics of the school textbook and how the requirements of the market constrain and influence what is published and thus the content of school textbooks (e.g. Apple and Christian-Smith, 1991; Apple, 1996). There has been less research that has focused on the market place at the university and academic level, but the influences are no less real. It is essential to recognize that, within a capitalist economy, academic publishing is not separated from any other form of publication. Publishers exist, and shareholders invest in publishing houses, because they wish to make a good return on their investment. Quality alone is insufficient to ensure publication; a manuscript has to have a large enough potential market for the publisher to recoup costs and make a profit.

The profit-related demands of publishing are most clearly seen in book publishing. Books are recognizable products that are traded and available in shops in a similar way to baked beans or breakfast cereals. The manufacturers of books wish to make as much overall profit as they can and price each book according to their expectations of how well it will sell. If they believe a book will have a narrow appeal, and the major part of the market is likely to be academic libraries, a decision might be made to produce only hardback copies. The price charged will be high but, even with small sales volume, a worthwhile profit can be achieved. In contrast, the expectation of a wider potential market may lead to a decision to print both hardback and softback, with the hope that a cheaper edition will lead to sufficiently large sales to achieve the maximum profit.

Just as baked beans or breakfast cereals have to be packaged in particular sized boxes, so books have to be of a certain length and structure. For example, few commissioning editors will think about publishing an academic monograph of 30,000 words or one of 150,000. One would be too thin to be priced cheaply enough to get sales, while the other too fat to be produced economically. For most publishers the ideal length is between 80,000 and 100,000 words, or about 200 or so pages. That is the rough 'size' that buyers expect 'a book' to be. That is the product that they have become accustomed to and socialized into buying; the product that has gradually been constructed by printers and publishers. The original physical limitations of printing and binding have led to a recognizable product that is within certain size and design limitations – a product that fits neatly on a bookshelf, a product that can be held in the hands relatively easily, a book that looks and feels like 'a book'.

The influence of the profit motive within book publishing is self-evident, yet similar, although more complex, considerations apply to publishing within academic journals. Journals are usually started by enthusiasts who wish to legitimize a particular developing field of knowledge. A new journal might be a by-product of meetings of a group of academics interested in similar issues, or it could be the entrepreneurial initiative of a small group wishing to enhance their own statuses or careers. Whatever the initial impetus, while the group itself may initially finance the journal, if it wishes the journal to expand its circulation, it soon has to convince an external body to invest.

In most cases educational journal publishing is just a part of the activities of a far larger publishing company, which is often, in turn, part of the activities of a multinational conglomerate. Journals are supported by these companies because they can make a profit. And academic journals have the potential for being a very profitable business. In contrast to popular journals, contributors to academic refereed journals are not paid for their articles, much of the work of producing each issue is donated free by editors, reviewers and the authors themselves, and the serial nature of the publications means that once the initial subscription has been sold, the buyers will usually continue to purchase the product. Brand name loyalty is high. While the details depend on pricing decisions and the peculiarities of particular markets, the sales level at which journals become profitable is surprisingly low. Once 300 or so subscriptions have been sold profits can usually start to flow.

Most academic refereed journals have an editor and an editorial board, with the editor having a vital role as academic gatekeeper (Simon and Fyfe, 1994). Generally, when a manuscript is sent to the editor she or he will quickly assess if it is relevant to the aims of the journal and looks worth reviewing. Two or three referees are then chosen (often including someone from the editorial board) and are sent copies of the manuscript. They then assess the article and write back to the editor with their views about the desirability of publication and any changes that they believe to be necessary before publication can proceed. It is common for there to be disagreement between reviewers and, when this happens, the editor will adjudicate with or without a further opinion being sought.

A straightforward decision to publish is rare. Much more common is the decision to reject the article or publish subject to changes being made. In the latter case the author will be sent copies of a selection of what reviewers have written about the paper and be asked to revise in the light of their suggestions. As is shown below, it is not uncommon for the comments from different reviewers at this stage to be somewhat contradictory. The author is left to try to make sense of multiple demands.

In a similar way to book publication, the decision about publication of articles in academic journals is not made purely on academic grounds. Editors work within the constraints and rhythm of the journal production process. They have to find sufficient articles to fill the planned number of issues each year. As with books, each issue has to be of an acceptable size – usually about 130 pages for Carfax or Taylor and Francis journals. This means that, at the margins, the decision to publish is influenced by the flow of articles submitted to the particular journal. Submitted articles compete with each other for space, so that when many articles are being submitted the standard of the papers accepted rises. In contrast, in times of scarcity, editors are forced to publish articles about which they may have considerable doubts. Most editors try to smooth the flow of articles by building a stockpile of articles ready for future publication, but authors object if the wait between acceptance and publication becomes too long. Few editors like to have more than about a year's worth of articles waiting to appear in print so there are bound to be periodic fluctuations in the standard of papers accepted in most journals.

My experience as Joint Editor of the *British Journal of Educational Studies* has made me more aware of the degree of both the power and the helplessness of the editor in this process. The editor certainly has some power in deciding whether an article is suitable for the journal. The *British Journal of Educational Studies* has a stated policy that: 'Reports of empirical investigations [will not be published] unless the report is used as illustration of a discussion of a major topic.' Yet authors still often send manuscripts which report small-scale investigations which have limited wider relevance. Some cases are clear, but other lie on the borderline and a judgement has to be made by the Joint Editors about whether to send the paper for review. There is also considerable power in selecting the reviewers, yet this is more limited than I expected. I have recognized that editors are at the mercy of their reviewers, and that they can be unpredictable.

One of the roles of an editor is to encourage academics to submit articles to the journal. At one international conference I heard what I felt was an excellent paper being given. I obtained a copy and invited the author to submit a revised version to the journal. The paper duly arrived and I selected two referees who I thought would be tough yet positive. Both returned reviews that were tough, but not positive. I had to write back to the author saying that, in the light of these reviews, we could not publish the paper. In this case the clear message from the reviewers led to a rejection. I do not know what decision would have been made had there been no other accepted papers in the pipeline for the journal.

WHY DO ACADEMICS PUBLISH SO MUCH?

While the publishing industry is structured around profit, monetary gain is certainly not the prime motivation for the academic author. A particularly generous publisher might give authors 10 per cent of the net price of a book. This might be about £1.00 per copy. As most academic books are rated highly successful if they sell more than 2,000 or 3,000 copies, the amount that an author gains cannot be a prime motivation. In terms of the rate of pay per hour of writing, most authors would do far better serving drinks behind a bar!

With academic journal articles, the authors are not paid anything at all. They spend time researching and writing, they produce manuscripts to set length and style requirements, they modify what they have written in accordance with referees' comments and even act as proofreaders for their printed article. Yet they receive not a penny from the publisher!

There are clearly other motivations. One is that most academic writing is done by people already in full-time work where there is at least an implicit contractual requirement that they publish. Academics are usually required to 'teach and conduct research' and publication is seen an essential part of the latter. Moreover, at least in the initial stages of a career, there is often perceived to be an overriding need to 'publish or perish'. The academic on a short-term contract is unlikely to have it renewed or to be able to find another academic job elsewhere unless he or she has several articles published or in press. Obtaining a permanent job or promotion within academia is highly dependent upon a substantial and significant record of publications. This direct pressure to write is at its most evident for academics at the early stages of their careers, but the regular Research Assessment Exercises within the British higher education sector have increased the pressure on established academics to continue to get published once they have obtained an established post. The current expectation for the Research Assessment Exercise is that every academic will produce at least four significant publications within each assessment exercise period of about five years.

But many established academics produce far more than this. Many well known academics within education are producing several books and dozens of academic articles within each assessment period. It is hard to believe that the pride of seeing one's name in print is sufficient to encourage such overproduction. There is a real sense in which this is 'compulsive writing behaviour' – it certainly is for me.

THE PUBLISHING PROCESS: SOME EXAMPLES

I have had colleagues approach me with an article they have written and ask me to suggest journals to which it might be submitted. I find this bizarre. To me, it is rather like writing a letter and, only after completing it, deciding who should receive it. While it may be true that ageing Aunt Joan may be interested in some of the same things as your bank manager, it is highly likely that both the content and style of letters to each of them will be substantially different.

My writing, and to a great extent the conduct of the research itself, is always structured around particular books and journal articles that I wish to write. I always have in mind a particular 'outlet' for everything I write, and it is only if a piece is rejected by that journal or publisher that I have to search for another that is as similar as possible to my original preference.

From the point when I received the Nuffield Foundation grant, I decided that I wanted to publish four or five academic articles about the work on Christian schools and then revise them and add some new material to form a book. In particular, the pressures of the regular higher education Research Assessment Exercise led me to feel that I 'needed' to have several publications in highly respected academic journals, but I also wished to have a complete book as an outcome. In my mind, as the research progressed, I divided the various parts of the research into articles, each linked to a particular journal.

Educational Studies

One article was straightforward. With Colin Poyntz (who was a social sciences undergraduate working with me for a year) I conducted a survey of the 60 or so new Christian schools then in membership of the Christian Schools Trust. This was a necessary preliminary to any further work and the results of the survey could be easily shaped into an article that presented both a quantitative and a qualitative description. This type of article almost writes itself and the structure broadly follows the physics reports of experiments that I wrote when I was 13. The traditional format of experiment, method, results, conclusion, was echoed in this paper by introduction, research methods, results, conclusion. The only slight development of structure was that the results were presented under four sub-headings covering different aspects. *Educational Studies* seemed an appropriate journal to aim for and, to my surprise, it accepted the article with no amendments required

(Poyntz and Walford, 1994). I later learned more of the unusual way in which the editor and editorial board of *Educational Studies* go about their task. In contrast to practically all other refereed academic journals in education, with this journal, if the Editor in Chief judges a manuscript to be worthy of refereeing a copy is sent to all members of the six strong editorial board. The board meets three times each year to decide which of the articles they have read since the last meeting should be included in the next issue. Their policy has since changed but at that time only very rarely was an article from the previous period held back for the next, so the law of supply and demand was starkly evident. While the articles published were each reviewed by many more people than in comparable journals, the decisions made about publication were highly dependent on the quality of the papers submitted during the last four-month period. In my case, I guess I was lucky. Mine was one of the eight papers selected for that issue, but then, unusually and for reasons unknown to me, was held over for the next issue.

Journal of Education Policy
The next article about the research was the result of an unexpected victory for the campaign during the passage of the 1992 Education (Schools) Act. The main purposes of this Act were to introduce the offices of Her Majesty's Chief Inspector of Schools for England and for Wales, to provide for regular inspection of schools and to give the Secretary of State powers to require schools to publish information. In practice, it was the Act that led to Ofsted (the Office for Standards in Education) and more detailed league tables of examination results. The Christian Schools Campaign saw the Act as another way of raising a debate about religious schools. Through contacts in the House of Lords, principally Lord North-bourne, they introduced amendments that related to the inspection of spiritual, moral and cultural values and to the publication by schools of information on the spiritual, moral and cultural values that each school was trying to promote. This was done to challenge what they had come to see as the 'myth of religious neutrality' (Clouser, 1991) which accepted the idea that schools could either be religious or religiously neutral. The campaign believed that it was not possible for schools to be religiously neutral, and that schools always present their own spiritual and moral values either overtly or covertly. Those involved in putting forward the amendments had no expectation that any of them had a chance of being accepted.

The more recent panic about declining values and morality, and the now widespread acceptance of the importance of teaching appropriate values in schools, makes it difficult to remember that in 1992 the idea that schools could and should be 'morally neutral' was widespread. This was the basis of the American ideal of separation of church and state, and many educationalists argued that it should be emulated here. What was interesting was that, quite unexpectedly, the Lords agreed with the amendments and there was about an hour of one-sided support for the Act to include the inspection of values. There were no speeches against and only three expressed any hesitations. Faced with such determination, and in spite of the perceived difficulty of inspecting values, the government of the day was forced to rethink. It eventually introduced its own rather similar amendments that led to a fundamental change to what was to be inspected.

What interested me was why this had happened. I decided to investigate and write an account that tried to understand that particular decision-making process. I soon recognized that I did not fully understand the procedures of the House of Lords and House of Commons, so I first had to read some elementary books on the British political system. Next, I had to delve into the Parliamentary Reports in the local law library and interview various people about their activities. I learned a great deal about the workings of Parliament that I had not known before. Then I attempted to relate what I had found to existing models of decision-making. Rational models clearly did not fit, but it seemed to me that two theories were particularly helpful: micro-politics, derived from Stephen Ball's (1990a) work, and the 'garbage can' model from Cohen *et al.* (1972). The latter idea is based on the metaphor of viewing the opportunity to make a choice as an open can into which participants can 'dump' problems or solutions. 'Solutions' are seen as products looking for choice opportunities and a group of problems to which to fit. In highly politicized settings, opportunities are seized as they present themselves and as events unfold. Here, I decided, the Lords were using the 'solution' of inspection of values to answer a 'problem' about school league tables. They wished to emphasize that education was to be seen as more than just examination results, and agreeing to the Northbourne amendments allowed them to express that view.

The article that I wrote for the *Journal of Education Policy* was largely a blow-by-blow narrative account with an additional section where I discussed the theoretical models of decision-making and argued that the 'garbage can' model gave considerable insights into the case. I gave the article the rather over-clever title of 'The Northbourne amendments: is the House of Lords a garbage can?' I now think it was an inappropriate title for two reasons. First, it does not tell the reader what the article is about. Only those readers who already have a deep knowledge of the topic will be guided to read it. Second, it assumes that readers know that I am playing with the idea of a 'garbage can' and that there is a theoretical model with that name. I was advised to not include the paper in my list of publications for the last higher education Research Assessment Exercise as readers might think that it was a flippant and highly critical article about the House of Lords.

In due course the editor of the *Journal of Education Policy* sent me comments from two reviewers. Although both reviews recommended publication subject to revision, they were very different. The first, unusually, was handwritten. It was about 200 words long and, although there were some helpful suggestions, there were several parts of the review that I simply could not decipher. The writing was so bad that I, and other people I showed it to, could not understand what was being suggested. I took account of what I could read and ignored the rest.

The second review was a stark contrast. The reviewer had clearly taken a great deal of time and effort to give suggestions and indicate areas where he or she believed changes should be made. In about 800 words the reviewer made several significant suggestions for improvement, as well as going through the paper page-by-page correcting errors, inconsistencies and unclarities. The tone of these comments can be judged from the opening words:

> I think this paper may be publishable subject to revision, although the case is not of great interest unless its theoretical side, and the link between theory and the case study, are both considerably strengthened. In particular, the interpretation (p. 19ff) is underdeveloped. ... The 'garbage can' model is not very well explained or applied. The case itself is not of sufficient interest, so the success of the article must rest on the theoretical insights to which it might give rise, and that is where the paper is weak. I will point this out later on in itemising where I think revisions should be made. The reason I am spending time on these details of wording, etc. is that I would like to encourage the author to resubmit the paper.

The last sentence of this introduction was important to me. Without it, the review would have felt very critical. As it was, although I felt that the case in itself was of considerable interest as a narrative account, I was more than willing to follow the suggestions made by the reviewer. There were more than 60 points of detail which included deleting an extra 's', instructions about how to address a Baroness and several pointers to where further explanation or clarification was required. There were also more substantive suggestions about the general content and structure of the article. I was genuinely very pleased to receive such full comments and wrote to the editor to ask that my thanks should be communicated to the reviewer.

I usually try to make any revisions to articles very quickly. Indeed, sometimes I have returned a revised manuscript the next day. In this case I took three months over it. I hope both reviewers were satisfied with the final product (Walford, 1995c).

British Educational Research Journal
The next article came from a gradual recognition of a contradiction that I saw as the research progressed. As I visited the various new Christian schools and talked with those involved in the Christian Schools Campaign, I saw the open and very positive way in which most of them viewed schooling. While these schools were technically private schools, they were far from being elitist and exclusive. Most served working-class families who were worried about the schooling that was locally available for their children. These parents simply sought what they believed was in the best interests of their children and were prepared to make considerable financial sacrifices for their children to attend these schools. More surprisingly, most of the schools were open even to children of different religions, and several Muslim parents preferred to send their children to schools where religious belief was respected rather than to what they saw as secular state-maintained schools. These parents and activists were not natural friends of the New Right, yet their activities were in accord with the desires of the New Right, and the Christian Schools Campaign was working with leading figures on the Right such as Baroness Cox, Stuart Sexton and John Marks to achieve their aims. I saw a severe contradiction here between ends and means which I believed would provide the basis for an interesting article. I thought that the *British Educational Research Journal* would be appropriate for an article of this nature that outlined the history of the campaign and highlighted the contradictions. By that time the 1993 Education Act had been

passed and the campaign could be seen as having been successful. Yet, while the immediate objectives had been achieved, I predicted that many of the potential results of the legislation would be in contradiction to the beliefs held by most of the parents and activists from the Christian schools.

Somewhat unusually I received only one set of comments from the reviewers. I assume that the other reviewer was prepared to have the paper published as submitted, but the first reviewer bluntly demanded some amendments before the paper was to be accepted. The paper could be published after:

1. More details of the research methodology are included.
2. The CSC is located in relation to other Christian initiatives, e.g. on p. 9 in relation to the ACE schools studied by O'Keefe.
3. Comparisons are made (e.g. p. 29) with European policies for funding religious and other schools of sub-cultural maintenance.
4. More references are made to relevant social theory.
5. The claims made on pp. 28 and 29 about inequality and deepening social and ethnic divisions are justified (at least by reference to other literature) rather than just asserted.
6. The paper's significance for wider debates about choice and diversity is clarified.

Some other minor, but very helpful, comments were made on detailed presentation.

This list of suggestions presented me with several difficulties. As someone who had taught research methods for about 16 years, it was the first point that gave me the most angst. It was easy to expand what I had written on methodology, but slightly shameful that I should have to be asked to do so. I also readily accepted point 5 and tried to put forward a more reasoned argument. In contrast I felt that points 2 and 6 were really asking me to write a slightly different article from the one I wished to write. I had already written about these issues elsewhere or had plans to do so. Reviewers' attempts to make authors write the article that the reviewer would wish to have written rather than the article that the author wishes to write are far from uncommon. Here I compromised and added a little on both issues. But I objected strongly to points 3 and 4 and was not prepared to compromise on them. After I had made the relevant changes I sent the paper back to the editor with an accompanying letter. I stated:

The only two points I have not dealt with are points 3 and 4. I have not dealt with point 4 because I have an aversion to 'add-on' theory, which many people seem to use as decoration to their papers. You can't just 'add on' some references to social theory – you are either using it or not. I have already referenced what I have used.

Point 3 is very interesting, because it strongly suggests that I do exactly what I think we should not do! I have just written another paper that looks at policy-borrowing from the Netherlands and argues that you cannot simply take bits and pieces from other countries' educational systems and apply them to your own. Simply making reference to the way other European countries fund their religious schools is likely to be completely misleading without a consideration of the whole social, economic and historical context.

Whether the editor was convinced by my arguments, or whether there was nothing better to fill the pages, I shall never know, but the paper was accepted without further comment (Walford, 1995b).

One of my more recent articles had less success with the *British Educational Research Journal*. This article related to the way the sponsored grant-maintained schools policy was implemented by successive Conservative and Labour governments. I was particularly interested in the similarities between the City Technology Colleges initiative and these sponsored grant-maintained schools, for there were interesting continuities and discontinuities between these two policies in terms of their origins, and the issues of selection and privatization. I wrote a paper that first described the two policies and then examined each of these three topics. I eventually received a letter rejecting the paper and enclosing three referees' reports. The first two were diametrically opposite in their evaluation. The first was complimentary, arguing that:

This article reminds us of the extent to which two key policy initiatives, developed under the last Conservative administration, are joined at the hip. Each of these policies was justified on the basis that it would promote diversity in the provision of education, each was founded on the belief that institutional autonomy was the basis of restructuring and revitalising education, each developed with the idea of private sponsors taking some responsibility for the fate of the policy, and ultimately each policy 'failed' to attract on-the-ground support.

This article carefully makes these connections. The author also articulates these policies to the larger concerns within Tory education policy, namely reduction in state forms of provision, the privatisation of public welfare services and attempts to introduce forms of academic selection within the education system. Moreover, the author seeks to explain how these policies have fared under a Labour government.

Underpinning the paper is a critical review of the relevant secondary literature and a judicious use of official documents, party political texts. These are employed to construct a coherent history of each of these initiatives and the reasons behind their demise. The key idea though, is the comparison of policies which rely on private sponsorship. This idea has since been extended to Educational Action Zones and the National Grid for Learning.

The paper is well written. It does illuminate an area of policy which has left its mark on the educational landscape and which foreshadows current, and important initiatives.

In contrast, the second reviewer starkly wrote (unusually, in written block capitals):

This is a rather dull re-hash of very familiar ground with some 'bringing up-to-date' (which hardly merits publication in a long descriptive paper). The single point of argument is rather weakly made – that CTCs were a fore-runner of other marketising/devolving change – and no more sturdily established than other interpretations. As a piece of policy analysis this is derivative and descriptive and lacking in insight and originality. It would merit a 'B' as an MEd essay.

In such cases the editor (or someone else) usually reads both reviewers' comments and comes to a decision. This reviewer wrote that:

I have read both of the reviews and the article concerned. I'm afraid that I agree rather more with the negative review. The author offers a mainly descriptive account of the development of CTCs and of grant-maintained schools. He/she is interested in these initiatives as reflections of 'market' strategies in English education, reflecting ideologies of 'choice' and 'diversity'. The account promises to identify similarities and differences between the two initiatives and to evaluate their longer term significance. His/her conclusion is that the two initiatives were precursors for later policy innovations and contained several of them in embryo.

I found the account too detailed and too descriptive. It did seem to be well-researched in a factual sort of way, but I came to the conclusion that it did not really contribute enough to warrant inclusion in BERJ.

Once the anger of receiving such referees' comments has subsided, the only possible reaction is laughter. The second referee seems hardly to have read the article at all. The 'single point' that s/he believed the article weakly made was not the point of the article at all. While the material on City Technology Colleges was obviously already in the public domain, the paper presented data on sponsored grant-maintained schools that had not been presented before. Finally, what I take to be a gratuitous insult at the end is hardly an appropriate comment. I am actually surprised that the editor did not delete this last sentence before sending the review to me.

The final reviewer does appear to have a better idea about the paper, but raises doubt by stating that the paper was about the development of grant-maintained schools, when it actually described a small group of sponsored grant-maintained schools, not grant-maintained schools as a whole. The implications of a negative stance towards an article that is 'well researched in a factual sort of way' are worth pondering. What else is research to be based on? But my purpose in reproducing these reports is not to take issue with their detail or even the final conclusion, simply to illustrate the type of reviews that are sometimes received. What is important is that when such disparate reviews are received, the paper is resubmitted elsewhere as soon as possible. The paper was later published in the *Oxford Review of Education*, where both reviewers were happy to accept it (Walford, 2000b). The delay sadly meant that the work was more dated that it should have been and its potential impact was reduced. It is also worth noting that at the time the article was being refereed by the *British Educational Research Journal*, I was actually a member of the Editorial Board. What is clear is that there was no favouritism in the way this article was dealt with! And I also do not think that I had made any potential enemies on the Editorial Board. The use of referees sometimes leads to odd decisions.

Book publishing
The accounts of publishing journal articles may read as if my publishing efforts always eventually lead to success. This is not true. My attempts to publish a book about the research show clearly the restrictions imposed through the need for publishers to produce a profit. The book I wanted to write was to be based on four previously published papers. Some of the book would simply reuse sections from these papers, but there would also be a great deal of new material. One of the advantages of word-processing is that, even where a chapter is based upon already published material, it can be reworked, edited, added to and shifted from place to place to form a new patchwork quilt of a book. A reading of the acknowledgements of very many academic books shows that publishers are not particularly opposed to authors doing this. The key question is: will it sell?

As I was already an established author I produced only a five-page outline of the book to send to publishers. Following an introduction and justification for the book, I sketched the contents of the nine proposed chapters. This was followed by an attempt to indicate the potential market. I suggested that 'the book should be of interest to sociologists, political scientists and all those interested in policy studies. This will include undergraduates and postgraduates on courses or doing research with a policy studies element, as well as academics and those themselves involved in the policy process.' Publishers were not convinced by my optimism.

In July 1993 I sent the proposal to Routledge as they had recently published one of my previous books. In August the editor replied that 'I do not think that it would be a viable book for us – it's simply too specialist. I could not with any certainty predict a wide enough audience to justify a paperback edition.' Cassell rejected it with the view that 'this title is probably too specialist for an education list as such'. Falmer Press decided that it was 'too far outside the main thrust of our list'. The editor at Open University Press stated, 'I believe this book would be rather too specialized for our list', while the one at Kogan Page expressed her doubts as: 'such a book would not fit in with the publishing strategy for our education list'. They were probably correct, but we can never be sure as a large publishing house might have been able to sell many more copies than have so far been sold by Avebury, who eventually became the publisher.

What is of note about the responses from the major education publishers is their unanimity. All the editors responded politely but firmly and indicated that, although they saw merit in the research, they did not believe it would sell. Looking back, I can't think why I tried so many different publishers – one at a time, of course – for not only were the responses clear, they were fast. A fast response from a publisher is not to be expected, yet these editors responded quickly. Evidently none of them thought it worthwhile even sending the outline to be reviewed. They decided themselves that a rejection was required, no matter what the academic merit might have been.

Faced with my small pile of rejections I could have simply given up, but I *wanted* to write the book. I decided to try Avebury. Now Avebury has a particular place in the market. It is not a vanity publisher (where the author pays to have something published) – I have my limits! – but its usual policy is to pay no royalties. It produces short-run hardback-only academic editions which, as the cover price is usually in the £30–40 range, are mainly sold to libraries. They are also 'roll-your-own' books, by which I mean that the author provides camera-ready copy from which the publishers print directly after adding a few titles. Such books provide a profit for the company, an outlet for academics with severe 'compulsive writing activity', and may even be read by a few students and other academics. In this case, I spent a wonderful five weeks (remember I already had four articles completed) producing the book. I cut and pasted, typed and retyped, and did practically nothing else other than eat and sleep for the five weeks. I buried myself in the data, read books and articles, wrote, rewrote and played with words. The feeling of satisfaction on sending off the camera-ready copy was far more significant than that felt on receiving the free copies of the book some four months later. For me, the satisfaction is *not* in seeing my name in print, but in completing the long process of researching, writing and publishing.

CONCLUSION

My aims in this chapter have been modest. I have tried simply to give an account of the process by which some of my 'compulsive writing behaviour' ended in publication. I hope that the account has helped to demystify that process and to lead readers to see how, in addition to academic constraints, the market for books and journals structures what is available for public consumption.

I hope to have also shown that academic writing is not a final stage of doing research that occurs once all the data construction, thought and analysis has finished. Text production is not just an automatic process that reports what has gone before. For me at least, the act of writing and the preparation of journal articles and books structure what I do during the research process. I research particular aspects (for example, the nature of a group of schools or the details of parliamentary procedures) because I have in mind something that I wish to write that demands that I conduct that aspect of the research. Of course, this does not mean that I am able to use all the data that I collect or that I do not waste effort on what turn out to be false trails. Much is discarded, but it can only be discarded because I have come to understand those data and have no further use for them in the argument I wish to present.

A further point worth making is that, for me, writing does not just improve my thinking, it allows me to think. It is only when a draft is finished that I begin to be clear about what I am trying to say – even if only at that particular moment. Writing forces me to confront at least some of my illogicalities, such that a temporary truce is constructed. What I write is always open to reassessment and development, and by the time an article eventually appears in print, I have frequently moved on from that position. I rarely read the final print version of anything I have written. My compulsion is for writing – it is for others to judge the value of what I have written.

Conclusion

In 1987, when I first edited a volume that collected together various reflexive accounts by sociologists of education of the research process, there were still not many similar volumes, and none devoted entirely to sociology of education. During the late 1980s and early 1990s there was a considerable rise in reflexive, semi-autobiographical accounts of the research process, and this led to the publication of more specialist volumes. Some concentrated on education evaluation (e.g. Adelman, 1984) or research ethics (Burgess, 1989), while others focused on researching education policy (Halpin and Troyna, 1994) or researching the powerful in education (Walford, 1994a). While these and similar books have been widely used by students and other researchers, they have not been without criticism.

One of the most important criticisms has developed from a growing interest in language use and representations within educational writing (van Maanen, 1995). For example, Atkinson (1996) discusses the genre of the autobiographical or 'confessional' account in which ethnographers, in particular, 'tell it like it was' and reveal the personal and practical issues they experience in the course of their own fieldwork. Such stories often recount hardships, deprivations, danger and fortitude but, Atkinson argues, such accounts are no less contrived or more authentic than any other genre of sociological reportage. He explains:

> It must be remembered that however 'intimate' and revealing confessionals may be, they are themselves artful products of writing. The genre is used by authors to invite particular kinds of readings and responses: the moral character and analytic acumen of the narrator are assembled out of the textual elements offered by the confessional. It would be quite wrong to assume that the 'confessional' embodies a 'true' and transparently unvarnished account, in contrast to the more

worked-up 'realist' ethnographic text. There is nothing uniquely privileged or authentic about the autobiographical story. The confessional is as conventional as any other style or genre. (Atkinson, 1996, p. 55)

Atkinson goes on to show that the accounts are shaped by narrative and other conventions. Their form is as culturally shaped as is other writing. One aspect of this is that such accounts often present the author as a strange mixture of 'hero' and 'anti-hero'.

There is the wry tradition whereby we rehearse the second-worst thing that ever happened to us in the field, the first being too painful or embarrassing. We paint ourselves in unflattering colours: we are by turns naïve, vulnerable and incompetent. Of course, we mean to present ourselves as 'socially acceptable incompetents' for the purpose of data collection. (Atkinson, 1996, p. 91)

In his edited collection of reflexive accounts, Barry Troyna (1994) has also raised several questions about such alternative accounts of research. He has three major reservations. His first echoes that of Atkinson, for he claims that the accounts tend to suffer from delusions of grandeur, and that they parade a pretence that it is possible to 'tell it like it is' in a way that is not done in conventional research methodology textbooks. Where accounts are presented in this way it helps to legitimize a realist view that there is 'something out there' that can be written about and transmitted to others. Troyna argues that, while these additional narratives about the research process may be of social, historical and intellectual interest, and may also demystify a researcher's particular experiences in the framing, execution or dissemination of a study, the methodological significance of such accounts cannot be taken for granted.

Troyna's second concern is about the effect that such reflexive accounts may have on the credibility of certain types of educational research. The particular problem here is the imbalance in expectations and practice that exists between qualitative and quantitative researchers. While there are now many reflexive accounts of qualitative research, and some researchers such as Ball (1990b) argue that methodological rigour demands that every ethnography should be accompanied by such an account, there are still relatively few comparable reports about the process of conducting quantitative research. Troyna argues that this imbalance may have serious negative implications for qualitative research. The result of the availability of alternative accounts of qualitative research processes could mean that non-qualitative researchers, policy-makers, researcher-funders and lay people may be less likely to take qualitative research seriously. The reflexive accounts available might be interpreted to show that qualitative research is subjective and value-laden, and thus unscientific and invalid. As there are few corresponding accounts of quantitative research, it is more able to retain its illusion of being objective, value-free, scientific and valid.

Troyna's third concern is with the impact of such 'confessional tales' within the power relations of the research community. He argues that the activity of writing such accounts is akin to self-appraisal. However, while self-appraisal is conducted in a highly structured and local environment, such reflexive accounts lead the researcher to open himself or herself to wider scrutiny by the research community. Troyna claims that while this is potentially threatening to anyone, it holds less danger for those already with established posts and reputations than it does to those on the fringes of the research community, such as postgraduate students and contract researchers.

This last concern has also been voiced by Paechter (1996), whose insightful article compares reflexive accounts of the research process with Bentham's Panopticon and the Christian ritual of confession. Using a Foucauldian analysis of the relationship between knowledge and power, she argues that the increasing imperative on researchers to produce reflexive accounts acts to control those with little power within the research community. For the powerless, the act of confession is an enactment of a power relation. She argues that Ball's exhortation for all researchers to produce a research biography alongside their ethnographic account should be ignored. For doctoral students, in particular, the inequalities of power between examiners and students are great, such that the practice becomes strongly coercive.

All three of Troyna's concerns are worthy of further examination, but it is first necessary to recognize that not all reflexive accounts serve a similar purpose or attempt to cover the same type of issue. Within any reflexive volume there is considerable variation in the nature of the accounts given in each chapter. However, the primary aim in practically all the chapters is to show other new and experienced researchers that the research process is rarely straightforward, and that personal, political and practical matters play significant parts in shaping what was done in particular research projects. In this book I have been able to give accounts that show some of the 'warts-and-all' nature of my practice. Of course, these reflexive accounts are separated in time and place from the original research reports, and the security of my academic position gives me considerable autonomy to admit the 'second worst thing that happened'. In answer to Troyna's third point, it is undoubtedly correct that the publication of such reflexive research accounts could potentially have a rather different impact on a doctoral student from that on an established researcher. But this does not mean that doctoral students should not write a reflexive account of their research – it just needs to be a different type of account.

The doctorate is, in part, a learning process, but I believe the doctoral thesis should be a record of successful learning and research rather than a blow-by-blow account of the whole learning process. In essence, the doctorate must be a 'contribution to knowledge' that can be used by others and not just a contribution to the student's self-knowledge. Thus, I do not believe that it is particularly useful for doctoral theses to record all the false starts, errors, disappointments, feelings of despair and so on that everyone who has actually done research already knows about. These aspects will have been important to the student, but an examiner or any other reader wishes to know about the research that has been successfully conducted as a result of the learning process. I find navel-gazing accounts from doctoral students that record every detail of their own learning process very boring to read, and I see them as the worst examples of 'vanity ethnography' (Maynard, 1993). For doctoral students, the reflexive account should certainly include consideration of the importance of the researcher within the research and a discussion of personal influences on the research process, but the essence of the account is to show that a successful piece of research has been conducted, and to explain where justifiable decisions were made. No novice researcher (or any other researcher for that matter) should feel obliged to emulate the type of reflexive account that details all the problems, mistakes and meanderings of their research process. However, in contrast to student accounts, accounts from experienced researchers are valuable simply because they are concerned with academic research that has been already accepted by the wider research community. They show that recognized researchers have difficulties, which may make the novice researcher's difficulties seem more manageable.

I am in broad agreement with Troyna's first and second concerns about reflexive accounts, but I believe that these potentially negative effects can be reduced. His first point was that they can tend to legitimize a realist view of research. However, I would argue that, while some of the early reflexive accounts may have been cast within the framework of 'telling it as it is', this is now a rarity. Most such accounts are now written by researchers who accept that their descriptions are selective and constructed according to narrative and other conventions. They recognize that they do not present a complete 'true' account of what 'really' went on, but offer another perspective. In themselves reflexive accounts do not necessarily support a realist perspective of educational research. Indeed, they may act to challenge such a view.

Troyna's second concern about the potential effects of reflexive accounts on the credibility of qualitative research is one that also concerns me. The particular effect of a bias towards more reflexive accounts in qualitative rather than quantitative research can be potentially corrected by editors encouraging more quantitative researchers to contribute to volumes such as those I have edited (Walford, 1987c, 1989, 1991a, 1994c, 1998a). This is far from easy to achieve. I have tried several times to encourage quantitative researchers to write more openly about their work, but I have been unsuccessful. I am very grateful for the few such researchers who have been prepared to write such accounts, but the balance in my own edited books and those of others is still far too much towards quantitative research.

However, the effect of such a balance might not be entirely positive. If it were possible to encourage more quantitative researchers to write reflexive accounts of their work, this might have the effect of reducing the credibility of *all* educational research rather than just qualitative educational research. But a more reasonable answer to the concern is that it probably overestimates the impact of such accounts. They are unlikely to be read by anyone other than those involved in research themselves – who will either already know about the uncertainties and vagaries of research or will very soon find out for themselves. If policy-makers, research funders and other powerful individuals do read them, it is likely that they will already have a wide-ranging knowledge of the practicalities of research. My feeling here is that the potential benefits to those conducting research outweigh the risks of reducing the wider credibility of research. The intention of this book and the many chapters collected together in my edited volumes is certainly not to devalue educational research. I believe that the first step towards improving the quality of educational research is to recognize its limitations, and I hope that the publication of such accounts will assist in that task.

Bibliography

Abolafia, M. Y. (1996) *Making Markets: Opportunism and Restraint in Wall Street*. Cambridge, MA: Harvard University Press.

Abolafia, M. Y. (1998) 'Markets as cultures: an ethnographic approach', in M. Callon (ed.) *The Law of the Markets*. Oxford: Blackwell.

Acker, S. (1980) 'Women: the other academics'. *British Journal of Sociology of Education*, **1**(1), 81–91.

Adelman, C. (ed.) (1984) *The Politics and Ethics of Fieldwork*. Beckenham: Croom Helm.

Aggleton, P. (1987) *Rebels without a Cause*. Lewes: Falmer.

Apple, M. (1996) *Cultural Politics and Education*. Buckingham: Open University Press.

Apple, M. and Christian-Smith, L. K. (eds) (1991) *The Politics of the Textbook*. London: Routledge.

Atkinson, P. (1996) *Sociological Readings and Re-readings*. Aldershot: Avebury.

Australian Research Council (1992) *Educational Research in Australia*. Canberra: Australian Government Publishing Service.

Baldridge, J. V. (1971) *Power and Conflict in the University*. New York: John Wiley.

Ball, S. J. (1981) *Beachside Comprehensive: a Case Study of Comprehensive Schooling*. Cambridge: Cambridge University Press.

Ball, S. J. (1984) 'Beachside reconsidered: Reflections on a methodological apprenticeship', in R. G. Burgess (ed.) *The Research Process in Educational Settings: Ten Case Studies*. Lewes: Falmer.

Ball, S. J. (1990a) *Politics and Policy Making in Education*. London: Routledge.

Ball, S. J. (1990b) 'Self-doubt and soft data: social and technical trajectories in ethnographic fieldwork'. *International Journal of Qualitative Studies in Education*, **3**(2), 157–71.

Barnes, J. A. (1979) *Who Should Know What?* Harmondsworth: Penguin.

Becher, A. and Kogan, M. (1980) *Process and Structure in Higher Education*. London: Heinemann.

Becker, H. S. (1964) 'Problems in the publication of field studies', in A. J. Vidich, J. Bensman and M. Stein (eds) *Reflections on Community Studies*. New York: Harper & Row.

Becker, H. S. (1968) 'Whose side are we on?' *Social Problems*, **14**, 239-47.

Becker, H. S. (1990) 'Generalising from case studies', in E. Eisner and A.

Peshkin (eds) *Qualitative Inquiry in Education*. New York: Teachers College Press.

Becker, H. S., Geer, B. and Hughes, E. C. (1968) *Making the Grade: the Academic Side of College Life*. New York: John Wiley.

Becker, H. S., Geer, B., Strauss, A. L. and Hughes, E. C. (1961) *Boys in White: Student Culture in Medical School*. Chicago: University of Chicago Press.

Bell, C. (1977) 'Reflections on the Banbury restudy', in C. Bell and H. Newby (eds) *Doing Sociological Research*. London: George Allen and Unwin.

Bell, C. and Newby, H. (eds) (1977) *Doing Sociological Research*. London: George Allen and Unwin.

Bell, C. and Roberts, H. (eds) (1984) *Social Researching. Politics, Problems and Practice*. London: Routledge & Kegan Paul.

Bernstein, B. (1971) 'On the classification and framing of educational knowledge', in M. F. D. Young (ed.) *Knowledge and Control*. London: Collier-Macmillan.

Bernstein, B. (1973) *Class and Pedagogies: Visible and Invisible*. Paris: OECD. Reprinted as Chapter 6 of *Class, Codes and Control, Volume 3*, 2nd edn. London: Routledge & Kegan Paul.

Bernstein, B. (1975) 'Introduction', in *Class, Codes and Control, Volume 3*. London: Routledge & Kegan Paul.

Bernstein, B. (1977) 'Aspects of the relations between education and production', in *Class, Codes and Control, Volume 3*, 2nd edn. London: Routlege & Kegan Paul.

Bertaux, D. (1980) *Biography and Society*. London: Sage.

Beynon, J. (1983) 'Ways-in and staying-in: fieldwork as problem solving', in M. Hammersley (ed.) *The Ethnography of Schooling*. Driffield: Nafferton.

Bogdan, R. and Taylor, S. J. (1975) *Introduction to Qualitative Research Methods*. New York: John Wiley.

Bryman, A. (1988) *Quantity and Quality in Social Research*. London: Unwin Hyman.

Burgess, R. G. (1983) *Experiencing Comprehensive Education: a Study of Bishop McGregor School*. London: Methuen.

Burgess, R. G. (1984a) *In the Field: an Introduction to Field Research*. London: George Allen and Unwin.

Burgess, R. G. (ed.) (1984b) *The Research Process in Educational Settings: Ten Case Studies*. London: Falmer.

Burgess, R. G. (ed.) (1985a) *Field Methods in the Study of Education*. London: Falmer.

Burgess, R. G. (ed.) (1985b) *Strategies of Educational Research: Qualitative Methods*. London: Falmer.

Burgess, R. G. (ed.) (1985c) *Issues in Educational Research: Qualitative Methods*. London: Falmer.

Burgess, R. G. (1985d) 'The whole truth? Some ethical problems of research in a comprehensive school', in R. G. Burgess (ed.) *Field Methods in the Study of Education*. Lewes: Falmer Press.

Burgess, R. G. (1987) 'Studying and restudying Bishop McGregor School', in G. Walford (ed.) *Doing Sociology of Education*. Lewes: Falmer.

Burgess, R. G. (ed.) (1989) *The Ethics of Educational Research*. London: Falmer.

Carmichael, A. (1994) *Four Square Selling*. London: Concept.

Carr, W. and Kemmis, S. (1986) *Becoming Critical*. Lewes: Falmer.

CERI (1995) *Educational Research and Development: Trends, Issues and Challenges*. Paris: OECD.

Clouser, R. A. (1991) *The Myth of Religious Neutrality*. Notre Dame, IN: University of Notre Dame Press.

Cohen, L. and Manion, L. (1994) *Research Methods in Education*, 4th edn. London: Routledge.

Cohen, L., Manion, L. and Morrison, K. (2000) *Research Methods in Education*, 5th edn. London: Routledge and Falmer.

Cohen, M. D., March, J. G. and Olsen, J. P. (1972) 'A garbage can model of organizational choice'. *Administrative Science Quarterly*, **17**(1), 1–25.

Collins, H. M. (1984) 'Researching spoonbending: concepts and practice of participatory fieldwork', in C. Bell and H. Roberts (eds) *Social Researching*. London: Routledge and Kegan Paul.

Convery, A. (1999) 'Listening to teachers' stories: are we sitting too comfortably?' *Qualitative Studies in Education*, **12**(2), 131–46.

Corey, S. M. (1949) 'Action research, fundamental research and educational practitioners'. *Teachers College Record*, **50**, 509–14.

Cox, C., Jacka, K. and Marks, J. (1977) 'Marxism, knowledge and the academies', in C. B. Cox and R. Boyson (eds) *Black Paper 1977*. London: Temple-Smith.

Cox, C. and Marks, J. (1988) *The Insolence of Office*. London: Claridge Press.

Crick, F. (1989) *What Mad Pursuit*. London: Weidenfeld & Nicolson.

Dalton, M. (1959) *Men who Manage*. New York: John Wiley.

Davies, P. (1999) 'What is evidence-based education?' *British Journal of Educational Studies*, **47**(2), 108–21.

Deakin, R. (1989) *The New Christian Schools*. Bristol: Regius.

Deal T. E. (1985) 'The symbolism of effective schools'. *Elementary School Journal*, **85**(5), 601–20 (reprinted in A. Westoby (ed.) (1985) *Culture and Power in Educational Organizations*. Milton Keynes: Open University Press).

Delamont, S. (1973) 'Academic conformity observed: studies in the classroom', unpublished PhD thesis, University of Edinburgh.

Delamont, S. (1976a) 'The girls most likely to: cultural reproduction and Scottish elites'. *Scottish Journal of Sociology*, **1**, 29–43.

Delamont, S. (1976b) *Interaction in the Classroom*. London: Methuen.

Delamont, S. (1984a) 'The old girl network: recollections on the fieldwork at St Luke's', in R. G. Burgess (ed.) *The Research Process in Educational Settings: Ten Case Studies*. Lewes: Falmer Press.

Delamont, S. (1984b) 'Debs, dollies, swots and weeds: classroom styles at St Luke's', in G. Walford (ed.) *British Public Schools: Policy and Practice*. Lewes: Falmer Press.

Delamont, S. (1990) *Sex Roles and the School*, 2nd edn. London: Routledge.

Delamont, S. (1992) *Fieldwork in Educational Settings*. London and Washington, DC: Falmer.

Denny, R. (1988) *Selling to Win*. London: Kogan Page (2nd edn 1997).

Denscombe, M. (1995) 'Teachers as an audience for research: the acceptability of ethnographic approaches to classroom research'. *Teachers and Teaching: Theory and Practice*, **1**(1), 173–91.

Denzin, N. (1989) *Interpretive Biography*. London: Sage.

Department of Education and Science (DES) (1986) *City Technology Colleges. A New Choice of School*. London: DES.

Derricourt, R. (1996) *An Author's Guide to Scholarly Publishing*. Princeton, NJ: Princeton University Press.

Dey, I. (1993) *Qualitative Data Analysis: a User-friendly Guide for Social Scientists*. London: Routledge

Dooley, P. (1991) 'Muslim private schools', in G. Walford (ed.) *Private Schooling: Tradition, Change and Diversity*. London: Paul Chapman.

Douglas, J. D. (1976) *Investigative Social Research*. London: Sage.

Economic and Social Research Council (1993) *Frameworks and Priorities for Research in Education: Towards a strategy for the ESRC*. Swindon: ESRC.

Edwards, T., Fitz, J. and Whitty, G. (1989) *The State and Private Education. An Evaluation of the Assisted Places Scheme*. Lewes: Falmer.

Eggleston, J. and Klein, G. (1997) *Achieving Publication in Education*. Stoke-on-Trent: Trentham.

Ehrenborg, J. and Mattock, J. (1993) *Powerful Presentations*. London: Kogan Page.

Elsbach, K. D. (2000) 'Six stories of researcher experience in organizational studies', in S. D. Moch and M. F. Gates (eds) *The Research Experience in Qualitative Research*. London: Sage.

Emmison, M. and Smith, P. (2000) *Researching the Visual*. London: Sage.

Evans, T. (1988) *A Gender Agenda*. Wellington and London: Allen & Unwin.

Felstead, A. (1993) *The Corporate Paradox: Power and Control in the Business Franchise*. London: Routledge.

Finch, J. (1983) *Married to the Job*. London: George Allen & Unwin.

Fine, G. A. and Sandstrom, K. L. (1988) *Knowing Children: Participant Observation with Minors*. Beverley Hills, CA: Sage.

Fisher, P. (1989) 'Getting down to business'. *Times Educational Supplement*, 13 January, 35.

Fitz, J. and Halpin, D. (1994) 'Ministers and mandarins: educational research in elite settings', in G. Walford (ed.) *Researching the Powerful in Education*. London: UCL Press.

Fletcher, C. (1974) *Beneath the Surface, an Account of Three Styles of Sociological Research*. London: Routledge & Kegan Paul.

Foster, P. (1999) ' "Never mind the quality, feel the impact": a methodological assessment of teacher research sponsored by the Teacher Training Agency'. *British Journal of Educational Studies*, **47**(4), 380–98.

Geer, B. (1964) 'First days in the field', in P. E. Hammond (ed.) *Sociologists at Work*. New York: Basic Books.

Gewirtz, S., Miller, H. and Walford, G. (1991) 'Parents' individualist and collectivist strategies at the City Technology College, Kingshurst'. *International Studies in the Sociology of Education*, **1**, 171–89.

Glaser, B. G. and Strauss, A. L. (1967) *The Discovery of Grounded Theory*. Chicago: Aldine.

Glassner, B. (1976) 'Kid society'. *Urban Education*, **11**, 5–22.

Goffman, E. (1961) *Asylums*. New York: Doubleday.

Gold, R. L. (1958) 'Roles in sociological fieldwork'. *Social Forces*, **36**, 217–23.

Gold, R. (1997) 'The ethnographic method in sociology'. *Qualitative Enquiry*, **3**(4), 387–402.

Goodson, I. and Ball, S. J. (eds) (1985) *Teachers' Lives and Careers*. Lewes: Falmer.

Goodson, I. and Mangan, J. M. (1996) 'Exploring alternative perspectives in educational research'. *Interchange*, **27**(1), 41–59

Graddol, D. (1994) 'What is a text?', in D. Graddol and O. Boyd-Barrett (eds) *Media Texts: Authors and Readers*. Clevedon, Avon: Multilingual Matters.

Gray, J. (1998) 'An episode in the development of educational research', in J. Rudduck and D. McIntyre (eds) *Challenges for Educational Research*. London: Paul Chapman Publishing.

Gribble, D. (1998) *Real Education. Varieties of Freedom*. Bristol: Libertarian Education.

Griggs, C. (1989) 'The new right and English secondary education', in R. Lowe (ed.) *The Changing Secondary School*. London: Falmer.

Halpin, D. and Troyna, B. (eds) (1994) *Researching Education Policy: Ethical and Methodological Issues*. London: Falmer.

Halsey, A. H. (ed.) (1972) *Educational Priority. Volume 1, Educational Priority Area Problems and Policies*. London: HMSO.

Hammersley, M. (1984) 'The researcher exposed: a natural history', in R. G. Burgess (ed.) *The Research Process in Educational Settings: Ten Case Studies*. Lewes: Falmer.

Hammersley, M. (1991) *Reading Ethnographic Research: a Critical Guide*. London: Longman.

Hammersley, M. (1992) *What's Wrong with Ethnography?* London: Routledge.

Hammersley, M. (1993) 'On the teacher as researcher', in M. Hammersley (ed.) *Educational Research: Current Issues*. London: Paul Chapman Publishing.

Hammersley, M. (1997) 'Educational research and teaching: a response to David Hargreaves'. *British Educational Research Journal*, **23**(2), 141–61.

Hammersley, M. and Atkinson, P. (1995) *Ethnography: Principles in Practice*, 2nd edn. London: Routledge.

Hammond, P. E. (1964) *Sociologists at Work*. New York: Basic Books.

Hammond, P. E. (1967) *Sociologists at Work*. New York: Doubleday Anchor (paperback).

Hargreaves, D. H. (1967) *Social Relations in a Secondary School*. London: Routledge & Kegan Paul.

Hargreaves, D. H. (1996) *Teaching as a Research-based Profession: Possibilities and Prospects*. Cambridge: Teacher Training Agency Lecture.

Hargreaves, D. H. (1997) 'In defence of research for evidence-based teaching: a rejoinder to Martyn Hammersley'. *British Educational Research Journal*, **23**(4), 405–19.

Hargreaves, D. and Beveridge, M. (1995) *A Strategic Review of Educational Research*. London: Leverhulme Trust.

Headmasters' Conference (1978) *Manual of Guidance*. London: HMC.

Hillage, J., Pearson, R., Anderson, A. and Tamkin, P. (1998) *Excellence in Research on Schools, Research Report RR74*. London: Department of Education and Employment.

Hillgate Group (1986) *Whose Schools?* London: Hillgate Group.

Hillgate Group (1987) *The Reform of British Education*. London: Claridge Press.

Housden, J. (1984) *Franchising and Other Business Relationships in Hotel and Catering Services*. London: Heinemann.

Humphries, L. (1970) *Tearoom Trade*. London: Duckworth.

Jackson, B. and Marsden, D. (1962) *Education and the Working Class*. London: Routledge & Kegan Paul.

Janes, R. W. (1961) 'A note on the phases of the community role of the participant observer'. *American Sociological Review*, **26**(3), 446–50.

Johnson, J. (1975) *Doing Field Research*. New York, Free Press.

Junker, B. H. (1960) *Field Research: an Introduction to the Social Sciences*. Chicago: Chicago University Press.

Kalton, G. (1966) *The Public Schools*. London: Longman.

Keddie, N. (1971) 'Classroom knowledge', in M. F. D. Young (ed.) *Knowledge and Control: New Directions for the Sociology of Education*. London: Collier Macmillan.

Kelly, A. (1978) 'Feminism and research'. *Women's Studies International Quarterly*, **1**, 225–32.

Kelly, A. (1985) 'Action research: what is it and what can it do?', in R. G. Burgess (ed.) *Issues in Educational Research*. Lewes: Falmer.

Kimball, B. (1994) *AMA Handbook for Successful Selling*. Lincolnwood, IL: NTC Business Books.

Klatch, R. E. (1988) 'The methodological problems of studying a politically resistant community'. *Studies in Qualitative Methodology*, **1**, 73–88.

Kulick, D. and Willson, M. (eds) (1995) *Taboo*. New York and London: Routledge.

Lacey, C. (1970) *Hightown Grammar*. Manchester: Manchester University Press.

Lambert, R. (1966) *The State and Boarding Education*. London: Methuen.

Lambert, R. (1968a) 'Religious education in the boarding school', in D. P. Jebb (ed.) *Religious Education*. London: Darton, Longman and Todd.

Lambert, R. (1968b) 'The future of boarding in modern society', in M. Ash (ed.) *Who Are the Progressives Now?* London: Routledge and Kegan Paul.

Lambert, R. (1975) *The Chance of a Lifetime. A Study of Boarding Education*. London: Weidenfeld and Nicolson.

Lambert, R., Bullock, R. and Millham, S. (1970) *A Manual to the Sociology of the School*. London: Weidenfeld and Nicolson.

Lambert, R., Hipkin, J. and Stagg, S. (1968) *New Wine in Old Bottles?* Occasional Papers in Social Administration, 28. London: Bell.

Lambert, R. and Millham, S. (1968) *The Hothouse Society*. London: Weidenfeld and Nicolson.

Lambert, R., Millham, S. and Bullock, R. (1973) 'The informal social system', in R. K. Brown (ed.) *Knowledge, Education and Cultural Change*. London: Tavistock.

Lambert, R. and Woolfe, R. (1968) 'Need and demand for boarding education', in *Public Schools Commission, First Report*, Volume 2, Appendix 7. London: HMSO.

Lareau, A. and Shultz, J. (1996) (eds) *Journeys through Ethnography: Realistic Accounts of Fieldwork*. Oxford: Westview Press.

Latour, B. and Woolgar, S. (1979) *Laboratory Life. The Social Construction of Scientific Facts.* London: Sage.

Lewin, K. (1948) *Resolving Social Conflicts.* New York: Harper and Row.

Lincoln, Y. S. and Guba, E. (1985) *Naturalistic Enquiry.* Beverley Hills, CA: Sage.

Llewellyn, M. (1980) 'Studying girls at school: the implications of a confusion', in R. Deem (ed.) *Schooling for Women's Work.* London: Routledge and Kegan Paul.

Lomax, P. (ed.) (1990) *Managing Staff Development in Schools: an Action Research Approach.* Clevedon, Avon: Multilingual Matters.

Lukes, S. (1974) *Power: a Radical View.* London: Macmillan.

Lutz, F. W. (1981) 'Ethnography: the holistic approach to understanding schooling', in J. Green and C. Wallat (eds) *Ethnography and Language in Educational Settings.* New York: Ablex.

Mac an Ghaill, M. (1988) *Young, Gifted and Black.* Milton Keynes: Open University Press.

McGaulley, M. T. (1995) *Selling 101.* Holbrook, MA: Adams Media Corporation.

McHugh, J.D. (1994) 'The Lords' will be done', in G. Walford (ed.) *Researching the Powerful in Education.* London: UCL Press.

McNiff, J. (1988) *Action Research: Principles and Practice.* London: Routledge.

McNiff, J. (1993) *Teaching as Learning: an Action Research Approach.* London: Routledge.

Malinowski, B. (1922) *Argonauts of the Western Pacific.* London: Routledge & Kegan Paul.

Malinowski, B. (1967) *A Diary in the Strict Sense of the Term.* London: Routledge & Kegan Paul.

Marks, J., Cox, C. and Pomian-Srzednicki, M. (1983) *Standards in English Schools.* London: National Council for Educational Standards.

Massey, A. (1999) 'Methodological triangulation, or how to get lost without being found out', in A. Massey and G. Walford (eds) *Explorations in Methodology. Studies in Educational Ethnography, Volume 2.* Greenwich, CT: JAI Press.

Massey, A. and Walford, G. (1998) 'Children learning: ethnographers learning', in G. Walford and A. Massey (eds) *Children Learning in Context. Studies in Educational Ethnography, Volume 1.* Greenwich, CT and London: JAI Press.

Maynard, M. (1993) 'Feminism and the possibilities of a postmodern research practice'. *British Journal of Sociology of Education*, **14**(3), 327–31.

Measor, L. and Sikes, P. (1992) *Gender and Schools.* London: Cassell.

Measor, L. and Woods, P. (1984) *Changing Schools: Pupil Perspectives on Transfer to a Comprehensive.* Milton Keynes: Open University Press.

Medawar, P. (1963) 'Is the scientific paper a fraud?' *Listener*, 12 September.

Michell, J. C. (1983) 'Case and situational analysis'. *Sociological Review*, **31**(2), 187–211.

Morrell, F. (1989) *Children of the Future.* London: Hogarth Press.

Moser, C. A. and Kalton, G. (1982) *Survey Methods and Social Investigation*, 2nd edn. Aldershot: Dartmouth.

Moyser, G. and Wagstaffe, M. (1987) *Research Methods for Elite Studies.* London: Allen & Unwin.

Myrdal, G. (1969) *Objectivity in Social Research*. London: Duckworth.

O'Keeffe, B. (1992) 'A look at the Christian schools movement', in B. Watson (ed.) *Priorities in Religious Education*. London: Falmer.

Olensen, V. and Whittaker, E. (1967) 'Role-making in participant observation: processes in the researcher–actor relationship'. *Human Organizations*, **26**(4), 273–81.

Open University (1972) *School and Society*. Course E282. Milton Keynes: Open University.

Paechter, C. (1996) 'Power, knowledge and the confessional in qualitative research'. *Discourse*, **17**(1), 75–84.

Peshkin, A. (1984) 'Odd man out: the participant observer in an absolutist setting'. *Sociology of Education*, **57**, 254–64.

Peshkin, A. (1991) 'Appendix: in search of subjectivity – one's own', in A. Peshkin, *The Color of Strangers. The Color of Friends*. Chicago: Chicago University Press.

Phillips, D. C. (1989) 'Subjectivity and objectivity: an objective inquiry', in E. W. Eisner and A. Peshkin (eds) *Qualitative Inquiry in Education: the Continuing Debate*. New York: Teachers College Press.

Plummer, K. (1983) *Documents of Life*. London: Allen and Unwin.

Poyntz, C. and Walford, G. (1994) 'The new Christian schools: a survey'. *Educational Studies*, **20**(1), 127–45.

Pring, R. (1984) 'Confidentiality and the right to know', in C. Adelman (ed.) *The Politics and Ethics of Evaluation*. London: Croom Helm.

Punch, M. (1977) *Progressive Retreat*. Cambridge: Cambridge University Press.

Punch, M. (1986) *The Politics and Ethics of Fieldwork*. London: Sage.

Rae, J. (1981) *The Public School Revolution*. London: Faber and Faber.

Ranson, S. (1995a) *The Future of Educational Research: Learning at the Centre*. Swindon: ESRC.

Ranson, S. (1995b) 'Theorising education policy'. *Journal of Education Policy*, **10**(4), 427–48.

Ranson, S. (1998) 'The future of educational research: learning at the centre', in J. Rudduck and D. McIntyre (eds) *Challenges for Educational Research*, London: Paul Chapman Publishing.

Rist, R. C. (1980) 'Blitzkrieg ethnography: on the transformation of a method into a movement'. *Educational Researcher*, **9**(2), 8–10

Roberts, E. (1984) *A Woman's Place. An Oral History of Working-class Women 1890–1940*. Oxford: Blackwell.

Roberts, H. (ed.) (1981) *Doing Feminist Research*. London: Routledge & Kegan Paul.

Robinson, N. (1993) *Persuasive Business Presentations*. Singapore: Heinemann Asia.

Robson, M. H. and Walford, G. (1988) 'UK tax policy and independent schools'. *British Tax Review*, **2**, 38–54.

Rosenhan, D. L. (1973) 'On being sane in insane places'. *Science*, **179**, 250–8 (reprinted in M. Bulmer (ed.) (1982) *Social Research Ethics*. London: Macmillan).

Rudduck, J. (1998) 'Educational research: the prospect of change ...', in J. Rudduck and D. McIntyre (eds) *Challenges for Educational Research*. London: Paul Chapman Publishing.

194 *Bibliography*

Sarsby, J. (1988) *Missuses and Mouldrunners. An Oral History of Women Pottery Workers at Work and at Home*. Milton Keynes: Open University Press.

Schofield, J. (1990) 'Increasing the generalizability of case study research', in E. Eisner and A. Peshkin (eds) *Qualitative Inquiry in Education*. New York: Teachers College Press.

Seale, C. (1999) *The Quality of Qualitative Research*. London: Sage.

Sexton, S. (1987) *Our Schools – A Radical Policy*. Warlingham, Surrey: Institute for Economic Affairs Education Unit.

Sexton, S. (1992) *Our Schools – Future Policy*. Warlingham, Surrey: IPSET Education Unit.

Shaffir, W. B., Stebbins, R. A. and Turowetz, A. (eds) (1980) *Fieldwork Experience*. New York: St Martin's Press.

Shipman, M. (1976) *The Organisation and Impact of Social Research*. London: Routledge & Kegan Paul.

Sikes, P. (2000) ' "Truth" and "lies" revisited'. *British Educational Research Journal*, **26**(2), 257–70.

Sikes, P., Measor, L. and Woods, P. (1985) *Teacher Careers*. Lewes: Falmer.

Silverman, D. (1993) *Interpreting Qualitative Data*. London: Sage.

Simon, B. (1988) *Bending the Rules*. London: Lawrence and Wishart.

Simon, R. J. and Fyfe, J. A. (1994) *Editors as Gatekeepers*. Lanham, MD: Rowman & Littlefield.

Smetherham, D. (ed.) (1981) *Practising Evaluation*. Driffield: Nafferton.

Spencer, G. (1973) 'Methodological issues in the study of bureaucratic elites: a case study of West Point'. *Social Problems*, **21**(1), 90–103.

Spender, D. (1980) *Man Made Language*. London: Routledge & Kegan Paul.

Spindler, G. (ed.) (1974) *Education and Cultural Process: Towards an Anthropology of Education*. New York: Holt, Rinehart and Winston.

Stake, R. (1995) *The Art of Case Study*. London: Sage.

Stanley, L. (ed.) (1990) *Feminist Praxis*. London: Routledge.

Stanley, L. and Wise, S. (1983) *Breaking Out: Feminist Consciousness and Feminist Research*. London: Routledge & Kegan Paul.

Stanworth, M. (1983) *Gender and Schooling*. London: Hutchinson.

Stenhouse, L. (1975) *An Introduction to Curriculum Research and Development*. London: Heinemann.

Thomas, W. I. (1928) *The Child in America*. New York: Knopf.

Thompson, P. (1978) *The Voice of the Past: Oral History*. Oxford: Oxford University Press.

Thorn, J. (1978) 'The new public schoolboy'. *Spectator*, 16 December, 15.

Thornely, N. and Lees, D. (1994) *The Perfect Sale*. London: Arrow Books

Thyer, B. A. (1994) *Successful Publication in Scholarly Journals*. London: Sage.

Tooley, J. and Darby, D. (1998) *Educational Research: an Ofsted Critique*. London: Ofsted.

Troman, G. (1996) 'No entry signs: educational change and some problems encountered in negotiating entry to educational settings'. *British Educational Research Journal*, **22**(1), 71–8.

Troyna, B. (1994) 'Reforms, research and being reflexive about being reflective', in D. Halpin and B. Troyna (eds) *Researching Education Policy: Ethical and Methodological Issues*. London: Falmer.

van Maanen, J. (1988) *Tales of the Field*. Chicago: University of Chicago Press.

van Maanen, J. (1995) *Representation in Ethnography*. London: Sage.

Wakeford, J. (1969) *The Cloistered Elite. A Sociological Analysis of the English Boarding School*. London: Macmillan.

Walford, G. (1978) 'Research in a university physics department'. Unpublished MPhil (sociology) dissertation, University of Oxford.

Walford, G. (1980a) 'Why physics students start doctorates'. *Studies in Higher Education*, **5**(1), 77–80.

Walford, G. (1980b) 'Sex bias in physics textbooks'. *School Science Review*, **62**, 220–7.

Walford, G. (1981a) 'Classification and framing in postgraduate education'. *Studies in Higher Education*, **6**(2), 147–58.

Walford, G. (1981b) 'Tracking down sexism in physics textbooks'. *Physics Education*, **16**, 261–5.

Walford, G. (1983a) 'Girls in boys' public schools: a prelude to further research'. *British Journal of Sociology of Education*, **4**(1), 39–54.

Walford, G. (1983b) 'Research state and research style: a sociological analysis of postgraduate education'. *Collected Original Resources in Education*, **7**(1), 1–108.

Walford, G. (1984) 'The changing professionalism of public school teachers', in G. Walford (ed.) *British Public Schools: Policy and Practice*. Lewes: Falmer.

Walford, G. (1985) 'The construction of a curriculum area: science in society'. *British Journal of Sociology of Education*, **6**(2), 155–71.

Walford, G. (1986a) *Life in Public Schools*. London: Methuen.

Walford, G. (1986b) 'Ruling-class classification and framing'. *British Educational Research Journal*, **12**(2), 183–95.

Walford, G. (1987a) 'How dependent is the independent sector?' *Oxford Review of Education*, **13**(3), 275–96.

Walford, G. (1987b) 'How important is the independent sector in Scotland?' *Scottish Education Review*, **19**(2), 108–21.

Walford, G. (ed.) (1987c) *Doing Sociology of Education*. London: Falmer.

Walford, G. (1987d) 'Research role conflicts and compromises', in G. Walford (ed.) *Doing Sociology of Education*. Lewes: Falmer.

Walford, G. (1987e) *Restructuring Universities: Politics and Power in the Management of Change*. Beckenham: Croom Helm.

Walford, G. (1988a) 'The Scottish Assisted Places Scheme. A comparative study of the origins, nature and practice of the APS in Scotland, England and Wales'. *Journal of Education Policy*, **3**(2), 137–53.

Walford, G. (1988b) 'The privatisation of British higher education'. *European Journal of Education*, **23**(1/2), 47–64.

Walford, G. (ed.) (1989) *Private Schools in Ten Countries: Policy and Practice*. London: Routledge.

Walford, G. (1990) *Privatization and Privilege in Education*. London: Routledge.

Walford, G. (ed.) (1991a) *Doing Educational Research*. London: Routledge.

Walford, G. (1991b) 'Researching the City Technology College, Kingshurst', in G. Walford (ed.) *Doing Educational Research*. London: Routledge.

Walford, G. (ed.) (1991c) *Private Schooling: Tradition, Change and Diversity*. London: Paul Chapman.

Walford, G. (1991d) 'City Technology Colleges: a private magnetism?', in G. Walford (ed.) *Private Schooling: Tradition, Change and Diversity.* London: Paul Chapman.

Walford, G. (1991e) 'The reluctant private sector: of small schools, politics and people', in G. Walford (ed.) *Private Schooling: Tradition, Change and Diversity.* London: Paul Chapman.

Walford, G. (1991f) 'Choice of school at the first City Technology College'. *Educational Studies*, **17**(1), 65–75.

Walford, G. (1992) *Selection for Secondary Schooling.* National Commission on Education, Briefing Paper 7. London: National Commission on Education.

Walford, G. (1994a) 'Weak choice, strong choice and the new Christian schools', in M. Halstead (ed.) *Parental Choice and Education.* London: Kogan Page.

Walford, G. (1994b) 'The new religious grant-maintained schools'. *Educational Management and Administration*, **22**(2), 123–30.

Walford, G. (ed.) (1994c) *Researching the Powerful in Education.* London: UCL Press.

Walford, G. (1994d) 'Ethics and power in a study of pressure group politics', in G. Walford (ed.) *Researching the Powerful in Education.* London: UCL Press.

Walford, G. (1994e) 'Political commitment in the study of the City Technology College, Kingshurst', in D. Halpin and B. Troyna (eds) *Researching Education Policy: Ethical and Methodological Issues.* London: Falmer.

Walford, G. (1995a) 'Faith-based grant-maintained schools: Selective international policy borrowing from The Netherlands'. *Journal of Education Policy*, **10**(2), 245–57.

Walford, G. (1995b) 'The Christian Schools Campaign – a successful educational pressure group?' *British Educational Research Journal*, **21**(4), 451–64.

Walford, G. (1995c) 'The Northbourne amendments: is the House of Lords a garbage can?' *Journal of Education Policy*, **10**(5), 413–25.

Walford, G. (1995d) *Educational Politics: Pressure Groups and Faith-based Schools.* Aldershot: Avebury.

Walford, G. (1997) Sponsored grant-maintained schools: extending the franchise? *Oxford Review of Education*, **23**(1), 31–44.

Walford, G. (1998a) *Doing Research about Education.* London and Washington, DC: Falmer.

Walford, G. (1998b) 'Reading and writing the small print: the fate of sponsored grant-maintained schools'. *Educational Studies*, **24**(2), 241–57.

Walford, G. (1998c) 'Research accounts count', in G. Walford (ed.) *Doing Research about Education.* London and Washington, DC: Falmer.

Walford, G. (1998d) 'First days in the field: whose agenda?' Paper given at the Ethnography and Education Conference, University of Oxford, 7–8 September.

Walford, G. (1999a) 'Selling your way in', in A. Massey and G. Walford (eds) *Explorations in Methodology. Studies in Educational Ethnography Volume 2.* Stamford, CT: JAI Press.

Walford, G. (1999b) 'Educating religious minorities within the English state-maintained sector'. *International Journal of Educational Management*, **13**(2), 98–106.

Walford, G. (2000a) 'A policy adventure: sponsored grant-maintained schools'. *Educational Studies*, **26**(2), 247–62.

Walford, G. (2000b) 'From City Technology Colleges to sponsored grant-maintained schools'. *Oxford Review of Education*, **26**(2), 145–58.

Walford, G. (2000c) *Policy, Politics and Education – Sponsored Grant-maintained Schools and Religious Diversity*. Aldershot: Arena.

Walford, G. and Jones, S. (1986) 'The Solihull adventure: an attempt to reintroduce selective schooling'. *Journal of Education Policy*, **1**(3), 23–53.

Walford, G. and Massey, A. (eds) (1998) *Children Learning in Context. Studies in Educational Ethnography, volume 1*. Greenwich, CT and London: JAI Press.

Walford, G. and Miller, H. (1991) *City Technology College*. Buckingham: Open University Press.

Watson, J. D. (1968) *The Double Helix*. London: Weidenfeld & Nicolson.

Wax, R. (1971) *Doing Fieldwork: Warnings and Advice*. Chicago: Chicago University Press.

Weinberg, I. (1967) *The English Public Schools*. New York: Atherton.

Whitehead, J. (1989) 'Creating a living educational theory from questions of the kind "How do I improve my practice?"' *Cambridge Journal of Education*, **19**(1), 41–52.

Whitty, G., Edwards, T. and Gewirtz, S. (1993) *Specialisation and Choice in Urban Education. The City Technology College Experiment*. London: Routledge.

Whyte, J. B. (1987) 'Issues and dilemmas in action research', in G. Walford (ed.) *Doing Sociology of Education*. Lewes: Falmer.

Whyte, W. F. (1955) *Street Corner Society*, 2nd edn. Chicago: Chicago University Press.

Wober, M. (1971) *English Girls' Boarding Schools*. London: Allen Lane.

Wolpe, A. M. (1988) *Within School Walls*. London: Routledge.

Woods, P. (1985) 'Conversations with teachers: some aspects of the life history method'. *British Educational Research Journal*, **19**(1), 3–5.

Woods, P. (1994) 'Collaborating in historical ethnography: researching critical events in education'. *International Journal of Qualitative Studies in Education*, **7**(4), 309–21

Woods, P. (1995) *Creative Teachers in Primary Schools*. Buckingham: Open University Press.

Woods, P. (1998) 'Critical moments in the *Creative Teaching* research', in G. Walford (ed.) *Doing Research about Education*. London and Washington DC: Falmer.

Woods, P. and Jeffrey, B. (1996) *Teachable Moments: The Art of Teaching in Primary Schools*. Buckingham: Open University Press.

Young, M. F. D. (ed.) (1971) *Knowledge and Control: New Directions for the Sociology of Education*. London: Collier Macmillan.

Yin, R. K. (1994) *Case Study Research*, 2nd edn. London: Sage.

Index